Theory and Practice o… …riented Psychotherapy

Advances in Focusing-Oriented Psychotherapy

Jessica Kingsley Publishers also publishes the companion volume, which looks forward to the future of focusing-oriented approaches, exploring recent innovations such as Focusing-Oriented Psychotherapy as a response to trauma, Wholebody Focusing, and how Focusing has been adapted in Japan and South Korea.

Emerging Practice in Focusing-Oriented Psychotherapy
Innovative Theory, Applications and Practice
Edited by Greg Madison
Foreword by Marion Hendricks-Gendlin
ISBN 978 1 84905 371 6
eISBN 978 0 85700 722 3

of related interest

Focusing-Oriented Art Therapy
Accessing the Body's Wisdom and Creative Intelligence
Laury Rappaport
ISBN 978 1 84310 760 6
eISBN 978 1 84642 852 4

Neuroscience for Counsellors
Practical Applications for Counsellors, Therapists and Mental Health Practitioners
Rachal Zara Wilson
ISBN 978 1 84905 488 1
eISBN 978 0 85700 894 7

The Hormone Factor in Mental Health
Bridging the Mind-Body Gap
Edited by Linda M. Rio
ISBN 978 1 84905 929 9
eISBN 978 0 85700 729 2

Mindful Therapeutic Care for Children
A Guide to Reflective Practice
Dr Joanna North
ISBN 978 1 84905 446 1
eISBN 978 0 85700 840 4

Theory and Practice of Focusing-Oriented Psychotherapy

Beyond the Talking Cure

Edited by Greg Madison

Foreword by Eugene Gendlin

Jessica Kingsley *Publishers*
London and Philadelphia

First published in 2014
by Jessica Kingsley Publishers
73 Collier Street
London N1 9BE, UK
and
400 Market Street, Suite 400
Philadelphia, PA 19106, USA

www.jkp.com

Library of Congress Cataloging in Publication Data
Theory and practice of focusing-oriented psychotherapy : beyond the talking cure / edited by Greg
Madison ; foreword by Gene Gendlin.
pages cm
Includes bibliographical references and index.
ISBN 978-1-84905-324-2
1. Brief psychotherapy. 2. Solution-focused brief therapy. I. Madison, Greg.
RC480.55.T48 2014
616.89'147--dc23

2013047025

British Library Cataloguing in Publication Data
A CIP catalogue record for this book is available from the British Library

ISBN 978 1 84905 324 2
eISBN 978 0 85700 782 7

Printed and bound in Great Britain

MIX
Paper from responsible sources
FSC® C013604

This volume is dedicated to Eugene Gendlin and Marion Hendricks-Gendlin. Their openness and generosity as teachers and colleagues have been a model for how to live a focusing-oriented approach.

CONTENTS

Foreword

Eugene Gendlin and Greg Madison

It is an honour to invite Eugene Gendlin, the originator of Focusing-Oriented Therapy, to write a brief foreword to open this volume, the first compilation sharing the work of Focusing therapists from around the world.

"Gene" Gendlin is fundamentally a philosopher. Although also a gifted therapist and theoretician within academic psychology, Gendlin's primary love and PhD research is in philosophy. This is of great benefit to us because he often peppers his philosophy with concrete examples from therapy, so his points are immediately alive and practical for our work with clients. Some years ago, after making major contributions in the world of psychotherapy, "Gene" returned to concentrate exclusively on his first love.

The kind of therapy described in these two volumes, *Theory and Practice of Focusing-Oriented Psychotherapy* and *Emerging Practice in Focusing-Oriented Psychotherapy*, is deeply rooted in Gendlin's philosophy; a philosophy which centers around the idea that living bodies "imply" their own way forward.

Gene's statement for the foreword comes directly from his philosophy. As he says:

> It seems to me that the most important central development is to become bodily sensitive to how the situation sits in the body, to let a bodily felt sense *come*. This is the spot where there is always an *implicit unfinished further implying*. If we permit it, it will expand and move from step to step, explicating and expanding our felt sense of the situation in which we find ourselves. More

> and more experience will come. The steps that come open the dilemmas that brought us into therapy.
>
> There is always a further implying and a still further implying. The bodily experience of the situation, the quality, like "agitated," "comfortable," "desiring," or "excited," supplies the dimension that can then develop towards new possibilities. Those new possibilities are always implicit in experiencing.
>
> Bodily experience is always incomplete, and always leads to further steps of development if we make room for it in our bodies. This requires particular skills in the therapist as well as a dawning sensitivity in the client. These two volumes describe many new angles for therapists to develop to help facilitate this unfolding process.
>
> The situational understanding that every animal has differs from the kind of experiencing we humans have, already divided between sounds and pictures and smells, tastes, and textures. The bodily situation is needed along with those already-symbolized sensations.
>
> One story I like to tell is when Einstein, after a long discussion with a group, said to them, "Now I will go a little think." He had these two different modes of thinking: he could be perfectly accurate in using already-existing knowledge, but he could also use experience to develop new steps from the bodily implying.

In recent years, the direct emphasis on the bodily dimension has reorganized the therapy process for more and more people. These two volumes illustrate how the practice of Focusing and the philosophy that underpins it can be integrated into a wide range of therapeutic modalities and applications. Therapists, counsellors, psychologists, and anyone in the caring professions will learn specific methods for increasing the sensitivity to bodily experience during sessions and will also discover new ways to *think* about their work and about themselves.

ACKNOWLEDGMENTS

I would like to offer a heartfelt thank you to each contributor who gave generously of their time and talent to make the two volumes on Focusing-Oriented Therapy possible. I would especially like to mention those authors whose first language is not English. I can hardly imagine the effort needed to communicate such complex ideas so clearly in a second language.

In addition to the contributors, I would like to mention the focusing-oriented therapists whose names do not appear here but who have supported us all with time-consuming editing and feedback in the preparation of our chapters. This book really does represent a community effort and I am proud to be a part of it. Special mention to Melinda Darer, Kye Nelson and all at The Focusing Institute who were helpful in the initial phase of the project.

My gratitude also goes to the editorial team at Jessica Kingsley Publishers, who have shown faith in what the Focusing approach offers and who have always been supportive and flexible. It has been a pleasure to work with them.

Finally, I would like to acknowledge those in my personal life who have born the brunt of the sacrifices required to breathe air into this beast.

PREFACE

In the initial stages of planning a book on the current state of Focusing therapy, it became apparent that it would be impossible to represent the range of developments in the field since the publication of Gendlin's *Focusing-Oriented Psychotherapy* in just one book. Expanding the project to two volumes immediately presents the issue of how to group the chapters into two cohesive offerings. After some deliberation, we have arrived at two balanced and unique volumes representing contemporary Focusing-Oriented Therapy around the world.

Volume One provides the reader with a necessary context for understanding FOT as a tradition, some cross-theoretical integration, modalities of practice, and a focusing-oriented perspective on current topics within the profession of psychotherapy.

Volume Two develops this basis in specific directions, emphasizing concrete applications of FOT, such as trauma work, as well as more personal accounts of the practice. These are complementary companion volumes emphasizing both depth of understanding and concrete practical application. As psychotherapists we need to have both sophistication in our knowledge and sensitivity in our practice.

The books have been prepared so that the reader can dip into topics of special interest or read the chapters consecutively cover to cover, proceeding from the fundamentals to integrations, modes of practice to further applications, and finally to more personal accounts of the experience of FOT. A prime ingredient of both volumes is the emphasis on practice, with each chapter offering insights into how therapists and clients actually explore issues and topics in focusing-oriented sessions.

These volumes were inspired by the desire to share our work with each other, certainly, but primarily we have written our accounts to share our work with readers who are new to Focusing and FOT. We are reaching out; something that as an international community we are now ready to do. We seek dialogue and cross-fertilization with other thinkers and clinicians.

Our hope is that you will immediately be able to take from these pages aspects of the approach that can be integrated into your sessions with clients and into your own personal life. Focusing is an "adding-to," not a "replacement-for." By reading about our work you might be inspired to combine aspects of the FOT approach with your current orientation to practice, and we might thereby discover new and exciting integrations that could be called "focusing-oriented." Let us know what you come up with.

Introduction

Greg Madison

In 1996 Eugene Gendlin produced the long-awaited text *Focusing-Oriented Psychotherapy*, introducing his approach to the profession of practicing psychotherapists. Many of us had already been integrating what we knew of Focusing into our practice with clients, based upon what we had gleaned from discussions of Gendlin's numerous articles on client work but also on what we had learned from our own personal Focusing practice.

Now, 18 years after that first publication, the world of Focusing-Oriented Therapy (FOT) has grown considerably.[1] Each contributor to this book, whether a psychologist, psychotherapist, or counsellor, represents the working-out of a unique elaboration of Focusing therapy, tested through years of clinical practice. The time is now ripe for Focusing therapists from around the world to share these applications and integrations with a wider audience.

It may sound like a paradox but, since its inception, Gendlin's work on Focusing therapy has had a profound effect upon the practice of psychotherapy *while remaining* a little-known practice in its own right. It is not uncommon to receive a brief introduction to Focusing: an afternoon lecture followed by a guided experience, for example, on many integrative, existential, or person-centered psychotherapy training courses. However, there still exist only a small handful of centers around the world where a student can find

1 "Focusing-Oriented Psychotherapy" is the full term used by Gendlin in the title of his book on psychotherapy. However, in common usage this is often abbreviated to "Focusing-Oriented Therapy" (FOT). In this volume the terms are used according to chapter authors' preference.

a comprehensive professional training in this approach. The result is that FOT has often been misunderstood as a stand-alone Focusing technique to encourage a client to deepen their experiencing, but within traditional therapy sessions that typically emphasize verbal content.

The subtitle of this book, *Beyond the Talking Cure*, refers to Dr. Josef Breuer's patient, Anna O, who called her early "therapy" sessions "the talking cure." The term, later adopted by Sigmund Freud, indicated the belief that in some way "talking" cured symptoms. Interesting to note that the facts of the case could just as well have lead to the term "the listening cure," which would have been much more consistent with the approach you will find in this book.

FOT rests deeply upon the importance of a sensitively attuned listening relationship. In Anna O's time it was utterly radical for a doctor to actually listen to a patient as she unfolds a narrative of her own making. Sadly, that may still remain largely true today. FOT transforms listening into *experiential* listening, taking it beyond just the verbal content of what is said and deeper into the body's feeling response to what is said; the feeling of being heard by another human being, and seeing the impact that the words and feelings then have in the listener. In these pages you will read how FOT goes well beyond "the talking cure" or even "the listening cure" conventionally conceived. In this sense, Focusing therapy depends fundamentally upon how the therapist is and not upon something the therapist is *doing to* the client.

In these two volumes the reader will discover that Focusing-Oriented Therapy is an experiential psychotherapy that boasts a unique integration of theory, method, and a radical philosophy of living process. FOT is far more comprehensive than the "six-step focusing procedure" as outlined in Gendlin's original book *Focusing* (1979). The contributors for both volumes integrate many aspects of other models of therapy, but always integrating experientially, so that the "focusing-oriented" aspect of practice is honored.

Selecting contributors for these new volumes has not been an easy task. There are a few long-established FOTs who felt unable, for various reasons, to accept the invitation to contribute. Also, there are numerous FOTs in the non-English speaking world whose work I would have liked to bring to a larger audience outside their own communities. Sadly, the limitations of the current project did not allow for those additions, or for input from various other countries, for example, South Africa, China, Afghanistan, Palestine, Portugal, and regions of Latin America. Asking for contributions from joint authors has been one way to include as many diverse voices as possible and to make the whole project feel more like a community endeavor.

Plan of this volume

This book, *Theory and Practice of Focusing-Oriented Psychotherapy: Beyond the Talking Cure*, proceeds through four parts. Each part opens with an introduction that briefly describes the topics of the chapters to follow. Part I provides the reader new to Focusing and FOT with a background and context for the practice. The first three chapters define many of the basic terms in FOT and, although each chapter in the book is meant to be able to stand alone, some of these early chapters provide a good basis for understanding later discussions.

Part II includes examples of integrations between focusing-oriented practice and various other contemporary therapeutic orientations. The third part describes different modes of therapy, group, couples, etc., and how to work experientially within these various formats. Part IV of the book returns to wider issues including a critique of the term "felt sense" and FOT views of philosophy, neuroscience, and research. The last chapter opens the theme of Focusing as an international movement and the whole volume then closes with a brief conclusion.

PART I

Understanding the Focusing-Oriented Approach

The first part of this book opens with three chapters designed to offer a comprehensive and engaging introduction to the theoretical and philosophical framework of Focusing-Oriented Therapy.

Opening the book is Akira Ikemi's chapter presenting Gendlin's essential facets of FOT, including a discussion of what constitutes "personality" and how the assumptions in FOT set it apart from other orientations to therapy.

Following on, Anna Karali and Pavlos Zarogiannis explore the fundamental topic of "change" within focusing-oriented theory and practice. Their chapter illustrates a combination of internal and external aspects of change, weaving together both conceptual and practice issues as well as a discussion of the positioning of the profession of psychotherapy in social-cultural context.

Finally in this first part, Kevin C. Krycka asks central questions about FOT and its future in relation to its own development and interaction with various developments in the profession of psychotherapy.

All three chapters set the stage for a deeper understanding of FOT and Part II, which moves into clinical integrations with other traditions.

CHAPTER 1

A Theory of Focusing-Oriented Psychotherapy

Akira Ikemi

Introduction

Conventional major theories of psychotherapy elucidate a specific set of assumptions about human living—what is optimally human, what is "normal" and "abnormal," or what personality "is" and how it developed. For example, Sigmund Freud portrayed the person as driven by unconscious, infantile, and libidinous impulses. In contrast, Carl Rogers portrayed the person as being on the way to actualizing her or his own self. A self to be actualized existed for Rogers, but not for Freud. These basic views of the person give rise to theoretical models of what psychotherapy is and how it works.

Is there such a coherent psychotherapy theory in Focusing? The Focusing literature is explicit with the practice of Focusing and its applications, but psychotherapy theory tends to remain implicit in the literature. Eugene Gendlin has written on this topic, most notably in the book *Focusing-Oriented Psychotherapy* (1996), but much of Gendlin's other writings since the late 1990s are in the field of philosophy, and these papers are difficult for many psychotherapists to follow and understand. It is the attempt of this chapter to weave together a somewhat coherent sketch of a psychotherapy theory from some of Gendlin's writings.

The enterprise of this chapter needs to be carried out with care and caution. The coherent theory, which this chapter hopes to arrive at, will not be like a "product" comparable to other products, that is, other psychotherapy theories. This is because Focusing assumes a different *kind of theory*. For instance, if classical psychoanalytic theory could be symbolized as an Audi engine, and person-centered theory as a Ford engine, Focusing theory would not look like an engine at all. It would be more like gasoline, which could make both Audi and Ford engines run. This is because Focusing is about *how we have experience*, and not about the contents of *what we experience*. So if one were to ask if one's experience is related to a Freudian libidinous unconscious or a Rogerian actualizing self, the reply would be that it can be one of the two, both or neither. Focusing is concerned with *how* it is that one finds libidinal forces, or an actualizing self, operating within experiencing. A close investigation of this process may reveal that it is indeed one of the two, or an entirely new and unique concept emerging from this investigation. In short, Focusing theory is not a *content* theory, it is a theory of the *process* with which contents arise and change. Nevertheless, this does not mean that there is no view of the person at all in Focusing. Thus far, we already have a view of the person as an experiencing subject from which concepts can emerge.

Gendlin (1990, p.208) writes of a need "to communicate how very different our philosophical assumptions are, compared to everything else in the field." According to Gendlin, this difference has resulted in some of the difficulty that Focusing approaches have in communicating with practitioners from other approaches. What exactly are these philosophical or theoretical assumptions that are so different from everything else? Gendlin *doesn't* write much about it in his psychological works. For example, the book *Focusing* is mostly practical, showing the readers how to *do* Focusing. It does include a "Philosophical Note" which is Appendix A, two pages only. Similarly, in *Let Your Body Interpret Your Dreams*, theory appears in Appendix A (Gendlin 1986, pp.141–162), not in the main text. In this appendix, Gendlin writes:

> If you don't like this theory, don't let it get in the way of the experiential steps the book describes. They are not based on theory. You don't need the theory for them. That is why it is an appendix, here... Theory does not ground what I described in the book. I love theory, but it does not ground life. Many people think everything is "based on" theory. If that were so, what would theory be based on? (p.141)

Yet the "Theory of the Living Body and Dreams" that appears in this appendix is 21 pages in length and very rich in content, requiring some background in philosophy to understand it.

"Theory does not ground life," Gendlin writes. Truly, most of what we do in our daily lives are not "based on" any theory. I love listening to jazz, but that is not "based on" any theory, for example. Yet theoretical concepts point to phenomena, they enable us to see things in ways that otherwise would be difficult or impossible to see. Moreover, with concepts, we can begin to see the relations between one concept and another, which is theory. Theory is not something that is to be "based on," but something to be "built." (I recall that Gendlin used to teach a course called "Theory Construction" at the University of Chicago. It has now developed into TAE, "Thinking at the Edge.") We cannot translate or reduce a person's life into theory, but a person can reflect on their lives and build theories that bring new light to their lives. Thus the attempt of this chapter is not to reduce, nor to "fit" a person into a set of concepts. Rather, the theoretical elaborations woven in this chapter may serve to see therapy, our lives, and our client's lives, in ways that are implicit in Focusing-Oriented Psychotherapy.

A view of "personality"

Psychotherapy orientations are often grounded in their personality theories, and these are usually mutually exclusive. One needs to adopt either a Freudian view of personality as basically regressive or a Jungian view of the progressive nature of the process of individuation, for example. One cannot have both, without making major revisions in the theories. As mentioned above, Focusing espouses a different kind of personality theory, which can make use of both Freudian and Jungian concepts and more. How is this possible? And what exactly is the personality theory that enables the use of supposedly mutually exclusive concepts?

For Gendlin, personality is "a theory of *how* people live, rather than *what* they are and do. People are their living, not the products, not the facts and the concepts they make… The existential view [which Gendlin advocates] denies that any theory can render what a human person is, since that is always in the making by living, and thus radically open. Theory is made by people, and can never be such that people can be derived from it" (1973, p.329). Further in this article, Gendlin writes: "to study the person apart from community, to conceive of 'personality' as purely internal machinery, are errors" (p.330). "Psychological maladjustment is not the classical neuroses, nor any 'bad content' inside..." (p.331).

To understand these assertions, we need to discard the classical view of personality as an "internal psychic apparatus." Together with this, the view of psychopathology as pathological contents "inside" that causes malfunctioning of the psyche must also be abandoned. If "personality" is not *inside* us, where is it then?

> Personality is not so much "what one is," as how one carries oneself forward in further living, further feeling and self-responding, and further interpersonal relating... Personality is not stuff inside, but the capacity to carry forward in words or acts what is experientially felt as focal and next. (Gendlin 1973, p.333)

Gendlin strongly upholds the philosopher Martin Heidegger's concept of *being-in-the-world* (Heidegger 1962). The hyphens in that term "are meant to indicate that one being, one event, is both the person and the situations (or environments and universe) in which the person lives. Human beings *are* encounterings in the world and with others... Sartre (1956) discussing sadness, says that it is '...a situation too urgent'" (Gendlin 1973, p.323). Thus, Gendlin cites the philosopher Jean-Paul Sartre in asserting that an emotion such as sadness is not a feeling inside, but a situation. Humans *are* the situation, the relationships.

When I feel frustrated in a relationship, the frustration is not inside me. The frustration is the way this relationship is. Thus to work on this frustration would not be a personal and internal process. Rather it would involve changing the nature of the relationship with the other person involved. Contrast this view with a more popular view, which I shall refer to as the "representationalist" view. In that view, the frustration I feel in the relationship *represents* another relationship of which I cannot recall, thus unconscious. That unconscious relationship must have occurred at a prior time, so the frustration must be a *manifestation* of an *earlier* frustration in a significant relationship. In this representationalist view, an "inner" world of contents is presupposed and an "internal psychic apparatus" that preserves memories and prevents certain memories from coming into awareness is assumed.

In the phenomenological and existential view of personality espoused by Gendlin as above, no such inner world is assumed. Personality, as quoted above, is about "how one carries oneself forward in further living," which is concretely our living, our *existence.* It is popularly assumed that the manner with which we project ourselves into further living must be determined by what we have learned in the past. Gendlin, however, would not agree to this. In an article entitled "Three assertions about the body," Gendlin asserts that "we have plant bodies," and the characteristics of a plant body are as follows:

> A plant does not have our five senses. It does not see, hear or smell. And yet obviously the plant contains the information involved in its living. It lives from itself; it organizes the next steps of its own body-process, and enacts them if the environment cooperates to supply what it needs. (Gendlin 1993, p.25)

In the first line of this excerpt Gendlin rejects the commonly held notion that what we know must have come into us from our senses. Commonly, we believe that information has to be put in, "inputted," through our five senses. In this popular view, there is no organization in human nature, unless information is inputted. Gendlin has repeatedly argued against this popular view. The body is in constant interaction with the environment, even before perception. Through this ongoing interaction, the plant knows exactly how to live, even though it has no perceptual input channels. Ikemi (in press) discusses this assertion with an example of a sunflower:

> The sunflower turns to the sun, although it does not have eyes to see the sun, although nobody has taught it to do so. It grows taller and sometimes a little sideways, so that leaves of other plants do not get in the way of the sun. If you go to a field of sunflowers (or any flowers) you will notice that each sunflower plant is a little different from the others... They are not identical to one another, like products produced in a factory. Each plant processes the various and delicate information of soil, water,

> sunlight, wind, temperature, insects and so forth, and they generate their own bodily living.

Memories, past events that we do not even recall, our language and culture, "historicity," are all involved in the body's generating of the further steps of living. They are like minerals in the soil for the plant. However, the plant's living is not totally "determined by" any one of these minerals. The plant organizes what it needs and uptakes just what is necessary for the living that it is generating. *Pre-reflexively*, that is, before we can reflect and think about it, our bodies organize whatever is available to them to generate the next moves to live further in the situation.

Ikemi (in press) discusses how, with each and every step of the walk that we take, the body generates a further living process.

> ...if you observe a crowd of people walking, you will notice that each person has a somewhat different way of walking. Persons have their own delicate balances of so many factors involved in walking. Weight and mass of different parts of the body; the length of the legs and arms; size and shape of the feet (which may even vary from left to right foot); muscle tones in the calves, thighs, hips, shoulders, neck, and other parts of the body; the structures and conditions of so many joints; respiration; circulation; digestion; the person's current emotion and schedule; the type and fit of shoes; bags and other items carried; climatic conditions as temperature, humidity, wind chill, wind velocity; results of modeling and learning...this list is probably inexhaustible. All these delicate and multi-faceted information affect the walk. More precisely, the walk is the processing-generating, the living-forward of all these information. Pain in some part of the body, or fatigue in the muscles of the thighs, indigestion, a slight elevation of the street, for example, result in an instant adjustment of the walk. Like plants, human bodies process and generate their own living, with every step that they take!

Much in our living happens *pre-reflexively*, that is, before we dwell on and reflect about it. I may feel like taking the afternoon off today to just relax. When asked why, all I may be able to say might be "I just feel like it." This does not indicate, however, that my feeling is dominated by an irrational unconscious motive produced by a "psychic apparatus" inside me. Rather my body is organizing and generating my afternoon living from as much information as it has. Moreover, when I *reflect* on this feeling, I may discover what *was implicit* in it. And the *explication* of what *was* implicit, may change the way I live my afternoon. For example, upon reflection, I may discover a certain tension in me that is making me feel heavy and tired. With this explication, I may now feel that I would like to talk to someone about this tension, rather than "just relaxing." We discover what *was implicit* by *reflection*, and expression changes what *was* there. Such expressions that change "what was" will be referred to as *explication*.

Theories can greatly help explication. In the book *Let Your Body Interpret Your Dreams* (1986), Gendlin puts forth a way of using different psychotherapy theories for explication, instead of reducing people's experiences (dreams) to theoretical constructs. Thus, instead of interpreting people's dreams by fitting them into theory, theoretical interpretations can be formulated as questions to be checked against the person's felt sense of the dream.

A client dreamed, four years before our session, that her tongue was cut off, like a sparrow in a Japanese folktale. The dream bothered her for four years. The therapist asked the client to recall the folk story. She told the gist of the story: an old man takes care of a sparrow but since it eats the fruits of their farm, his wife, the old lady, cuts the tongue off the sparrow. The sparrow goes away... The therapist asked her if the following made any sense to her: your father takes good care of you, but your mother is aggressive to you. "Wow!" she said, and let out a loud sigh of relief. "Yes," she said, "that really feels right!" This part of the dreamwork took only five minutes and yet the uneasiness about the dream she had had for four years dissolved instantly. More work was done about what came from the dream in the later portion of the session, exploring the way she lived her relationships, particularly with her parents.

Rivalry with the parent of the same sex and the love and caring experienced with the parent of the opposite sex is an Oedipal theme, first articulated by Sigmund Freud. Asking the client to tell the Japanese folktale is an application of a method used by Carl G. Jung called "amplification." These usually mutually exclusive theoretical models can be combined when they are used in the service of the client's experiential explication. Rather than fitting the client into a theoretical schema, these theoretical concepts and methods are checked against the client's felt sense to see what is brought forth when their experiencing is crossed with the theory. When the meaning of the dream is carried forward with these concepts, it is actually the client's living that is being carried further.

A view of psychotherapy

Reflexive awareness and the manner of experiencing

If personality is the person's living, how does it change? A person changes "by living differently" writes Gendlin (1973, p.341), a seemingly tautological but obvious answer. And how does a person live differently?

Persons live differently, first, by reflecting on the ways they live. The first step to change is to become reflexive about oneself and one's living in the situation. As a result of this reflexive endeavor, the person may visit a psychotherapist, or any other types of professionals, to aid them in their reflection and in their generating of a different living. For example, I may realize that I am out of shape and out of energy and decide to seek advice from a gym trainer to prescribe specific workouts for me. As a consequence of training, I may start to feel healthier, more energetic, more outgoing and my living and relationships may begin to change. The first step here is the reflection that I am out of shape and in need of exercise, from which gym training ensued. If there were a lack of such reflexive awareness, there would have been no change, and living differently would not have happened.

Psychotherapists aid the client in their *reflections* of life. Psychotherapists do not give answers or "explain away" symptoms, or solve the issue in place of the client. The therapist explores together with the client, and attempts to understand each step of the client's reflection.

Sometimes, clients do not seem to enter a reflexive mode of awareness even when they are in therapy. It has been my experience that some patients in hospitals take a "doctor-centered" position, assuming that the doctor will give them solutions. "What's wrong with me, doctor? Can you cure me?" is the kind of verbalization that such patients mention. Psychotherapy is difficult in such cases because of the lack of reflective awareness on the part of the client.

The Experiencing (EXP) Scales, which are research measures that played an important role in the development of Focusing, actually measure the degree to which clients are able to be reflexive about themselves and their situations. Table 1.1 shows the characteristics of the stages of the EXP Scales, from Klein, Mathieu and Kiesler 1969 and Miyake, Ikemi and Tamura 2008. Studies using the EXP Scales found that clients who had low EXP levels tended not to be successful in therapy, while clients who were rated higher on the scale showed successful outcomes. The differences between these two groups were evident from very early in therapy. A detailed review of the literature of these studies appears in Klein, Mathieu-Coughlan and Kiesler (1986).

EXP levels 1 through 3 in Klein *et al.*, and LOW in Miyake *et al.*, portray a mode of awareness where clients are not reflexive about their feelings, situations or their living. "I suddenly had this pain here and I went to a doctor and she told me I had gastritis," may be an example of level 2 experiencing, or VERY LOW level in Miyake *et al.* When asked "What do you feel about that?" or "What do you think led up to the gastritis?" the client may say "Oh, I don't know. I'll just do what the doctor says, I'll be alright."

As in this example, clients may fail or refuse to reflect on what was going on in their lives that might have led up to the problem. In this condition therapy is difficult, as predicted in studies using the EXP Scales. This does not mean that successful therapy is impossible with low EXP clients. The manner of the relationship between therapists and clients affects clients' reflexive capacity. Active or experiential listening is powerful in engaging the clients' reflexive awareness. Ikemi (2011) articulated a *reflecting mode of consciousness* that is elicited when symbols used to explicate one's experiencing are reflected back through listening. Other responses made by the therapist attempt to engage the client's reflexive capacity in some way or another. Particularly, responses originating from the therapist's felt sense, sometimes called "genuine" responses or "personal resonance" (Schmid and Mearns 2006) are also effective in eliciting the client's reflexive awareness. We will return to this in a later part of this chapter.

Table 1.1 Characteristics of EXP stages

Stages	Characteristics (Klein *et al.* 1969)	Stages	Rating criteria (Miyake *et al.* 2007)	Overview
1	Content or manner of expression is impersonal (e.g. abstract, journalistic account of events)	VERY LOW	External events with no reference to feelings	Event-centered
2	Association between speaker and content is explicit, but no reference to the speaker's feelings			
3	Description of the speaker in behavioral terms with added comments on feelings	LOW	External events are narrated; feelings are reactions to events	
4	Clear presentation of feelings. Feelings or experiences of events, rather than the events themselves	MIDDLE	Feelings are used not as reactions to events but to express the self. Characterized by richness of feelings	Feeling-centered
5	Purposeful exploration of the speaker's feelings and experiences	HIGH	Feelings are used as referents for self-exploration, or as a hypothesis for understanding the self	Creative
6	A synthesis of accessible, newly recognized, or more fully realized feelings and experiences to produce personally meaningful structures or to resolve issues	VERY HIGH	A new facet of the feeling arises as in an inspiration. Laughter and excitement are often seen, indicating confidence in the newly emerging meaning	
7	Expanding awareness of immediately present feelings and internal processes. Speaker can move from one inner reference to another, altering and modifying concepts of self or feelings			

Note: This table shows the author's summary and translations of the EXP Scales. Klein *et al.*'s 1969 version is a relatively early version of the EXP Scale. Later versions, notably the 1970 and 1986 versions, exist, but the 1969 version is chosen here for relatively easy comparison with Miyake *et al.*'s scale.

Felt sense

Attending to, and letting words (symbols) arise from the *felt sense* is vital, and is characteristic of Focusing and FOT as seen throughout this book. In level 4 of Klein *et al.* and in the MIDDLE stage in Miyake, the person is attending to a bodily felt sense that is more than what is captured in a word. "It's not really anger, it's..." is an example to indicate that what the client is sensing is more than what the word "anger" can carry. This expression is not a reaction to an event, but explores what it feels like to be oneself in this situation.

Explicitly exploring what might arise from the felt sense is level 5 in Klein *et al.* and HIGH in Miyake *et al.* This level is observed in Focusing sessions, when the focuser asks the felt sense, "What might this felt sense need?" "What is the crux of this?" or any one of the "asking responses" in Focusing.

When symbols (words) arise newly from the felt sense, a breakthrough results with a newly emerging understanding, accompanied by a physical sense of relief. This is called a *felt shift*, or an *experiential step*. The felt sense changes or may undergo a series of changes with each experiential step. This is levels 6 and 7 in Klein *et al.* and VERY HIGH in Miyake *et al.* "It's not really anger, it's... wait a minute, maybe it's loneliness. Yes! That's what it is! I *was* feeling lonely all this time!" This sentence is an example where the felt sense is *carried forward* with the word "lonely." In this *explication* a new understanding arises that changes the way one "was" before. *Now*, the client realizes that it was not anger, it *was* loneliness. As Gendlin (1997a) points out, this "was" is a carried forward kind of "was," because the "was" emerges only after explication. The forward movement of explication changes what one "was" before. Hence, a new person, a new and different living results. Now, here is a lonely person, not the angry person we had a few minutes before.

Attending to the felt sense is actually a *re-experiencing* (*nacherleben*) of situations in life. (*Nacherleben* is a term from Willhelm Dilthey, a philosopher who Gendlin took up in his master's thesis (Gendlin 1950). *Re*-experiencing may not be an accurate translation, the Japanese translation is *tsui-taiken*, or *follow*-experiencing.) It is a special kind of reflexive activity, where one "re-experiences" a situation while being mindful of how one is in the situation, or how the situation is felt in the body. While the client re-experiences the situation, the therapist also re-experiences the client's re-experiencing. This will be discussed in more detail in Part II.

How therapists can carry forward clients' experiencing

What difference does the therapist's presence make to clients' explications? How can clients carry forward their experiencing with therapists in ways which they could not have done alone? The role of the therapist needs to be articulated in relation to the process of experiencing. Gendlin refers to the philosopher Dilthey in this interesting passage:

> Dilthey said that we can understand the authors only if we understand them better than they understood themselves, and this happens only if we carry their experiencing forward with our further understanding, when the author's experiencing is reconstituted by our experiencing—accurately but enriched by ours, as ours is enriched by theirs. Or, as I would say it: these cross so that each becomes implicit in the other. (Gendlin 1997b, p.41)

If we substitute "clients" for "authors" in the passage above, a view of the interactive nature of understanding unfolds. Therapists can understand clients only when therapists understand clients better than clients understand themselves, and this is achieved when clients' experiencing is carried forward with the further understanding of the therapists, when clients' experiencing is reconstituted by therapists' experiencing. Gendlin introduces the term *reconstituting* in his famous 1964 article "A theory of personality change." He describes it as: "in whatever respects it does not function (is structure bound), responses are needed first to *reconstitute* the interaction process of experiencing in these respects" (Gendlin 1964, p.132). Thus "reconstituting" signifies regaining the interactional nature of experiencing through the responses of the other. The therapists' experiencing can reactivate clients' experiencing, when they *cross*, by which Gendlin means: "each becomes implicit in the other."

Ikemi (2013) uses this model to understand what Carl Rogers meant by "presence." In the therapy demonstration where Rogers discusses presence (Rogers 1989), Rogers can be seen as *crossing* with his client Jan. In so doing, he refers to an aspect of Jan (a naughty girl) that strikes Jan as a particularly important aspect of her, yet unrecognized as such until Rogers pointed it out. Ikemi (2013) describes his own experiences in a session where the focuser who was new to Focusing voices a similar surprise:

> After the session, when we shared our experiences of the session with the whole group, she said: "You know, this person (me) is a total stranger! I only met him a couple of hours ago. How can it be that he knows so much about me!"

In a transcript of a session with a different client provided in Ikemi (2011), the client says in several instances, "How did you know that?" These instances are often described as "intuition." However, an alternative explanation is possible. In these instances, the therapist *re-experiences* the clients' re-experiencing. In so doing, what was implicit in the client becomes implicit in the therapist. When that which was implicit in the client is carried further by the therapist's explication, the client's experiencing is carried forward. Just as "each becomes implicit in the other," *each is carried forward by the other.*

From the discussion above, two directions of therapists' engagements can be indicated. One direction is to enhance the reflective capacity of the client. Reflective listening is particularly powerful for this purpose. The other direction is where therapists carry forward their own experiencing of their clients' experiencing. This may happen with "genuine responses," "personal resonance," or Focusing along with the client in the therapy session.

Instead of a model of therapy where the therapist "analyzes" the client's past to make sense of their relevance to present events, or instead of the model of cathartic discharge, FOT illuminates a model where the client's understanding is enriched in the experiential interaction *with* the therapist. Again, analyses, catharsis and many other "avenues" *can* carry forward the client's experience, as seen in the book *Focusing-Oriented Psychotherapy* (Gendlin 1996). Yet, as shown abundantly in that book, FOT sees carrying forward as central, that is, analysis, catharsis, and other processes may work in the service of carrying forward. When experiencing is carried forward, a person's *living* is carried forward. From there, life continues to generate itself newly.

References

Gendlin, E.T. (1950) "Willhelm Dilthey and the Problem of Comprehending Human Significance in the Science of Man." Master of Arts dissertation submitted to the Department of Philosophy, University of Chicago.

Gendlin, E.T. (1964) "A Theory of Personality Change." In P. Worchel and D. Byrne (eds) *Personality Change*. New York: John Wiley & Sons.

Gendlin, E.T. (1973) "Experiential Psychotherapy." In R. Corsini (ed.) *Current Psychotherapies*. Itasca, IL: Peacock.

Gendlin, E.T. (1986) *Let Your Body Interpret Your Dreams*. Willmette, IL: Chiron Publications.

Gendlin, E.T. (1990) "The Small Steps of the Therapy Process: How They Come and How to Help Them Come." In G. Lietaer, J. Rombauts and R. Van Balen (eds) *Client-Centered and Experiential Psychotherapy in the Nineties*. Leuven: Leuven University Press.

Gendlin, E.T. (1993) "Three assertions about the body." *The Folio 12*, 1, 21–33.

Gendlin, E.T. (1996) *Focusing Oriented Psychotherapy*. New York: Guilford Press.

Gendlin, E.T. (1997a) "The responsive order: A new empiricism." *Man and World 30*, 383–411.

Gendlin, E.T. (1997b) "How Philosophy Cannot Appeal to Experience, and How It Can." In D. Levine (ed.) *Language beyond Postmodernism: Saying and Thinking in Gendlin's Philosophy*. Evanston, IL: Northwestern University Press.

Heidegger, M. (1962) *Being and Time*, trans. John Macquarrie and Edward Robinson. New York: Harper & Row.

Ikemi, A. (2011) "Empowering the implicitly functioning relationship." *Person-Centered and Experiential Psychotherapies 10*, 1, 28–42.

Ikemi, A. (2013) "You Can Inspire Me to Live Further: Explicating Pre-reflexive Bridges to the Other." In J.H.D. Cornelius-White, R. Motschnig-Pitrik and M. Lux (eds) *Interdisciplinary Handbook of the Person Centered Approach: Research and Theory*. New York: Springer.

Ikemi, A. (in press) "Sunflowers, sardines and responsive combodying: Three perspectives on embodiment." *Person-Centered and Experiential Psychotherapies*.

Klein, M., Mathieu, P. and Kiesler, D. (1969) *The Experiencing Scale: A Research and Training Manual Volume 1*. Madison: Wisconsin Psychiatric Institute.

Klein, M., Mathieu-Coughlan, P. and Kiesler, D. (1986) "The Experiencing Scales." In L. Greenberg and W. Pinsof (eds) *The Psychotherapeutic Process: A Research Handbook*. New York: Guilford Press.

Miyake, M., Ikemi. A. and Tamura, R. (2008) "Five stage experiencing scale: Rating manual." *Japanese Journal of Human Psychology 25*, 2, 115–127. (In Japanese.)

Rogers, C. (1989) "A Client-Centered/Person-Centered Approach to Therapy." In H. Kirschenbaum and V. Henderson (eds) *The Carl Rogers Reader*. New York: Houghton Mifflin.

Schmid, P. and Mearns, D (2006) "Being-with and being-counter: Person-centered psychotherapy as an in-depth co-creative process of personalization." *Person-Centered and Experiential Psychotherapies 5*, 174–190.

CHAPTER 2

The FOT View of Change

What Is Therapeutic about Therapy?

Anna Karali and Pavlos Zarogiannis

Introduction

Focusing-Oriented Therapy (FOT), an inner experiential process, centers its attention on the inwardly felt body that knows how life should be lived. Its essence is therefore largely beyond the talking cure. In fact, the theory and practice of FOT incorporate pre-linguistic or non-linguistic factors that facilitate the client's carrying-forward process. As a consequence, we differentiate between internal aspects (e.g., felt sense, implicit, interaction, felt shift) and external conditions (e.g., socio-political, philosophical) to illuminate the therapeutic aspects and the process of change itself in FOT.

Part I: FOT practice

Anna Karali

> I am a weak, ephemeral creature made of mud and dream. But I feel all the powers of the universe whirling within me... (Nikos Kazantzakis, "Ascesis")

One might briefly outline Focusing-Oriented Therapy (FOT) as having its roots in the findings of two important studies (Kirtner and Cartwright 1958a, 1958b), which strongly suggested that it is possible to predict, from the first few sessions, whether a client was likely to be successful in therapy. Much seemed to depend on the personality of the client and "on how the client *related* to their own experiencing" (Purton 2004, p.55; emphasis added).

The sine qua non of this research led to a fundamental change: the shift from the *content* (*what* is discussed during the session) to *how* the clients talked. Based on these results, Eugene T. Gendlin's major contribution is his pointing to the relation of the individual with his/her felt meaning (as he initially called it), coining later the term *felt sense*. Gendlin (1996, p.63) described the *felt sense* as a bodily sensation, not a merely physical sensation, like a tickle or a pain, but a sense of a *whole* situation, or problem, or concern, or perhaps a point one wants to convey. Not *just* a bodily sense, but rather a bodily sense of the [...].

Gendlin uses the device [...] ("dot, dot, dot") to depict the *implicit* that has not yet been made explicit; sometimes he also refers to the implicit as "the more," while the process is stated as *experiencing*, to stress its fluid, active qualities. Hence, in Gendlin's words, "a good client-centered response formulates the felt implicit meaning of the client's present experiencing" (1961, p.241).

Therefore, it is argued that FOT is quite different from psychoanalytical approaches, as it is not concerned with "making the unconscious conscious" but with "making the implicit explicit" (Purton 2010, p.89). Accordingly, Gendlin contends, "Every experience and event contains implicit further movement. To find it one must sense its unclear edge" (1996, p.15).

To accomplish this effect of moving experience forward, an FOT therapist has to keep the client gently in his/her experiencing process. Still, for one to go further, and engender a new experiential step, a series of FOT therapeutic basics have to be pursued. I will present these only briefly, to leave room both for the FOT key constructs (terminology) and my commentary. In Gendlin's language, this commentary will come from the *crossing* of his thinking, through my own experience, acquired through 23 years as a psychotherapist.

Therapeutic basics

1. THE RELATIONSHIP

a) Within the therapeutic process

Carl Rogers (1951) was the first to point at the importance of the therapeutic relationship; nowadays almost all of the contemporary approaches consider it as the core of successful therapy. The FOT therapist also relates to the person; not to *his/her experiencing process* but to the person attending to his/her experiencing process. On the other side of the relationship it is the therapist's felt sense of the therapeutic situation that determines how he/she responds, and to which aspect of his/her experience and knowledge he/she can best draw (Purton 2007, p.60).

b) In the client's inner interaction

In FOT nothing is more important than the "person inside." Therapy exists for the person's inner being; it has no other purpose. When that inner being comes alive, or even stirs just a little, it is more real and important than any diagnosis, or evaluation (Gendlin 1996, p.23). That is to say, the felt sense is the "client" inside (the "client's client"). Our usual conscious self is the "therapist," often a crudely directive one, who gets in the way of our inward client all the time (Gendlin 1984).

2. THE PRESENCE OF THE THERAPIST

According to Daniel Siegel (2010, p.34), "presence" is our openness to the unfolding of possibilities; by attuning to others and taking their essence into our own inner world, the other will sense our attunement and will experience "feeling felt" by us. Furthermore, Gendlin deeply touches into the human core when he claims, "The essence of working with another person is to *be present as a living being*" (1990, p.206; emphasis added). As a person-centered and focusing-oriented therapist, I have deeply experienced, acknowledged, and learned to trust the outcome of both interactive and inner friendly *presence.* This falls in line with my view that Rogers' six therapeutic conditions (1956, pp.827–832) are critical in creating a pertinent atmosphere in therapy and this usually initiates a process of constructive personality change.

3. THE "REVOLUTIONARY PAUSE"

For a client to go *inside* and ask, "What is 'my sense' of this situation?" he/she needs the ability to pause the ongoing situation and create a space in which a felt sense can form (Hendricks-Gendlin 2003). This pause may often initiate the possibility of an inner dialogue.

4. DISIDENTIFICATION

To avoid the client's tendency to over-identify with his/her experiencing, the FOT therapist needs to reflect the client's feeling in a way that points towards his/her felt sense. This encourages the client to attend to their felt sensing in a way that facilitates an experiential step. This therapist reflection is called *experiential response*. Example:

C: My mother has driven me crazy again...

T: *Something* in you is feeling driven crazy...

C: Well, yes, crazy...though it might also feel a bit worried...a sort of uneasiness...

5. "CLEARING A SPACE"

In this procedure, the FOT therapist takes a kind of inventory of the client's concerns (i.e., what is—just now—in the way of feeling good in the middle of one's body). To do this, the client attends to their body experientially rather than cognitively, and senses what is in the way of feeling good. Every acknowledged blockage is addressed gently and then "placed" somewhere close to oneself. A physical relief emerges in the center of one's body as soon as each of those blockages gets named and externalized. In the resulting free internal space the client may then invite a felt sense to form unencumbered by other concerns.

6. "HERE AND NOW" PRINCIPLE

According to Gendlin (1996), the *here and now* process affirms that the past is not a single set of formed and fixed happenings. Every present does indeed include past experiences, but the present is not simply a rearrangement of past experiences. The present is a new whole, a new event. It gives the past a new function, a new role to play.

Before reviewing the fundamental FOT terminology, note that Gendlin, owing to his philosophical origin, has drawn on the work of a rich and diverse array of thinkers to develop his experiential phenomenological approach for the understanding of the human body. His readings of Merleau-Ponty, Dilthey, Husserl and others have deeply influenced his work in psychotherapy.

Key constructs

- *Implicit:* This construct refers to the *implicit* (present but unspoken) texture of experience.
- *Interaction first:* This principle asserts that what each person is within an interaction is already affected by the other (Gendlin 1997b).
- *Carrying forward:* In such an interaction, what occurs when the "implicit" changes is called *carrying forward*, so that what was implied is no longer implied, because "it" has occurred (Gendlin 1997b).
- *Felt shift:* It denotes the "opening" of the felt sense, its "shift," which is experienced physically and always has a freeing quality to it, even when something painful unfolds.
- *Structure-bound:* This refers to psychological disturbance, due to the client being caught in specific forms of thought and emotions that are not open to modification by his/her immediate lived experiencing. His/her experience has been *frozen* into specific forms, so that in certain areas of his/her life the creative interplay between form and feeling has ceased (Purton 2004).

Clinical application

An FOT therapist attempts to assuage the client's suffering by gently encouraging him/her to relate, in a friendly manner, to his/her own experiencing. We have to remember that clients struggle to be congruent with "their own" organismic self.

This core process of relating is exceptionally well portrayed by the *I and Thou* tenure of Martin Buber (2004), who argues for two basic ways of relating, which he called I-It and I-Thou. In the I-It mode, the other is an object or a means to an end. In the I-Thou encounter, the other ceases to be an object and we are drawn into a deeper kind of relationship. When we relate to another as an It, Buber adds, the I that goes forth is very different from the I that goes forth to meet a Thou. In my understanding this suggests that therapists can only "heal" the other when they themselves are in contact with their own inner selves. We can encounter our clients only as deeply as we come from within ourselves.

Commentary

From the many different contexts I have worked with over the years, I have chosen to concentrate on my work with cancer patients. I would like to describe an approach that is counterintuitive to the general public's attitude towards this disease and which attempts to challenge the reluctance to nurture a "friendly" encounter with the body part being assaulted by the disease.

My practice covers both private sessions and group therapy. In both situations I initiate therapy by allowing space for the clients to share their own feelings and personal "stories" (no traditional clinical interview). Most of the time, they become overwhelmed by their feelings at some point, so I invite them to take a moment and create a little pause for turning inside, in the torso area. From here I engender the disidentification process by saying: "Something therein seems to be feeling much pain (...feeling lost, being frightened, trembling, etc.). Would it be possible for you to welcome it, stay by it and keep it company?" The wording of this request is strongly affected by culture and language. In Greek, I had to change the friendly "welcome" invitation (almost no one acknowledged it) to the phrase: "Would you like to attend to 'it,' from a safe distance, and make an effort to 'comprehend' it?" (Although this language may sound strange, it is central to FOT.)

Some clients may accept this invitation, pause and turn their attention to the space of the "border zone" between the conscious and the unconscious. As soon as the client allows the space for the felt sense to be formed, an inner dialogue may be initiated between the client's interactions with the bodily sense of the situation and the words that arise from it, as the [...] is full of possibilities that are not yet realized.

According to Gendlin (1961), genuine psychotherapy begins at this point, beyond an intellectual approach, when the patient is facilitated to attend to an immediate, present experiencing of his/her condition. Indeed, the client does more than just become familiar with emotions and experiences; he/she is being mindful to observe the emergence of something new. When this directly sensed, but cognitively unclear *felt sense,* makes the experiencing moment a defining one, the client experiences a physical relief (i.e., felt shift) and a movement may carry him/her forward into a new step of holistic change (i.e., change-steps arising from the felt sense).

I may then gently invite him/her to sense: "What difference has that movement caused?" or "How is this new 'thing' for you?" This might enable a successive step. This is, in Gendlin's words, a "zigzag" process that consists of new steps of movement. Eventually these steps will bring one closer to being oneself.

Keeping clients in their experiencing process of the moment primarily depends on their therapist, as we are not just working together, we are an ensemble. Only if the presence of, and relationship with, the therapist is a trusted one, will they follow his/her invitations. By doing so they will hopefully attain a feeling of self-empathy for "whatever" emerges inside there that is uniquely *theirs.* This is significantly related to therapeutic outcome. Yet the clients do well as a result of what they themselves do, not only because of what the therapist does. I strongly muse, therefore, that when they find this inner thread, they are led to themselves, their dear, though at the moment incongruent, selves.

One might assert that the major strength of this approach is the "wholeness" that the clients may experience, as a result of their inner relationship; a *sense,* that all of their "parts" are there to underpin their wounded part, and to unconditionally accept it. This acknowledgment often brings vulnerability and a courageous compassion that enhances the perception and consequently the behavior of the clients towards their "disease," or their blockages in general. Now, they are no longer "fighting" this assaulted part, instead they are caring and looking for new positive life energy to support it.

Obviously, not every client is well suited for this approach. For some clients it can be difficult to attend to their experiential process so that a felt sense may be formed. This could be considered as a limitation of this approach.

In summary, the basis of FOT is that *change-steps* arise from the *felt sense*, followed by the client's "zigzag" process. The critical therapeutic element of FOT is founded on the *inter- and intra-relating* of each, the client and therapist.

Part II: FOT as Heterotopia

Pavlos Zarogiannis

> Zeus, who guided mortals to be wise, has established his fixed law—wisdom comes through suffering. (Aeschylus, *Agamemnon*)

Beyond these "inner-therapeutic" variables (Part I), which FOT recognizes as important conditions responsible for therapeutic change, there are also "outer-therapeutic" factors, that is, a priori conditions that may not explicitly belong to the narrative of FOT, but nevertheless make FOT's presence and existence possible, as they make possible psychotherapy per se. Furthermore, these external conditions influence FOT; they contribute implicitly to its therapeutic outcome and guarantee to some point its validity.

In this part of the chapter is illustrated what is therapeutic in FOT (and probably in every psychotherapy) from such an "outer-therapeutic" point of view by exploring the socio-political space of FOT. FOT, as clinical practice, is first and foremost a socio-political "institution."

The location of psychotherapy

A short, epigrammatic Foucaultian genealogy (Foucault 1994) of psychotherapy would describe several historic-political circumstances (modern society, bio-power, bio-politics), concrete sovereign discourses (literature, philosophy/aesthetics, medicine, theology) and established discursive practices (Socratic dialogue, confession, medical interview) as those constitutive conditions which gave rise, at a certain historical time, to psychiatry/psychology (eighteenth to nineteenth century) and psychotherapy (nineteenth to twentieth century). However, while psychiatry and psychology "easily" institutionalized themselves and found their place in universities as sciences, psychotherapy as the practical application of those disciplines—being a relatively new practice—needed to find and define its own social space (Cresswell 2004; Lefebvre 1991). This space didn't exactly pre-exist; it had to be "construed" or "invented" accordingly to the unique nature of psychotherapy, which can be described in the following way.

Psychotherapy is presumably neither just science (theory) nor just an ordinary activity in everyday life (the phenomenological *Lebenswelt*/lifeworld). Thus, its "application-space" cannot be either quite public or just private. It must be something else, a wholly new social space, which is actually created when these two different spheres meet/cross. Exactly in the inter-space, in the marginal *intricate crossing* between pure theory (science, psychology, language) and ordinary life (reality, mundane life, action, speech) psychotherapy found its suitable existing-place and dwelled, offering from now on a new place, wherein both spheres (theory and life) can further interact, cross, encounter and suspend each other, can be confirmed and/or changed. In this new created, liminal, multilayered psychotherapeutic inter-space theory grounds itself, finds application, proves its validity and becomes a living experience, while life—at the same time—becomes subject to observation, reflection, questioning and reorganization. This space is an in-between, transitional, temporary, different, better, ideally real space; real, as long as one resides in it—imaginary, when one goes away from it; a space which exists and at the same time doesn't; a space which therapist and client create anew every time they meet. This space is another space, a heterotopia (*hetero* = other; *topos* = place) (Foucault 1967, 1994, p.xviii; Lefebvre 1972, p.138).[1] By appropriating the liminal space

1 There are doubtless many other ways to symbolize, classify, and describe this other place, such as the *in-between* space (Bhabha 2005, pp.1, 38), *third Space* (Bhabha 2005, pp.36–39; Soja 1996) and *non-places* (Auge 2009). However, in this article I'll focus on Foucault's *heterotopias*, since these other concepts have come after heterotopia and are influenced by it, with a lot of similarities and analogies, despite their differences.

between theory and life, psychotherapy becomes itself a liminal space—a heterotopia.

Heterotopias are "real places—places that do exist and that are formed in the very founding of society—which are something like counter-sites, a kind of effectively enacted utopia in which the real sites, all the other real sites that can be found within the culture, are simultaneously represented, contested, and inverted. Places of this kind are outside of all places, even though it may be possible to indicate their location in reality" (Foucault 1967). They have the property "to suspect, neutralize, or invert the set of relations" that they happen "to designate, mirror, or reflect" (Foucault 1967). Furthermore, they have a double functionality: they are producers of knowledge as well as sites of resistance. "By juxtaposing and combining many spaces in one site, heterotopias problematize received knowledge by destabilizing the ground on which knowledge is built" (Topinka 2010, p.54).

Conceptualizing psychotherapy as a heterotopia, it wouldn't be an exaggeration to assume further that its therapeutic value lies exactly and essentially in its heterotopic quality: psychotherapy functions really and truly therapeutically, because it is, in principio, a heterotopia.

Only as such does psychotherapy have the power or possibility to question, transcend, and change old structures and generate new ones: by transforming in its own space already existing facts and conditions (architectural place, conventional discourses, concrete practices…), psychotherapy establishes/generates within the given socio-political status quo (fixed, predominant, one-dimensional rules, behaviors, emotions…), an-other space, a new socially acceptable safe space wherein this status quo can be questioned, reversed, criticized, so that (personal) transformation/change can occur.

In other words, by interrupting ordinary life (the repetition of the same/given), psychotherapy creates a necessary interstitial distance (Critchley 2007, p.114; Topinka 2010, p.66), that is, a space wherein usual ordinary life can be…suspended, contested, and inverted. And so can our suffering (everything that happens to us) lead us, through reflection, questioning, and reconsideration, to increased wisdom: to new meaning, to a real and more truthful knowledge about ourselves.

However, describing psychotherapy as heterotopia doesn't necessarily mean that psychotherapy always remains one. As we know, psychotherapy has by now institutionalized/instrumentalized itself and become (often) another normalizing mechanism. In this case psychotherapy seems to be rather satisfied with a superficial version of itself, even at the expense that it betrays its fundamental essence and becomes just a normalizing practice, a technocratic managerial contact, an administrative operation, some advice-providing agency, that is, a "technology of self" (Foucault 1988; Rose 2000). Only if psychotherapy undertakes the demanding status of a heterotopia does it remain a liberating social activity, an emancipating practice, aesthetics of existence (Dreyfus and Rabinow 1987, p.267).

FOT as heterotopia

> The world is large, but in us
> it is as deep as the sea
>
> *(R.M. Rilke)*[2]

What is valid for psychotherapy in general applies especially to FOT. FOT is (could be) an experiential, socio-political heterotopia. Heterotopia—par excellence. FOT is, accordingly, neither theory nor ordinary life; neither entirely social, nor just personal. It's both and at the same times something else, different, more: a carried forward possibility of their *crossing*, their fusion, their *intricate interaction.*

Furthermore, by inserting a rupture/pause within the same (given social order, old structures, repetitive convention), FOT as heterotopia creates a new space, an-other space and by becoming itself this other place allows the other (new structures, the new, fresh, personal) to emerge (Gendlin 2012). But "otherness" in FOT is not just an "external" quality, only a socio-political condition/potentiality that FOT, as psychotherapy, actualizes (or not). Otherness resides inside FOT, in the core of its philosophy, theory and practice. It's called *implicit intricacy*. FOT is, thus, not just an "external" heterotopia. Moreover, in FOT the therapeutic process/interaction/crossing, by

2 From opening quote of the essay "Intimate Immensity" (in Bachelard 1994, p.181).

creating an (inner) experiential distance (Ikemi 2000), points to the (possible) existence of an "internal" heterotopia characterized by the implicate order of intricacy.

As known, FOT puts in the center of its therapeutic efficacy the *carrying forward* or the *reconstitution* of the relationship with *experiencing*, that is, the interaction of feeling with symbols (words, events...), in cases when this interaction has been either distorted, interrupted or even blocked from the very beginning (Depestele 2000, p.78; Gendlin 1962, pp.242–244, 1964, p.22; Purton 2004, pp.56, 96, 125, 177), so that (new) meaning/understanding can occur. But experiencing doesn't have only this reflective dimension. Experiencing is a complex, dynamic concept including simultaneously two distinctive levels: the explicit, linguistic, cognitive, reflective level with a symbolized corporeal materiality *and* the implicit, pre-conceptual, pre-reflective feeling level with an immaterial situational corporeality. Experiencing is, thus, always an interaction, a double process, that is, unseparated multiplicity *and* distinctive singularity (Gendlin 1997a, p.16), implicit meaning *and* symbolization, experience *and* language, immediacy *and* passage, immanence *and* transcendence.

Although both levels of experiencing are important and interconnected, the "implicit" is the most significant level for FOT. In a broader sense, the term "implicit" points to the intricacy of life; it refers to the immediacy of our being, the primordial wholeness, the *pure experience* (Davis, Schroeder and Wirth 2011; Nishida 2001), the potential of our existence, which can never be entirely actualized, that is, transformed by symbols, because it is always more than its *explication*. Furthermore, the implicit is present although absent; incomplete, yet meaningful; mute, yet with sentient voice; intricate, yet potentially precise. It inhabits us; inscribes itself in our bodies, leaves traces behind as *felt senses*, that is, "incarnate meanings, materialized significations" (Castoriadis 1984, p.10). It is body and language together, undivided; our pre-conceptual, pre-social, quasi pre-linguistic side; our not-yet manifested, explicated, actualized potentialities, which *can* carry our life *forward*. To put it another way, the implicit is a dimension of our other/whole side, of our intricacy—a dimension of an "internal" otherness/heterotopia, of an "internal" *(third) space*, of an intermediate area of experiencing

(Winnicott 1951, p.230). Therein resides our potency and freedom (Agamben 2000); the potential of our existence, that is, the intricacy of our being and life, which has the power to carry forward the fixed conceptual, social, linguistic norms and give birth to/generate new concepts, behavior, words, society.

FOT, based on its theoretical/philosophical background, constitutes, accordingly, in its clinical practice an alternative place wherein the experiential occurrence of the implicit intricacy as the other is possible. That means, FOT creates the most adequate environment to meet this other, accept it, symbolize and understand it, and (eventually) be healed by it, exactly because it is something else, new, different, personal: that is, the implicit/intricate side of life; our not-yet symbolized possibilities; our very own meanings/ethics/ truth (Agamben 2007, p.10). It offers therefore a necessary frame to experience this implicit intricacy, this "internal" heterotopia, this otherness and start living through it—otherness in every possible form or expression: other space, speech, time, body, self/identity.

Within the FOT therapeutic space an-other speech (not the language of the others) is possible; a speech in and beyond language, experiential, unique, personal, private, metaphorical, perhaps even unintelligible outside the therapeutic setting, wired, crazy, with voids, pauses, silences, close to the immediate experiencing: a heterology or—otherwise—a micro-hermeneutics of words/ sentences/everyday life. In addition, a heterochrony arises gradually. Time (chronos) becomes Kairos (experienced or experiential time) and as such it transcends the usual time categories and limitations and includes everything: memories, events, passed traces, present references, hopes, dreams, wishes. FOT time is never stable; it never repeats itself exactly the same way. In every meeting, in every FOT session time has its own experiential duration which either expands or shrinks. Past invades present, present invades future and vice versa.

The body that inhabits such a space can neither be the pure biological body, the utopian body (Foucault 2006), nor the unconscious body of psychoanalysis (Dolto 1992; McDougal 1981). It's rather a "heterotopic body," that is, a body which confirms, transcends, questions, suspends, negates, and expands its own biological limits. It's the other body within the body, "inner space," "inner" world, real enacted utopia, materialized possibility, architectonics of sense (Nancy 2008). This is the body as potentialities that actualizes/materializes itself beyond its sociopolitical construction, its gendered performative normativity (Butler 2006), its textuality/signification (political, linguistic, social, historical, behavioral, psychological...). The heterotopic body, as the situational, phenomenological Leib (Waldenfels 2000), is neither signifying machine, nor signified essence, but, most likely, the zero point of meaning, which—being that—makes every meaning possible; *pure existence*, or "the plastic material of spacing...where existence takes place" (Nancy 2008, p.63); an *event* that comes to presence in the heterotopic space of FOT. It is the body which carries implicitly all life-intricacy, is life-intricacy (Gendlin 1992).

Finally, "therapist" and "client" could be described, within this therapeutic context, as "heterotopic" or *hybrid* identities (Bhabha 2005), that is, liminal, open, fluid, processual, changeable, provisional, interactive, inter-subjective positions.

Conclusion

The therapeutic in FOT lies exactly in its heterotopic quality (nature, power, possibility). This quality should be understood as a dialectical relationship, a parallel carrying-forward process: while FOT as a social practice becomes an "external" heterotopia, as a clinical practice it facilitates us to discover our "internal" heterotopia, our internal third space, our implicit intricacy. This is the intricacy as the potential of our existence: possibility, ethics, contingency, freedom.

References

Agamben, G. (2007) *Infancy and History: On the Destruction of Experience.* London: Verso.
Auge, M (2009) *Non-Places: Introduction to an Anthropology of Supermodernity.* London: Verso.
Bachelard, G. (1994) *Poetics of Space.* Boston, MA: Beacon Press.
Bhabha, H.K. (2005) *The Location of Culture.* New York: Routledge.
Buber, M. (2004) *I and Thou.* London: Continuum.
Butler, J. (2006) *Gender Trouble: Feminism and the Subversion of Identity.* New York: Routledge.
Castoriadis, C. (1984) *Crossroads in the Labyrinth.* Cambridge, MA: MIT Press.
Critchley, S. (2007) *Infinitely Demanding: Ethics of Commitment, Politics of Resistance.* London: Verso.
Cresswell, T. (2004) *Place: A Short Introduction.* Malden, MA: Blackwell Publishing.

Davis, B.W., Schroeder, B. and Wirth, J.M. (eds) (2011) *Japanese and Continental Philosophy: Conversations with the Kyoto School.* Bloomington & Indianapolis, IN: Indiana University Press.

Depestele, F. (2000) "Der therapeutischer Raum aus experientieller Sicht." In H-J. Feuerstein, D. Mueller and A. Weiser Cornell (eds) *Focusing im Prozess.* Cologne: GwG-Verlag.

Dolto, F. (1992) *L'image inconsciente du corps.* Paris: Seuil.

Dreyfus H.L. and Rabinow P. (1987) *Michel Foucault. Jenseits von Strukturalismus und Hermeneutik.* Frankfurt: Athenaeum.

Foucault, M. (1967) *Of Other Spaces, Heterotopias.* Available at http://foucault.info/documents/heteroTopia/foucault.heteroTopia.en.html, accessed November 12, 2013.

Foucault, M. (1988) "Technologies of the Self." In L.H. Martin, H. Gutman and P.H. Hutton (eds) *Technologies of the Self.* Amherst: University of Massachusetts Press.

Foucault, M. (1994) *The Order of Things: An Archaeology of the Human Sciences.* New York: Vintage Books.

Foucault, M. (2006) "Utopian Body." In A.C. Jones (ed.) *Sensorium: Embodied Experience, Technology, and Contemporary Art.* Cambridge, MA: MIT Press.

Gendlin, E.T. (1961) "Experiencing: A variable in the process of therapeutic change." *American Journal of Psychotherapy 15*, 2, 233–245.

Gendlin, E.T. (1962) *Experiencing and the Creation of Meaning.* New York: Free Press of Glencoe.

Gendlin, E.T. (1964) "A Theory of Personality Change." In P. Worchel and D. Byrne (eds) *Personality Change.* New York: Wiley.

Gendlin, E.T. (1984) "The client's client: The edge of awareness." In R.L. Levant and J.M. Shlien (eds) *Client-Centered Therapy and the Person-Centered Approach: New Directions in Theory, Research and Practice.* New York: Praeger.

Gendlin, E.T. (1990) "The Small Steps of the Therapy Process: How They Come and How to Help Them Come." In G. Lietaer, J. Rombauts and R. Van Balen (eds) *Client-Centered and Experiential Psychotherapy in the Nineties.* Leuven: Leuven University Press.

Gendlin, E.T. (1992) "The primacy of the body, not the primacy of perception: How the body knows the situation and philosophy." *Man and World 25*, 3–4, 341–353.

Gendlin, E.T. (1996) *Focusing-Oriented Psychotherapy: A Manual of the Experiential Method.* New York: Guilford Press.

Gendlin, E.T. (1997a) "How Philosophy Cannot Appeal to Experience, and How It Can." In D.M. Levin (ed.) *Language beyond Postmodernism: Saying and Thinking in Gendlin's Philosophy.* Evanston, IL: Northwestern University Press.

Gendlin, E.T. (1997b) *Process Model.* New York: Caversham Books.

Gendlin, E.T. (2012) "Process generates structures: Structures alone don't generate process." *The Folio: A Journal for Focusing and Experiential Therapy 23*, 1, 3–13.

Hendricks-Gendlin, M. (2003) *Focusing as a Force for Peace: The Revolutionary Pause.* Available at www.focusing.org/social_issues/hendricks_peace.html, accessed November 12, 2013.

Ikemi, A. (2000) *Presence, Existence and Space: Key Concepts in Focusing-Oriented Psychotherapy (VHS).* Canada: NadaLou Productions.

Kirtner, W.L. and Cartwright, D.S. (1958a) "Success and failure in client-centered therapy as a function of client personality variables." *Journal of Consulting Psychology 22*, 259–264.

Kirtner, W.L. and Cartwright, D.S. (1958b) "Success and failure in client-centered therapy as a function of initial in-therapy behavior." *Journal of Consulting Psychology 22*, 329–333.

Lefebvre, H. (1972) *Die Revolution der Staedte.* Munich: List.

Lefebvre, H. (1991) *The Production of Space.* Oxford: Blackwell.

McDougal, J. (1981) "Corps et metaphore." *Nouvelle revue de psychoanalyse 23*, 57–81.

Nancy, J.L. (2008) *Corpus. Perspectives in Continental Philosophy.* New York: Fordham University Press.

Nishida, K. (2001) *Ueber das Gute. Eine Philosophie der Reinen Erfahrung.* Frankfurt: Insel Verlag.

Purton, C. (2004) *Person-Centred Therapy: The Focusing-Oriented Approach.* London: Palgrave.
Purton, C. (2007) *The Focusing-Oriented Counselling Primer: A Concise, Accessible, Comprehensive Introduction.* Ross-on-Wye: PCCS Books.
Purton, C. (2010) "Introduction to the special issue on Focusing-Oriented Therapy." *The Person-Centered and Experiential Psychotherapies Journal 9,* 2, 89.
Rogers, C.R. (1951) *Client-Centered Therapy.* London: Constable.
Rogers, C.R. (1956) "The necessary and sufficient conditions of therapeutic personality change." *Journal of Consulting and Clinical Psychology 60,* 6, 827–832.
Rose, N. (2000) *Power in Therapy: Techne and Ethos.* Available at www.academyanalyticarts.org/rose2.html, accessed November 12, 2013.
Siegel, D.J. (2010) *The Mindful Therapist.* New York: W.W. Norton.
Soja, E.W. (1996) *Thirdspace: Journeys to Los Angeles and Other Real-and-Imagined Places.* Oxford: Blackwell Publishing.
Topinka, J.R. (2010) "Foucault, Borges, heterotopia: Producing knowledge in other spaces." *Foucault Studies 9,* 9, 54–70.
Waldenfels, B. (2000) *Das leibliche Selbst: Vorlesungen zur Phaenomenologie des Leibes.* Frankfurt: Suhrkamp.
Winnicott, D.W. (1951) "Transitional Objects and Transitional Phenomena." In D.W. Winnicott (1975) *Through Pediatrics to Psycho-Analysis.* London: Hogarth.

CHAPTER 3

Thinking and Practicing FOT in the Twenty-First Century

Challenges, Critiques, and Opportunities

Kevin C. Krycka

In this chapter I explore central questions regarding Focusing-Oriented Psychotherapy (FOT) in contemporary times. As the title suggests, my aim is to sketch out the influence of FOT in the professional psychotherapeutic community and the forces involved in keeping FOT at the margins of contemporary psychotherapy practices. A secondary but no less important aim is to respectfully challenge FOT by marking what I see as our most potent possibilities for a future that is sustaining and engages other theoretical positions and professionals.

To date there has been no systematic study of FOT as an approach to psychotherapy that might help us to understand why this amazing process appears to have little standing in the marketplace of therapeutic practices. Possibly the only published commentary on why Focusing is little understood today comes from Weiser Cornell (2005, pp.253–256). A respected and well-known teacher of Focusing, Weiser Cornell outlines five simple reasons why so many have not yet heard of Focusing: it isn't flashy, it is too general, the original steps are frozen as they were when *Focusing* was first published (Gendlin 1978/2007), it is too radical, and it appears in a person's life somewhat mysteriously, "when needed," not as a "tool" or skill.

Recently Gendlin has encouraged the building of bridges between Focusing and other theories and groups that hold similar humanistic values (Gendlin and Johnson 2004). He refers to all those ideas and practices that hold the person as central to be members of a "Town" (Gendlin 2006). Focusing is but one neighborhood in this town, as are Non-Violent Communication (NVC), relational psychoanalysis, Dynamic Facilitation, and so forth.

However, Focusing continues to "hide out" in the corners of what appear to be fresh and exciting developments instead of being recognized as foundational to many of these same emerging approaches.

Psychotherapeutic zeitgeist: then and now

I suggest that we can "read" FOT against the backdrop of the social and cultural themes of the mid-twentieth century when Gendlin laid out his major philosophical and psychological works. It was a period that saw a fomenting populace getting ready to unleash itself upon an unsuspecting "establishment"—and this included the established psychotherapies. By reading FOT in this way we open up a richer territory for its assessment and critique. It will help us understand how FOT may realize its potential to influence psychotherapy in the future.

The emergence of Gendlin's seminal philosophical works, most notably *Experience and the Creation of Meaning* (Gendlin 1962), occurred within a cultural zeitgeist marked in particular by pragmatism and secular humanism (Tarnas 1991). The doors were opened for an intellectual, spiritual, and sexual revolution that ultimately redefined power, freedom, and ethics. The establishment (or hope) of new societal, political, and academic views that embraced a liberated personhood and the rise of the self-awareness and human potential movements (Elliott and Farber 2010) are deeply part of FOT.

Carl Rogers (1902–1987) is undoubtedly key to understanding FOT and its place in contemporary psychotherapies. Rogers and Gendlin came together at the University of Chicago during a very interesting period. It was without doubt a time of profound change for American psychology and the wider global community that would challenge how we regard equality, fairness, power, and the political, economic, religious, and professional structures maintaining the therapeutic status quo (Tarnas 1991). Of particular importance to understanding Rogers, Gendlin, and FOT is the hard fought struggle for civil and human rights that took hold and flourished while what we know today as Focusing (Gendlin 1968, 1969) and Focusing-Oriented Psychotherapy (Gendlin 1968, 1970, 1996) were being developed.

We see humanistic values throughout FOT; the values of acceptance, congruence, and positive regard that are at the core of Rogers' client-centered (later person-centered) psychotherapy (Rogers 1951, 1959). Rogers, and it is fair to say Gendlin, were deeply concerned about social change. Rogers finally withdrew from his work in the person-centered movement to work for years outside the United States to help generate new thinking about peace building and the building of small-scale egalitarian communities (Elliott and Farber 2010, pp.18–20).

Rogers' core ideas are in part a reaction to the over-controlling approaches to psychotherapy found in psychoanalysis and behaviorism. Gendlin, not surprisingly, infused FOT with a similar spirit of hope and radicalism, helping to establish The Focusing Institute in the early 1980s, based upon minimal procedural rules, the protection of diverse training models, organically emerging applications, and a leadership who value local independent decision-making.

Contributions that FOT makes to the field of psychotherapy: a distinctive practice

I have pared down the many significant contributions to a few representative ones. From here we will explore the challenges and promises in more detail:

1. The felt sense
2. The client's change process
3. The experiential process philosophy

The felt sense

By far the chief contribution FOT makes is bringing the felt sense to the field of psychotherapy. Gendlin describes the felt sense in this passage from *Focusing-Oriented Psychotherapy*, "The felt sense is the wholistic [sic], implicit bodily sense of a complex situation. It includes many factors, some of which have never been separated before. Some of those factors are different emotions" (Gendlin 1996, p.58).

The felt sense is a living touchstone, which we sense in the here and now. It is the feeling we have of what we're saying and experiencing in the present moment, even before we can put it into words. Ann Weiser Cornell defines it similarly: "A felt sense is a fresh, immediate, here-and-now experience that is actually the organism forming its next step in the situation the person is living in" (2013, p.11).

There are two key elements to the felt sense that add something distinctive to psychotherapy practice: intentionally sensing the immediacy of bodily felt experience with its initial lack of accompanying symbols (e.g., words, emotions, gestures, etc.) accompanied by its potential to then *generate* those same symbols (also including concepts and actions).

Described as "the client's client" (Gendlin 1984), the felt sense freshly forms as we direct our attention inward and pause to let it form. In other words, the felt sense only comes into existence when we take a little pause to pay attention to our inner experiencing. It is a deliberative act that entails attention and pausing. Once formed, the felt sense constitutes the client's best inner guide.

Felt senses are not to be confused with somatic experience, mere emotion or thinking. Rather, the felt sense is a multivocal feel we have of this moment prior to symbolization. Emotions, words, gestures, and the like are already "cut"—symbolized—from the more basic level of our ongoing experience of this moment. It is the attention paid to ongoing experiencing and the therapist's support to contact it that constitutes a significant addition to psychotherapy.

In a way, the felt sense is nothing new—human beings have been having felt senses all along. Yet it was Gendlin (1968) who first named it after nearly a decade of research on what makes for successful psychotherapy. It wasn't until Gendlin and his team came along that a clear articulation of how the felt sense functions in therapeutic change entered into the field of psychotherapy.

The client's change process

FOT offers a unique understanding of what facilitates client change. To clearly understand and appreciate this claim it is important to note that it is based upon several tenets embedded in the values of humanistically oriented psychotherapies. First is the notion that people are the best judge of their own lives and should be empowered to gain the confidence needed to make important life decisions. Second, persons are irreducible to the sum of their "parts." Third, humans are creative and can evolve under the right circumstances (Greening 2006). Gendlin further clarifies and expands upon these broad principles in the practice of FOT (1997b) where acceptance, curiosity, and "welcoming" are foundational.

In contrast to other models of therapy that emphasize the expression of feelings or rationally exploring thoughts, FOT works quite differently. FOT practitioners encourage the felt sense to form, rather than any particular emotion, thought, or memory. FOT therapists by and large don't actively pursue intensity of somatic states either. Gendlin explains it this way:

> People change through feelings they *have not consciously felt and expressed before.*
>
> The steps of change and process do not come directly from the recognizable feelings as such.
>
> They come, rather, from an unclear, fuzzy, murky "something there," an odd sort of direct datum of awareness. But most often there is no such datum at first, when people turn their attention inward. Typically one finds the familiar feelings and no indefinable sense. (Gendlin 1984, p.77; emphasis added)

A new bodily sensed datum of experience is found freshly, not as something familiar or "from the past." Change comes from the *unclear.* This insight into what constitutes change in therapy is key to understanding FOT and what it brings to psychotherapy.

The *bodily sensed datum of experience* or felt sense involves a great many aspects of our past, including the social conditions in which we have lived and live currently, our age, gender, sexual identity, the person(s) we are with, etc. and is yet more than these. When I speak of a joy in my life, for instance, the words I choose include the many memories, feelings, thoughts, and ideas about that happiness but are not limited by these.

The FOT practitioner recognizes that the symbols (e.g., words, gestures, concepts, etc.) our clients use to represent their experiences often get in the way of the change they wish to *be*, particularly if they are repetitious emotions and cognitions. When a client uses her finger to point (a symbolizing of something as yet unclear) to that place in her chest that aches when she thinks of a lost loved one, she is using the gesture to literally point to something much broader in her experience than a single feeling or memory.

The experiential process philosophy

Gendlin's great philosophical accomplishment has been to articulate how a process of symbolization accompanying genuine present moment experiencing actually opens up new steps in life. His is an actively lived philosophy.

The primary philosophical home for the FOT approach is phenomenology (Gendlin 1973), which can be defined as the philosophical study of present moment embodied human subjective experience and consciousness. Gendlin's phenomenology includes existential thought, and is highly influenced by the American pragmatist Dewey and pluralist McKeon. This rich foundation underlies FOT and gives intellectual basis to the essential principles of the practice of FOT.

FOT is an outgrowth of Gendlin's mutual interest in philosophy and psychology (Gendlin 1961, 1996, 1997a). His philosophy emphasizes that human beings are not separable from the environment, including the people, places, and situations in which they find themselves. As Gendlin succinctly puts it, all living things are interactions first (Gendlin 2004). Parker states it this way, "Human beings, including you and me, *are* ongoing interaction. We don't exist separately from our environment and then start interacting with it. We *are* interaction between body and environment" (Parker 2007, p.10).

Gendlin has described his philosophy as having a process orientation, which understands human life and meaning making, including the bodily sense we have of our inner world and the extended world, as one ongoing reflexive development. A process approach can be contrasted to procedural approaches found commonly in the marketplace of contemporary psychotherapy theory and research. A procedural approach emphasizes a rational-linear way of understanding consciousness and human development. Gendlin's approach offers two unique facets that distinguish FOT practice.

UNIQUE ASPECTS

FOT requires us to adopt a fairly strange starting position. The practitioner and client must start with being comfortable with not knowing what will elicit change. The therapist has to be accepting of the client's process as valid as it is revealed, to refrain from advice giving, to let go of knowing what should happen. We must be able to dispose ourselves to the client's world as they experience it—even though it may be quite unusual to us, even alarming.

Second, for the FOT practitioner the notion of interaction first is critical because it frees us from having to be a psychological detective. In framing the client's lived world as interaction first, FOT practitioners rarely concentrate on the contents of the client's history, for instance. Without question other therapeutic approaches employ many of these same principles, but it is the FOT philosophical grounding that provides additional rationale for asserting such principles as essential to successful therapy outcomes (Gendlin *et al.* 1968) and how they are of use in areas beyond therapy.

Challenges to FOT's place among other psychotherapies: double-edged conditions

Some of what makes FOT a unique worldwide approach brings with it a set of conditions to which other therapeutic approaches appear exempt. FOT's unique organizational and certification structure encourages pedagogical training diversity and responsiveness to local conditions (needs, economies, political realities, racial, ethnic, and religious conditions). Creating and supporting such worldwide presence has not come without its challenges.

Decentralized

FOT has an organizational and professional training structure unlike most of its counterparts. This is largely due to FOT having embedded in it a social-transformative advocacy for a profoundly heterogeneous, non-hierarchical, non-ideological, and secular approach. This has lead to a prolonged period where FOT has remained at the margins of psychological practice.

Offered to the world marketplace of therapeutic ideas, FOT could be hobbled by its very roots, for example the absence of visible leadership (a president or chairperson at the helm of a non-existent governing organization). Who is the face of the approach? Simply put, there are many faces. But this is a shortcoming only if assessed from a vastly different worldview where theoretical approaches are treated and promoted as a form of commerce.

This situation has changed in the past decade whereby now there are more and more crossings between FOT and other established approaches. Nonetheless, there are many new therapists in training programs that will likely never hear of FOT because their training has come from a homogeneous model that has tended to sideline process approaches.

The difference decentralization makes in a "marketplace" of practices is profound. While The Focusing Institute clearly honors the creation of localized training models and organizations, its foundational identity as an anti-organization has hindered FOT in becoming recognized as important among other more traditionally organized approaches. However, it is double-edged. After all, this dilemma also expresses the deeply held conviction of the *centrality of personhood* over structures, and the *acceptance of all persons as they are* over the tendency to reify and conform what is "normal" to what is conventional.

Diverse FOT training models and mixing with others

Protecting the diversity of training models while simultaneously crossing FOT with various practices such as Somatic Experiencing (SE), NVC, or relational psychoanalysis creates an unintended problem for FOT. The intention to create new bridges to other, like-minded approaches could dilute the FOT method or its values.

To guard against dilution other approaches have developed more centralized training and rigid certification processes, a very unlikely road for FOT. While The Focusing Institute has consistently supported diversity in the training of Focusing professionals and FOTs, this laudable stance may contribute to FOT's lower visibility among other professional organizations and therapeutic approaches. It is possible that FOT is in danger of losing its distinctiveness through cross-fertilization as much as through standardization. Once again, it is worth noting that this is a double-edged situation. At this moment, the movement is toward creating more bridges to other approaches with the hope that FOT will gain recognition and be a continuing force in the field.

The felt sense is universal and is hard to describe

In one important way the felt sense, the core of FOT practice, is ubiquitous to being human and yet it remains elusive and difficult to describe. Talking about something so pervasive in human experience to other professionals or to our clients is not easy. In one sense, the felt sense is always potentially there ready to be touched. In another sense, it is unclear, hidden, fuzzy and without any standard way for describing it to others. Describing the process and its benefits to clients constitutes an ongoing problem for the FOT practitioner. It is odd, isn't it, to describe a process that is by definition occurring without words, with words?

This reality makes it very difficult for FOT to find and hold a place in contemporary theory and practice because, although many might be genuinely interested, it is simply too difficult to grasp the approach without continued experiential practice with a teacher or therapist.

FOT trades in the uncertain

To the FOT practitioner, acknowledging uncertainty renders useful a powerful vulnerability that paradoxically transforms the perceived "weakness" of vulnerability. As with Focusing, FOT developed in an era where certainty and predictability were highly sought and prized. This cultural context offers a primary source of challenge and also the promise for FOT in the twenty-first century.

As a psychological and philosophical practice, FOT encourages and engages us in a life-long curiosity about what is implicitly present yet "not-yet-known." As I've mentioned earlier, this stands in stark contrast to the current psychotherapeutic zeitgeist that prefers methods and approaches driven by theoretical expectations, rather than by subjectively grounded practice. In truth, it may be years, even decades, before the subjectivity of persons is again honored in mainstream psychotherapy. A shift will take time because of the dominating adherence to a mechanical view of life where there is suspicion of any approach that prioritizes the unknown and elusive.

Related to the emphasis on implicit experiencing is the fact that speaking and conceptualizing in a way congruent with the felt sense often produces non-standard language. This is fine for most as long as this odd way of speaking from the felt sense stays in the therapy room. However, FOT theorists writing about therapeutic practice also produces meaningful, but "idiosyncratic" descriptions of their work. This is yet another double-edged sword as the FOT theorist's orientation demands that words "fit" the experience but the conceptual-professional language expected by other schools of psychotherapy and other disciplines leaves FOT writing in the margins at best.

Opportunities for the future

In this part you will notice that several themes mentioned as challenges above appear here as opportunities. Below I first lay out what I see are the foundational promises for FOT from which more specific areas of development may arise.

Foundations

DIVERSITY

In most organized approaches in psychotherapy there is a tendency to codify practices early on so as to protect the original ideas from too much interference and to trademark "the brand," thus securing intellectual property rights. I have mentioned earlier the FOT disinclination to embrace a single authority/leader and its support of new FOT groups that are self-organizing and determining their own training structure as appropriate. This ideal keeps at the fore the person-to-person interaction in a profession otherwise overly constrained by impersonal structures, obsession with regulation, and dehumanizing approaches to mental health care. In this way, FOT remains a standard bearer for the retention and inclusion of the human element in all aspects of health care and the protection of diverse approaches to the theory, research, and delivery of that care.

VALUING

A second promise lies in the valuing of human experience. The philosophy behind FOT maintains that history or culture does not constitute humans. Rather, humans are originally occurring in the present. This means that FOT emphasizes the possibility of change regardless of the psychological issue or whether one conceives of treatment solely as a response to disorder or socio-cultural conditions. The possibility of change is not only a humanistic value, but stems from the existential-phenomenological perspective as outlined by Gendlin (1964). In this manner, FOT profoundly respects the rights of the other in the service of forming a deep understanding of that person's living. This will always remain central to FOT and be the foundation for its promise in the future.

Futures

EVIDENCE AND RESEARCH PRACTICES

The contemporary striving for evidence-based practice and empirically supported treatments, while arguably necessary, has resulted in the myopic push for narrowly defined, mechanical kinds of research protocols.

FOT has the capacity to be an alternative voice, yet, like all practices that hold a different epistemology and philosophical stance, it is challenged to conform to conventional standards. There is a strong possibility in FOT for championing what amounts to a correction to the overwhelming preference for verification through objectivity. Insisting that the co-subjectivity of practitioner and client be part of any evidence for treatment success is increasingly put forward by some researchers (Elliott, Greenburg, and Lietaer 2004; Greenberg and Pinsof 1986). Bringing co-subjectivity into the fore of the verification process of research could place FOT within the center of progressive change in the profession going forward.

As Hendricks (2001) reports, there have already been over 50 complementary studies at the time of her review and there have been many more since. It will be the central role of bodily felt sense awareness that will distinguish FOT researchers from other contemporary research. However, this has yet to fully take root in the general psychotherapy audience, much less the governmental funding agencies that control funding of most innovative research (Krycka 2012).

FIRST-PERSON SCIENCE

Gendlin outlines a proposal for first-person research practices that help articulate the subtle levels of human experiencing (Gendlin and Johnson 2004). He calls for what is essentially a paradigmatic shift from favoring *content* to pursuing knowledge of and about human *processes*. This shift entails finding unique, purposeful ways to give voice to the implicit, sensing self.

LISTENING AS A HUMAN TECHNOLOGY

Our profession is at risk of forgetting the value and importance of listening. It is unfortunately rarely taught in training programs outside the "humanistic" traditions. The FOT practitioner listens in order to hear and understand rather than categorize and circumscribe. Listening in this manner supports the dignity of persons no matter what their situation or problems are, nullifying the trend to homogenize. Having a listening foundation doesn't preclude "listening to diagnose" but it clearly directs diagnostic listening as a further articulation of listening-that-hears. Listening as praxis is thereby less about skills acquisition and more about supporting a way of being that raises the dignity of the persons we treat (Fiumara 1995).

Listening requires embracing dignity, valuing, and caring. Recently, listening is re-emerging within psychotherapy as a powerful force resisting the leveling of human experience to a few, narrowly construed approaches to treatment and research. Listening is a quintessential *human technology*, one that will outlast the treatment manuals we create. Listening is already part of FOT practice, epistemology, and research and should be emphasized in our communications about FOT. Here FOTs excel and should not be shy about claiming this expertise.

Final comments

I conclude this chapter with a question I believe is central for the future of FOT practice and research: why isn't FOT better known? It is critical that we ask whether it is the primary aim of psychotherapeutic practice and research to formulate and then test hypotheses or to be involved in discovery. FOT is a practice that *is* a form of discovery that holds openness, attentiveness, vulnerability, and humility at its core. FOT practitioners make few truth-claims due to the fact that FOT does not embrace the authority of truth-tellers or truth-sellers in the typical sense. FOT stays open to the field of possibilities, of objective and subjective personal truths, instead of forestalling discovery and dialogue with the rubrics of certainty. And in this lies its biggest problem in the marketplace of ideas and practices. Having a preference to refrain from the absolute truth statements seen in evidence-based practices, or from copywriting its training models, FOT presents as a powerful counter-narrative that may simply still be too counter-cultural.

Why isn't FOT better known?

You can see how the FOT approach, grounded as it is in philosophical reasoning and an era of deep societal and personal change, may not find an easy home in the current marketplace of therapeutic ideas and practices. FOT prefers praxis that is relationally savvy and process-oriented. FOT is a challenge to trends in psychotherapy management and research practices that have become entrenched. However, FOT is not averse to forming bridges with these practices. It will never likely be an approach that defines its processes to the exclusion of others, thus encumbering its marketability in the competitive world of psychotherapies.

Let's recall that Gendlin and his colleagues created Focusing and FOT out of concern for understanding human change. Early research provided something radical in the sense that it challenged the predominant paradigms influencing psychotherapy research and practice and offered an entirely original way of conceiving of and speaking about human change (Gendlin 1964). There are many contemporary pioneers in psychotherapy who take Gendlin's work and create new avenues for practice in our field. Weiser Cornell (2013) discusses several current therapeutic approaches informed by Gendlin's work (e.g., somatic, cognitive, empathic, relational, etc.), several which refer directly to Focusing. But by philosophically dwelling on fundamental issues about meaning-making and the processes of experiencing and symbolization of experience, the Focusing approach continues to inspire a whole new generation of thinking about psychotherapy. This is the nexus where FOT can shine.

References

Elliott, R. and Farber, B. (2010) "Carl Rogers: Idealist, Pragmatist, and Psychotherapy Research Pioneer." In L. Castonguay, J. C. Muran, L. Angus, J. Hayes, N. Ladany, and T. Anderson (eds) *Bringing Psychotherapy Research to Life: Understanding Change through the Work of Leading Clinical Researchers.* Washington, DC: American Psychological Association.

Elliott, R., Greenburg, L. and Lietaer, G. (2004) "Research on Experiential Psychotherapies." In M.J. Lambert (ed.) *Bergin & Garfield's Handbook of Psychotherapy and Behavior Change,* 5th edition. New York: Wiley.

Fiumara, G.C. (1995) *The Other Side of Language.* New York: Routledge.

Gendlin, E.T. (1961) "Experiencing: A variable in the process of therapeutic change." *American Journal of Psychotherapy 15,* 233–245.

Gendlin, E.T. (1962) *Experiencing and the Creation of Meaning; A Philosophical and Psychological Approach to the Subjective.* New York: Free Press of Glencoe.

Gendlin, E.T. (1964) "A Theory of Personality Change." In P. Worchel and D. Byrne (eds) *Personality Change.* New York: John Wiley & Sons.

Gendlin, E.T. (1968) "The Experiential Response." In E.F. Hammer (ed.) *Use of Interpretation in Therapy: Technique and Art.* New York: Wiley.

Gendlin, E.T. (1969) "Focusing." *Psychotherapy: Theory, Research & Practice 6,* 1, 4–15.

Gendlin, E.T. (1970) "The Significance of Felt Meaning." In R. Cornier, E. Chinn, and R.H. Lineback (eds) *Encounter: An Introduction to Philosophy.* Glenview, IL: Scott, Foresman.

Gendlin, E.T. (1973) "Experiential Phenomenology." In M. Natanson (ed.) *Phenomenology and the Social Sciences.* Evanston, IL: Northwest University Press.

Gendlin, E.T. (1984) "The Client's Client: The Edge of Awareness." In R.F. Levant and J.M. Shlien (eds) *Client-Centered Therapy and the Person-Centered Approach: New Directions in Theory, Research, and Practice.* Westport, CT: Praeger Publishers/Greenwood Publishing Group.

Gendlin, E.T. (1996) *Focusing Oriented Psychotherapy: A Manual of the Experiential Method.* New York: Guilford Press.

Gendlin, E.T. (1997a) *A Process Model.* Chicago: Focusing Institute.

Gendlin, E.T. (1997b) "The Use of Focusing in Therapy." In J.K. Zeig (ed.) *The Evolution of Psychotherapy: The Third Conference.* Philadelphia: Brunner/Mazel.

Gendlin, E.T. (2004) "Five philosophical talking points to communicate with colleagues who don't yet know focusing." *Staying in Focus 4*, 1, 5–9.

Gendlin, E.T. (2006) "The town and human attention." Paper presented at The Focusing Institute Summer School, Garrison, NY. Available at www.focusing.org/gendlin/docs/gol_2180.html, accessed November 13, 2013.

Gendlin, E.T. (1978/2007) *Focusing*. New York: Bantam Books.

Gendlin, E.T. and Johnson, D.H. (2004) "Proposal for an international group for a first person science." Gendlin online library. Available at www.focusing.org/gendlin/docs/gol_2184.html, accessed November 18, 2013.

Gendlin, E.T., Beebe, J., III, Cassens, J., Klein, M. and Oberlander, M. (1968) "Focusing Ability in Psychotherapy Personality, and Creativity." In J.M. Shlien (ed.) *Research in Psychotherapy, Vol I*. Washington, DC: American Psychological Association.

Greenberg, L.S. and Pinsof, W.M. (eds) (1986) *The Psychotherapeutic Process: A Research Handbook*. New York: Guilford Press.

Greening, T. (2006) "Five basic postulates of humanistic psychology." *Journal of Humanistic Psychology 46*, 239.

Hendricks, M. (2001) "Focusing Oriented/Experiential Psychotherapy Research." In D. Cain and J. Seeman (eds) *Humanistic Psychotherapy: Handbook of Research and Practice*. Washington, DC: American Psychological Association.

Krycka, K.C. (2012) "Incorporating research into your experiential and FOT practice: Midwifing the implicit." *The Folio: A Journal for Focusing and Experiential Therapy 23*, 1.

Parker, R. (2007) "Making peace from the inside." *The Folio: A Journal for Focusing and Experiential Therapy 20*, 1, 36–45.

Rogers, C. (1951) *Client-Centered Therapy: Its Current Practice, Implications and Theory*. London: Constable.

Rogers, C. (1959) "A Theory of Therapy, Personality Relationships as Developed in the Client-Centered Framework." In S. Koch (ed.) *Psychology: A Study of a Science, Vol. 3: Formulations of the Person and the Social Context*. New York: McGraw Hill.

Tarnas, R. (1991) *The Passion of the Western Mind: Understanding the Ideas that Have Shaped Our World View*. New York: Crown Publishers.

Weiser Cornell, A. (2005) *The Radical Acceptance of Everything: Living a Focusing Life*. San Francisco: Calluna Press.

Weiser Cornell, A. (2013) *Focusing in Clinical Practice: The Essence of Change*. New York: W. W. Norton.

PART II

Integrating with Other Orientations

Now that the theoretical and professional context of Focusing-Oriented Therapy has been established, we can move on to consider various integrations of the focusing-oriented approach with other therapeutic traditions and models of practice. Integrations occur when Focusing "experientializes" what other orientations offer so that the moment-to-moment felt sensing of the client and therapist becomes a guide to what happens in each session.

This part opens with Bala Jaison's integration of FOT and Solution Focused Brief Therapy, including her suggestion that the integration needs to be a good fit for the person of the therapist. Following on, Larry Letich and Helene Brenner bring insights from attachment theory to show how these can enrich the experiential work of the focusing-oriented practitioner.

The last two chapters continue to sketch how FOT can be practiced as a radically relational form of psychotherapy. Lynn Preston brings together her years of experience as both a psychoanalytic self-psychologist and focusing-oriented therapist to form Focusing-Oriented Relational Therapy. Preston emphasizes that as therapists we are entrusted with offering our clients a new interaction within which the client can become a new person. The part comes to a close with my own chapter questioning what I experience as a "positive bias" within FOT and how an experiential-existential stance attempts to address this. Again, the shared human predicament between client and therapist lies at the heart of this integration.

CHAPTER 4

Focusing with Solutions

How to Do Brief Therapy Deeply

Bala Jaison

Introduction

The practice of psychotherapy has evolved. There are now so many clinical approaches to working with clients that the list would take up an entire chapter in itself. The main point is that probably all of them work—some of the time—and, depending upon the nature and character of the client, some approaches work better than others.

The importance of the above is the *implication* regarding the phrase "some of the time." Every client is different. Every client responds differently. Every client responds differently to various approaches—even within the course of a single session! How often do we find that, depending upon the day, the mood of the client, the content of the session, we're suddenly shifting gears—because what we did last week isn't working today.

I believe that in order to practice psychotherapy well, we need to first find our own organic "style" and way of working that suits who we are and what we gravitate to naturally, then be ready to adapt to the person(s) sitting before us—sometimes on a moment's notice. This so-called ability to adapt is even more crucial when we've got more than one client in the room: a couple, a whole family. That said, this chapter is about weaving and blending two particular models of psychotherapy, both of which *feel* resonant, *fit* my therapy-style, and therefore I gravitate to naturally: Focusing-Oriented Therapy, the work of Eugene T. Gendlin, and Solution Focused Brief Therapy, the work of Insoo Kim Berg and Steve de Shazer. First, some background on each of these highly effective models:

Focusing-Oriented Therapy

Focusing was developed unexpectedly and organically in the therapy room. Eugene T. Gendlin, PhD, a professor at the University of Chicago in the 1960s was, with his colleagues, conducting a most a most fascinating research project. What they wanted to know was: Why does psychotherapy work for some people and not for others? Does psychotherapy really make a lasting difference in people's lives, or not? And when it does succeed, *why* does it succeed? Is it something the therapist is doing? Is it something the client is doing?

After taping and studying thousands of hours of therapist–patient interactions, Gendlin and his team unexpectedly discovered that they were able to recognize—sometimes within the first few minutes of the session—which clients would have a successful therapy experience—or not. What was it that the successful therapy clients were doing—or doing differently—from those who didn't have a successful therapy experience?

They were *listening inside of themselves, internally* and *naturally* (often without awareness) yet organically/intuitively checking to see if what the therapist was *saying* actually "fit" or "matched" what they were *feeling*. For example, the therapist says: "It sounds like this issue is related to your early interactions with your mother..." The client (automatically) pauses for a moment, *taking in* the therapist's words and responds with, "No, that doesn't feel right...it's more like..." and *self-corrects* with the exact right words or phrases that fit his/her experience, instead of deferring to "authority."

Over time, Gendlin discovered that he could actually teach clients how to better listen to what he termed the *felt sense* or *bodily felt sense* of one's direct experience. First he taught his clients how to do it, then his psychology students, and eventually developed a whole teachable process/model (for people from every walk of life) called *Focusing* (1979/1981), a magnificently simple yet profound process of *listening inside,* with *attention* and *presence* to one's inner experience.

So what exactly is Focusing?

First, in terms of theory, Focusing is based on the premise that everything that we experience, from the moment of birth to the present, is *registered in the body* in a cellular way—whether we consciously remember *it* (an event/occurrence) or not.

This *bodily registered experience* of a situation or issue, past or present, is an organic bodily remembering—a *felt sense*—that might be internally registered as *different* from our current cognitive experience, for example, the mind says: "It's no big deal, forget about it..." and concurrently, a knot forms in the gut screaming, "It's a very big deal...! I can't forget about it...!" Focusing pays attention to what the gut is saying.

In Focusing (speaking of the "gut") we also make a distinction between emotions and the felt sense. An emotion is a very specific feeling: anger, fear, sadness, etc. When we talk about the *felt sense of...* (anger, fear, sadness), Focusing often uses the term, "the more," "the bigger," the holistic sense of the totality of the problem or issue, in other words, "the whole thing!"

Hence, Focusing encourages a gentle, friendly "attitude" that encourages the focuser to "pay attention to" and "keep company with" the organic, holistic felt sense of any experience, (1) because the felt sense can give us information that has *more* to it than just relying on the intellect and cognitive mind alone, and (2) because through *deep listening* to *what the body has to say,* we are able to have a bodily felt *shift* in how we *carry the issue* around (inside)—what focusers often refer to as the *aha!* experience.

Solution Oriented (Brief) Therapy

Due to a number of factors: more limited funds from insurance companies for long-term therapy, people's busy schedules, and lack of time, there has been an ever-growing movement toward more short-term, constructive, solution-based approaches to creating change and movement in psychotherapy, especially in the field of Brief Therapy.

At the same time, for those clinicians who practice longer term experientially based psychotherapy, there is some concern that the Brief Therapy models may be more of a quick fix and less of a cure for long standing and deep psychological issues, that is, not taking the necessary time to explore and delve into the causes, affective states, and recurring or ongoing problems presented by clients.

A wonderful/doable "solution" comes in the form of a *both/and* approach, rather than an *either/or* position. There is choice. There is a way to *make room for both*, by integrating Experiential/Focusing components into the Brief Therapy models, or the reverse, using a Solution Oriented approach in an experiential way. The integration of the two models is both natural and harmonious—in both *process* and *outcome*—and in fact, supports very effectively the ever-increasing trend toward a holistic mind/body approach to psychotherapy.

This chapter is designed as a guide to begin thinking more creatively and constructively about new possibilities for therapeutic change by comparing, contrasting, and showing how Focusing and Solution Oriented Brief Therapy are similar, different, and ultimately complimentary.

(An oxymoron): brief evolution!

The evolution in the field of Brief Therapy over the past 35-plus years has been both considerable and noteworthy, taking slightly different twists and turns over time depending upon the applications and uses of the various modalities, upon the therapeutic orientation of the founder of a particular model, and the context in which he or she was/is practicing.

Jay Haley (1973) and Cloe Madanes (Madanes 1981) developed the now famous method called Strategic Therapy, based in part on prescribing some outrageous paradoxical interventions, including prescribing the problem or symptom, for example, "Every Monday, Wednesday, and Friday plan to be depressed for exactly one half hour each day."

Insoo Kim Berg (Berg and Miller 1992) and Steve de Shazer (1991) developed a compelling and very effective model of therapy called Solution Focused Brief Therapy. While their model has now been adapted worldwide, it was initially tailored, in part, for a variety of disorders, frequently adjusted to emergency situations: the borderline criminal element, alcoholics, welfare recipients, and extremely dysfunctional and/or abusive families. The work has proven to be very effective, in terms of making *immediate change.*

William O'Hanlon (O'Hanlon and Weiner-Davis 1989), a colleague of Berg and de Shazer, added his own particular slant to the model having initially been trained by Carl Rogers (1951, 1961), the founder of client-centered (experiential) therapy. O'Hanlon termed his model Solution Oriented Brief Therapy, which has evolved and transformed into what he now calls Possibility Therapy, continually broadening his focus.

Both Kim Berg and O'Hanlon have had a profound influence on my development as a therapist, and my own evolution in this work. (Note: I now call what I do Solution Oriented Therapy (SOT) integrated with Focusing-Oriented Therapy (FOT).)

To give credit where credit is due, it is important to recognize that behind all Brief Therapy models, including NLP (Neuro Linguistic Programming) is the genius of Milton Erickson, whose work has been suitably called "Uncommon Therapy." He did not found any of these models—he simply *did* them! Everything after Erickson is an adaptation of his natural precocity.

So, in expanding the idea/process of integrating a longer-term experiential approach (FOT) with Brief, shorter-term Solution Oriented Therapy (SOT) the most important word for me in terms of *combinability* is "oriented."

The both/and

Both models are *oriented* in a similar direction, geared toward change and movement in how the client *views* (Solution language) or *carries inside* (Focusing language) the problem or issue.

Both models could accurately be characterized as *wellness work* (verses emphasizing pathology) hence, each model is concerned with (Solution language) what *will be* creative, life-enhancing, and positive for the client. In Focusing parlance we say looking for what *feels like* "fresh air." Focusing looks for *what feels right*; Solution looks for *what works.*

Eugene T. Gendlin, author of *Focusing* (1979/1981), frequently uses the analogy of an elevator. He talks about *bringing one's attention down into the body* (between the throat, chest, stomach, and lower abdomen) and then going *down the elevator* to a particular "floor" (throat, chest, lower abdomen) to where the Focusing experience takes place.

A brief experiential *aha* moment

I had my own major epiphany—*aha* experience—on the very first day of my Brief Therapy training. Every time one of the teachers explained the "why" or "how" of what we were about to learn in the upcoming year I'd keep thinking: *This is exactly like focusing...but on a different level.* Then suddenly, I got a *bodily felt image* of Gendlin's elevator. I imagined riding an elevator in a hotel, and the hallways (of course) on each floor were identical—as was the placement of the rooms. At the very end of the long hall (on each floor) was a floor-to-ceiling window revealing a huge tree. Depending upon the floor, the view of the tree, of course, changed (the fullness of the leaves being on the upper floors and the big brown trunk more visible on the lower floors). And that is when the *aha* came: No matter what floor you were on, you still saw the same tree—just a different perspective. The two models were like that! The perspective was different (depending on "the floor") but each shared the same tree! I knew on that day that I had the *both/and*—I had to integrate/marry the two models.

It was vibrantly clear to me that the two models belonged together, worked together, complemented each other, and, most important, each gave the other what I viewed as *missing pieces.* Hence, my ongoing commitment (for more than 20 years now) to integrate FOT and SOT (with thanks to Glenn Fleish, PhD of California for the perfect acronym) into the SOFT approach: *Solution Oriented Focusing Therapy.* My goal has been nurturing a marriage of the two models into a complementary partnership by:

- First, keeping the integrity of the experiential Focusing model intact, so that clients have a rich inner understanding, remaining in touch with their moment-to-moment experiences and feelings.
- Second (and often simultaneously), streaming questions in a Solution Oriented manner (but in an experiential-style) as a way to help the session progress more quickly, facilitating the change process at *all levels.*

Comparisons/similarities/differences

One of the foundational concepts shared by both the SOT and FOT approaches is that the client has/holds *within* enormous resources, strengths, natural competencies, and life experience that can and should be drawn upon in moving "stuck places" *forward toward change.* Through the use of skillful *listening* on the part of the therapist, and validating what the client already *knows internally,* clients can be taught to value and access their own innate capabilities.

SOT centers around the concept of change: what makes change, breaking the patterns that inhibit change, co-creating with clients new *actions/ action steps* that will support change—different patterns of thinking and consequent behavior. The so-called "steps" in both models are always small, manageable, and built upon progressively, according to the clients' sense of *what works* (Solution approach) or *what feels right* (Focusing approach).

Both models observe and point to what the client is already doing that works: FOT, by "reflecting back" the positive: "It sounds like doing...x...feels really helpful and right" and SOT, by amplifying what the client is already doing that *works,* then building upon concrete action steps: "So from now until the next time we meet, how many times can you agree to do x?"

The significant difference between the Brief and Experiential models is that brief work is primarily interested in change. Focusing also looks for change, but with the desire for *experiential understanding* that is *bodily felt*—the *aha* sense of the *knowing* experience, or "Gestalt" (Perls 1969), as well.

Another significant feature of SOT is around the concept of clearly defining current and future goals and expectations. Much time and care is taken to set out and develop "doable," manageable goals—whether it be for the future, or for this particular session: "What would you like to see happen? When it is happening what will it look like? What will be different for you when this is happening?" The orientation of these questions is always pointing toward creating and building a more positive future: How it *will* be *when* [change takes place]?

Conversely, FOT is more attuned to staying connected to the present moment: What you are experiencing *right now... in the body,* for example, "Can you take a minute to sense what's there for you, right now..." or "See if you can you sense which is the most alive for you, right now." The purpose of this phraseology is to support the client in finding the issue *freshly* and *with aliveness*, as the body carries it *now*—rather than recounting to the therapist how you thought about it yesterday.

Another hallmark of SOT is in finding *exceptions* to the problem: "When was the last time this wasn't happening?" "What were you doing differently, then?" or "What was different, then?" "Given the incredible stress you've been under...I can't help wondering...how you've coped so well up to now?"

Both approaches look for "what's right." FOT calls it *finding fresh air*. SOT finds "the exception to the problem"—what small ray of light, what situation/example/experience can be built upon to create a glimmer of hope and a more positive vision and expectation of the future?

The point of all Experiential models is to help clients *experience, in the moment*, what they are feeling. The emphasis in experiential work is oriented to personal growth and inner change rather than symptom relief—important, but holding second place to what we call *being true to oneself* or having *inner integrity*: helping clients experience *congruency* between what they say and think, in relation to what they feel. In the Experiential models, they *must match*. I call this "think/feel."

Use of language

The specific use of language and phrasing is an essential component in each model, and studying the intricacies of each often feels like being bilingual!

Solution Oriented language is very specific, specifically used, and geared toward change and positive expectation about *how* it *will be when* these new changes occur. There is an emphasis on words like *will*, *when*, *yet*, and *then*: "How *will* it be for you *when* you are less depressed and more positive?" "Although it hasn't happened, *yet*, imagine a time in the future *when* the problem is solved...what you will be doing, *then*..."

SOT, which evolved out of a marriage and family therapy context, includes in its language the presence of others, whether or not they are in the room, and is also future-oriented: "So who will be the first to notice the changes you are making?" "Who else?" or "What will let you know that your wife has noticed these changes?" "What will she be telling you, then, that she is not telling you now?"

FOT takes place in the present with an orientation to what the client is experiencing *inside, right now.* Experiential language therefore, is quite opposite to the Solution model, which is very specific, and geared toward the future, for example, "What exactly will be happening when…?" Conversely, the language of Focusing is oriented to the present: "How does this feel inside of me, *right now*?" For example, a client says: "There is a real sinking feeling for me with this issue."

An Experiential response might be, "Can you just let that sinking feeling know that it's OK for it to be here, right now?" or "Can you tell that sinking feeling that you want to hear more about what it has to say?" The point: time is taken to allow feelings and felt senses to develop more fully. The Solution approach might ask, "So when you're not experiencing this sinking feeling" or "When this sinking feeling is less than it is now, what do you imagine you will be experiencing instead?"

A further interesting point regarding *precision vs. imprecision* of language: the Experiential approach often uses language that is specifically vague, fuzzy, and unclear: "So it's something like…", allowing the client to fill in the exact right word (perhaps anger, sadness, or heaviness). Without interfering or questioning, the therapist simply reflects, for example, "So there's a feeling of sadness…there…" (the word "there" is pointing to the *felt sense*). And the client might respond, "Well yeah, it's something like sadness…" The experiential therapist will stay with "the more"… until the client "gets it" exactly right, in a bodily felt way. Therapist: "So it's *something* like sadness…but that's not quite it…can you just spend some time with that *something-like-sadness* place and see if there is a word or image that exactly *fits* with…what you are *feeling…inside*?"

The value of utilizing vague and fuzzy language is the scope it gives to the client, allowing him/her to search and *internally grope* for the exact-right-fit that invites congruency between thought and feeling. Interestingly, the exactness of language in the Solution model achieves a similar result by *pinning down* what the action steps will be:

"What exact steps will be taken between now and the next session to move toward change?" The experiential approach is less concerned with action steps and more focused on internal realization. FOT and SOT can interface wonderfully, at this juncture.

Dialoguing

Another FOT/SOT integration spot is in the area of *dialoguing*, meaning:

- dialoguing with one's self
- dialoguing interactionally with couples and families
- dialoguing in imagery with "parts" (child-part, critical-part, hurting-part)
- dialoguing with people who don't happen to be in the room, but are either *there* in consciousness—or part of the problem!

Focusing tends to *internalize* the direction of the dialogue, particularly asking practitioners to avoid asking direct questions, and instead, asking the client to *ask him or her self.* For example, let's imagine that the real question in the therapist's mind is: "So what do you want to do about it?" In FOT the question might be phrased, "Can you *ask yourself*...what is *my sense* of what needs to happen, right now...a right next step *that fits for me*?" In another example, the therapist might think to him/her self, "Umm...what is really at the bottom of all this...? What is this pain really connected to...?" However, to remain unobtrusive, keeping the client in contact with the felt sense, the question (articulated as a statement) might be verbalized as: "Maybe you can you ask this *inside place* to sense... 'What is this pain connected to in my life, right now?'" or "Ask yourself...'What is it that makes all this discomfort there?'" Again, patiently waiting... following...while the client gropes for just the right *felt word* or *image* that fits his/her uniquely personal *felt meaning*.

The value in this gentle approach is the sense of empowerment given to the client, along with the implicit message that somehow *they know the next right step*; *they know the way*, and *they know the next right steps along the way*.

The Solution model accomplishes *exactly* the same thing (sometimes more quickly...) by having the client dialogue either directly with the therapist (who is asking very direct questions) or *externalizing* the dialogue with a person who is not there. "So if your husband was here with us now, what do you imagine he might say?" And perhaps the client says, "He would say that I nag him too much." And the therapist says, "Oh...I see...so can you ask him now, how it would make a difference to him if you were nagging him less?" And the clients says, "He says he wouldn't avoid me so much and would be more attentive" (the presenting problem in the first place!). Hence, this dialogue continues in a "circular" fashion until the client arrives (often seemingly magically) to an *aha* place—which happens in both models.

This type of externalized circular questioning can also be used with inner-parts. "So if the insecure part could speak, right now, what would she say she needs from you?" or "What would she say that you could do, that would be helpful to her?"

Which model is more effective?

The argument for whether change needs to happen from the outside in, or the reverse, is a moot debate at best. *It doesn't matter.* Both orientations work. The success of either is entirely dependent upon 1) the natural orientation/training of the therapist, and 2) the natural orientation/inclination of the client (couple or family) and what they respond to best in therapy. If the outer condition changes, something inside will most certainly change, as well. Conversely, if the inner viewing of the issue changes, consequent outer changes will occur. Therefore, rather than promoting any particular theory of change, my own inclination is to work in whatever way works best in the moment with a particular client and his/her natural affinities and proclivities.

The process

The Focusing process inclines toward following the client's *process*, in whatever direction that process happens to go. While the Brief/Solution orientations respect the client's process, the therapist takes greater responsibility for keeping the sessions "on track" through *directionality* in the type of questions asked, ever aware of the client's *stated goals*—whether it be for this session only, or for the whole course of therapy in general.

The Focusing orientation allows clients to direct the theme and structure of the session, encouraging more autonomy regarding the direction the session will take, and whatever the client *feels-to-do* with the therapy hour.

The up-side of this approach is in the philosophy that stands behind it: clients, if respected and gently coaxed by the professional, will find their *own right way*. The down-side: if the work/session is not progressing, change is not happening, the dialogue between the therapist and client is stuck in the same old territory, the clinician needs to step in and *do something different*, offering some skilled direction to move the process forward.

What keeps both models on track is that they are based on firm philosophical foundations of respect: Valuing, acknowledging and believing that the client has within a wealth of inner resources, experience and competencies. Hence, in theory, both models are somewhat client-centered.

The biggest gap between the two models, and the most interesting to try to interface is in the area of affect:

- The Experiential/Focusing approach takes the time for *processing* and *felt experiencing*.
- The Solution approach sometimes bypasses affect and keeps the client focused on the *action steps* necessary to reach the desired goals.

Note: Paradoxically, the two models can be particularly complementary in this area.

This seeming dichotomy might be best understood if we think in terms of parallel universes or parallel planes (think hotel floors!) The Solution work tends to be cognitive and imaginative, using the mind to *see* new possibilities. Similarly—or in parallel—the Focusing approach is specifically attentive to how one *feels* about *all that*. Therefore, we might say that we can ask the same questions, but on a "different floor."

Being bilingual

Solution: What do you *imagine* you will be *doing* when it's all OK?

Focusing: Try to *sense* what it will *feel like* when it's all OK...

Solution: When was the *last time* you were successful at handling that issue?

Focusing: Maybe *sense* how it *felt* when you were successful at handling that issue...

Solution: What were you *doing differently* then?

Focusing: See if you can *sense* what it *felt like* when you were doing it differently...

Solution: What is it like when the problem is *not happening...*?

Focusing: Take some time to *sense* how *you feel* when the problem isn't happening...

Note: Focusing always includes the bodily felt component.

Which model to use when?

There is no right or only way. It's a therapeutic hunch based on the practitioner's intuition in-the-moment. Sometimes clients are *talking about* the issue, but not really *experiencing* what they're talking about. Here may be the juncture to *stop, slow down,* and take the time to: *be with, process, pay attention to, sit with,* and not immediately try to *fix the problem.* Something fresh and new may need to come from the *deeper inside place* in the client.

Conversely, if the client is experiencing the *same-old, same-old* that you've been over many times before, a question phrased in Solution language can be very useful for pattern interruption: "How will this look...feel...be...when it is right, and no longer a problem?"

Finally, the client is also the expert in knowing which direction to take. I have experienced clients actually asking for what they need from both sides. Using solution-type questions (at the wrong moment) a client might say, "I'm not ready to find a solution, yet. I just want to explore this more..." Alternatively, offering an experiential time-to-be-with moment, the client says, "You know what? I'm sick to death of this, I don't really care what it's about anymore, I just need a solution."

Helpful tips for the practitioner

Over time, the goal is to become fluid/fluent in both languages so that the bilingual (or multilingual if you are using other models as well) becomes seamless. Next is trusting your own therapeutic style: how you speak; how you naturally connect with each of your clients. Some clients are more naturally cognitive/cerebral, and experiential work/language needs to be introduced slowly and over time—lest they be "turned off" or worse, think that you are weird! Others are more naturally experiential, and take to processing easily; then Solution Oriented language, phrased in an experiential way, is highly effective allowing time for processing and experiencing, yet done in a streamlined way that keeps the session on track.

- *The ultimate guide:* Flexibility, adaptability, and deeply trusting the resources of the client. Either way, each model honors the process of *taking small steps.*
- *The beauty of Focusing:* Gentleness, respectfulness, and explicit teaching of an *attitude* towards *self* that permits and allows, in a free and safe space, whatever wants to unfold, honoring the wisdom of the felt sense and working actively with various parts toward integration into the whole.
- *The beauty of the Solution Oriented model:* Respectfulness, positive, non-problem-focused orientation, and skillful use of language allowing clients to access, in a brief and time-efficient way, what they *do want* (rather than what they don't want).

The integration of the two allows for the gentle process of Focusing with a directional intention, and the sense-of-hopefulness in finding workable and manageable solutions to seemingly impossible situations.

The purpose of this integrative or SOFT approach is in *making room for both*!

References

Berg, I. and Miller, S. (1992) *Working with the Problem Drinker: A Solution Focused Approach.* New York: W.W. Norton.
de Shazer, S. (1991) *Putting Difference to Work.* New York: W.W. Norton.
Gendlin, E.T. (1979/1981) *Focusing,* 2nd edition. New York: Bantam Books.
Haley, J. (1973) *Uncommon Therapy.* New York: Norton.
Madanes, C. (1981) *Strategic Family Therapy.* San Francisco, CA: Jossey Bass.
O'Hanlon, W.H. and Weiner-Davis, M. (1989) *In Search of Solutions: A New Direction in Psychotherapy.* New York: W.W. Norton.
Perls, F.S. (1969) *Gestalt Therapy Verbatim.* Lafayette, CA: Real People Press.
Rogers, C.R. (1951) *Client-Centered Therapy.* Boston, MA: Houghton Mifflin.
Rogers, C.R. (1961) *On Becoming a Person.* Boston, MA: Houghton Mifflin.

CHAPTER 5

Applying Attachment Theory and Interventions to Focusing Therapy

Larry Letich and Helene Brenner

Gendlin has conceptualized psychopathology as "stopped process," and has written that, "According to my theory a 'pathological content' is nothing but the lack of a certain further experiencing. … When the missing further experiencing happens, I call it 'carrying forward'" (Gendlin 1996, p.38). This leaves many questions unanswered. What causes "stopped process"? Is it necessary and sufficient for the therapist to invite and encourage the client to access and express her direct inner experience, and to facilitate the unfolding of the client's own inner process and the subsequent "felt shifts" that emerge from it? What about those clients who simply can't manage this yet, or who won't? Does the process of following a felt sense through to resolution and the implied step forward automatically lead to a sustained social-emotional-behavioral change? Or do lifelong patterns of affect and behavior frequently need something more?

This chapter will attempt to bring the insights of attachment theory to Focusing-Oriented Therapy, showing how the profound insights into human emotions, behavior, and psychopathology engendered by attachment theory can inform and enrich the experiential process work of the focusing-oriented therapist. It will also attempt to show how the intrapsychic resolution facilitated by Focusing can be enhanced, and indeed, may at times need to be enhanced, by an interaction with the therapist that explicitly uses the therapist–client relationship to repair early attachment injuries. In the process, it will attempt to describe a working model of an explicitly attachment-oriented and Focusing-Oriented Therapy, melding two important contemporary experiential modalities.

The development of attachment theory

Attachment theory is the brainchild of John Bowlby (1902–1990), a British psychoanalyst who began his career working with delinquent children at a residential center and then the London Child Guidance Center. It's hard for us to imagine now, but the prevailing developmental theories of that era propounded that a baby's attachment to its mother was nothing more than a positive association to the source of food, and paid little attention to the quality and nature of parent–child interactions (Bretherton 1991). Hospitals of the time limited visiting hours with hospitalized children (who were frequently in the hospital for weeks) to one-to-two hours per week—or even no visitation whatsoever—with the fewest visitation hours often for children under three (Munro-Davies 1949).

By the early 1940s Bowlby was already convinced that major disruptions in mother–child interactions were precursors to later psychopathology. In 1948 Bowlby teamed up with John Robertson to study the effects of mother–child separation in hospitalized children. Their findings, published in 1952, along with a powerful film documentary shot by John Robertson the same year called *A Two-Year-Old Goes to the Hospital*, had a profound impact on the treatment of hospitalized and other institutionalized children (Bretherton 1991).

Bowlby and Robertson identified three phases in a baby's or small child's response to separation from its primary attachment figure: "protest," reacting with anxiety and anger and crying out for her to return, followed by despair and grief, and, eventually, detachment or denial (Robertson and Bowlby 1952). Yet there was no theory yet developed for why any of this would be so.

Bowlby looked beyond psychoanalytic theory to ethology (behavioral biology) and theorized that attachment was a mammalian evolutionary adaptation. In order to survive, mammals evolved the "attachment behavioral system" that caused the young to seek the proximity of their attachment figure at times of need or danger. Concurrently the caregiving behavioral system evolved complementary to the attachment system, since all the cries of a baby would be useless if the mother didn't feel "driven" to respond to them.

In three volumes—*Attachment* (1969), *Separation: Anxiety and Anger* (1973), and *Loss: Sadness and Depression* (1980)—Bowlby described attachment bonds as having four defining features: proximity maintenance (wanting to be physically close to the attachment figure), separation distress, safe haven (retreating to caregiver when sensing danger or feeling anxious), and secure base (exploration of the world knowing that the attachment figure will protect the infant from danger). Bowlby saw play and exploration—the process of growing, learning and discovering the world, and engaging in social interactions—as one of the behavioral systems within the mammalian brain, but one that was predicated on feeling safe and secure.

In his second volume, Bowlby (1973) refined his definition of the set goal of the attachment behavioral system. It was clear to him that as children get past the age of three or so, they aren't always trying to establish physical proximity. Bowlby concluded that the set goal of the attachment behavioral system is to get attachment figures to be accessible and responsive at times of need. As long as the child feels that the caregiver is readily accessible and responsive, he or she feels securely attached.

In the same volume Bowlby added that children develop an "internal working model of social relationships" based on their experiences with their caregivers from earliest childhood onward that guide what they expect from other people and what they think about themselves. This allows the world to become predictable. The child learns to avoid behaviors that don't work to maintain a positive attachment (Bowlby 1973).

Attachment styles

In 1969 Mary Ainsworth, a colleague of Bowlby's, studied a baby's first year of life in 26 different families. This study was the first to document the value of what we would call today "attuned parenting." Near the end of the project she developed a laboratory experiment, called the Strange Situation Protocol, to measure attachment and exploratory behaviors, where the now one-year-old babies came in with their mothers to a playroom and then were left for three minutes, first with a strange woman, and then alone. What Ainsworth found were three distinct responses when the mothers returned: one was that the baby cried upon seeing its mother, sought contact and was easily soothed; the second was the baby sought contact, but seemed especially angry at the mother and had a difficult time being soothed; and the third were babies who acted indifferent to the mother's return. Ainsworth called these attachment behaviors "secure," "anxious-ambivalent," and "avoidant" attachment. Analysis of the data showed that the babies in the latter two categories had less attuned and pleasurable relationships with their mothers at home (Ainsworth *et al.* 1978).

Later, Mary Main and Judith Solomon (1986) identified a fourth pattern: "disorganized" behavior that seemed erratic and odd, a result of having a mother who was experienced by the baby as unsafe. More important, in 1984 Main began asking mothers about their own attachment histories, developing what is now called the Adult Attachment Interview. Her research led to slightly different names for attachment styles that nonetheless correspond to that of Ainsworth's babies: "Autonomous" (corresponding to "secure"), "Preoccupied" (corresponding to "anxious"), "Dismissing" (corresponding to "avoidant"), and "Unresolved/Disorganized."

What is most remarkable is that numerous studies have shown that the Adult Attachment Interview predicts, with as high as 80 percent reliability, the attachment style of the woman's child (van Ijzendoorn 1995). In addition, Main's research showed that people who had had traumatic childhoods but who for some reason were able to talk coherently about it—who had somehow made sense of it so that they could "share their story" in a coherent way—were "earned-secure," and their children were just as secure as those whose mothers had a secure childhood (Main and Goldwyn 1984).

Attachment as emotion regulation

Why, exactly, do babies and children need attuned, responsive, and loving interactions in order to feel secure? Why does a baby need human connection almost as much as it needs food? Over the past 25 years, research in the fields of developmental psychology and neuroscience has shown that babies' brains cannot develop alone, nor can they regulate the storm of sensations and emotions that swirl through them without the help of at least one responsive and consistent person with whom they feel connected (Schore 1994). Babies and their caregivers are engaged in a dance of "affect regulation" that is the basic building block of the self. The holding and soothing responses to a baby's cries are necessary for the infants' healthy neural development. So are the little games adults play with babies—blowing into their belly buttons, smiling in exaggerated ways, moving their faces close and then far apart—which are all games of attunement, in which the caregiver responds appropriately moment-to-moment to the baby's reactions and expressions—moving away, for example, when the baby breaks contact by looking away, signaling that he feels overstimulated, then moving towards him again when the baby turns his head and looks expectantly forward, signaling "I'm ready to play again!" (Siegel 1999; Stern 1985; Tronick 1989).

This "dyadic regulation of emotion" has been deemed the most essential element of attachment (Sroufe 1995). It is this synchronization of affect states, this constant adjustment between hyper-arousal and hypo-arousal, this endlessly repeated cycle of disruption followed by repair, facilitated by right-brain-to-right-brain communication of facial expressions, nonverbal sounds and body language, that forms the basis for affect regulation and all relationships. It is in each case a dyadic interaction—this is not a baby addressing a committee. It is what Daniel Siegel (1999) calls "contingent communication"—the caregiver's behavior is in response to the baby's action, which in turn will now affect the baby's state of being and next action, calling for a new response. It is in the process of being able to affect caregivers in this way that a baby gets to experience its existence and value (Schore 1994; Siegel 1999; Sroufe 1995; Stern 1985; Tronick 1989).

The process of emotion regulation through contingent communication continues throughout childhood and adolescence (Schore 1994; Siegel 1999). Corollary to attachment theory, a theory of the development of psychopathology has emerged, in which disruptions to attachment bonds in childhood, whether through absence, neglect, withdrawal of love, or abuse, when not followed by sufficient repair, are experienced as literal threats to the organism's survival. These experiences leave a lasting effect on the autonomic nervous system and limbic system of the brain, and are encoded as both explicit and implicit procedural memories—memories which cannot be consciously remembered. These memories contribute both to the formation of an internal working model of the self that may be maladaptive as an adult and to a hyperreactivity to events that are emotionally resonant to the attachment injuries of the past (Schore 1994, 2003a, 2003b; Siegel 1999). In addition, lack of adequate soothing and nurturing in childhood has been theorized to leave the autonomic nervous system less equipped to handle the emotional demands of life (Porges 2011).

Models of attachment-oriented therapy

Despite all the research into attachment theory, a specifically attachment-oriented therapy was slow in coming. Meta-analyses of decades of research had already showed that the most powerful factor determining therapeutic success was a positive client–therapist relationship (Wampold 1997, 2000, 2001). But how could therapists be more effective in healing primal attachment wounds, beyond being the warm, attentive, and non-judgmental professionals that training already taught them to be?

The first therapy modality that explicitly employed attachment theory in its formulation was Emotion-Focused Couples Therapy (EFT). Beginning in the mid-1980s, Susan Johnson, a couples therapist and research psychologist at the University of Ottawa, overturned prevailing psychological theories of marriage with her theory that marriages were full-fledged attachment bonds, and the emotions and behavioral patterns evidenced in her office by distressed couples—protest, withdrawal, anxiety, panic, despair, and detachment—were the emotions activated when attachment bonds are lost or threatened.

> Ways of regulating primary attachment emotions are finite, and individual differences in emotional regulation and expression are predictable. In secure relationships the connection to the partner

> is used as a form of comfort and creates a sense of emotional homeostasis. In insecure relationships there are only limited ways of coping with a negative response to the questions, "Are you there for me?" "Will you respond when I need you?" "Can I depend on you?" "Do you value me and the connection with me?" (Johnson 2009, p.264)

EFT brings together structural-systems theory, client-centered experiential theory, and attachment theory to design a therapy that restructures relationships that are caught in patterns that prevent positive attachment signals being sent and received and repairs attachment wounds that prevent such restructuring. EFT categorically rejects the Western notion of "mature" adults being autonomous and without attachment needs in favor of Bowlby's (1988, p.62) view that "[a]ll of us, from the cradle to the grave, are happiest when life is organized as a series of excursions, long or short, from the secure base provided by our attachment figure(s)."

The first individual therapy modality that includes attachment theory centrally in its formulation is Accelerated Experiential Dynamic Psychotherapy (AEDP), developed by Diana Fosha (2000). Like Focusing-Oriented Therapy, AEDP is an experiential therapy that relies on the tracking of the moment-to-moment experience of the client, and that believes that the client's own process in the therapy room contains the seeds for a transformation in their state of being. Central to the theory behind AEDP is the "dyadic regulation of affect," the way in which an attuned therapist can mimic the emotional attunement that the client had not received adequately as a child.

One of the major innovations of AEDP is that it explicitly elicits reflection upon the feelings engendered by the therapist–client interaction. We have come a long way from the tabula rasa of the classic psychoanalyst. Virtually every therapist in practice today, at least in North America, is "Rogerian" in the sense that he or she seeks to be warm, empathic, reflective and non-judgmental. Implicit in this stance is that we strive to be unobtrusive so that our clients feel safe to explore their own inner processes and conflicts.

But, from an attachment perspective, our warmth, empathy, and unconditional acceptance are only half the equation. The other half is how the client, with her internal working model of relationships, processes our empathic presence, and how she expresses that reaction in session. In AEDP, the unit of experiential intervention is not the therapist's therapeutic response to the client, but an interaction: the therapist's response followed by the eliciting of how the client experienced what the therapist has said, and the therapist's subsequent contingent reaction.

This particular insight is one we've particularly adapted to our focusing-oriented practice. In her seventh session, "Cindy," a withdrawn woman in her early thirties, shared memories from her childhood of her mother getting angry at her and then not speaking to her for days. She related this in a sad quiet tone, while the therapist, hearing this, felt his own heart breaking for her.

T: It makes me so sad to hear that your mother did that to you. What a terribly painful thing for a child to have to go through! [Short pause] What is it like for you to hear me say that it makes me sad you went through that?

C: I don't know what you mean.

T: [Slowly] What's it like for you to hear me say...how sad it makes me...that your mother did that to you...cut you off like that... did something so painful?

C: [A long pause, then the client looked directly at the therapist with a deeply pained expression] Honestly, the truth is, I hope you're not upset with me if I say this, I mean it's not you, but I can't really believe you feel that way... 'Cause I know it doesn't make sense, I mean I know it in my head, but, I still feel, I still, like, I must have deserved it, you know? [Her voice cracked, and she covered her face, ashamed]

T: No you didn't deserve that, Cindy, you didn't. What's it like for you to hear that from me right now?

C: It's hard for me to believe...

This led to more tears, more painful memories and the conclusions she drew from them, more regulating responses from the therapist, and eventually:

C: Wow, I really believed that, I really believed what a crummy, stupid little kid, you knew this would happen, or you should have known, you can do better, you can do better, yeah, you can always...do...a little...better. I really really really believed it.

T: What's it like for you not to believe it anymore?

C: OH MY GOD! It's really...different!

This is a moment of dyadic regulation, where toxic shame and an internal working model of "I'm a person who deserves to be totally shut out by people I love if I do anything wrong" begins to be undone.

AEDP, however, does not have a model for using intrapsychic processes for healing, as FOT does. In the deep emotional work we do, there is a complex interplay between the eliciting of the implicit (i.e., the calling forth of the felt sense of "all that"); the fostering of the self-soothing and self-regulating aspects of the Inner Relationship Focusing developed by Ann Weiser Cornell; and the use of the dyadic-experiential "healing moment" to restructure internal working models and solidify felt shifts into deeply felt "markers" that can serve as reference points to create behavior changes.

Applying an attachment-oriented framework to Focusing-Oriented Therapy

Many clients come to therapy in a state of pain, feeling essentially that something must be "wrong" with them to be in the situation they're in and feeling the way they do (Brenner and Letich 2003). We have found that an attachment orientation involves extra affirmation of the "carrying forward" implicit in a client from the very first session, explicitly affirming any sign of the client's courage and competence, if only for coming to therapy, while being careful not to discount their pain and self-doubt. The therapist must enter into the client's own world as he or she sees and constructs it (Kohut 1977, 1981). The therapist must also, from the start, "take delight" in the client (Fosha 2003). The client's own purpose and goals for therapy must be elicited and welcomed, and their story of how and why they arrived in therapy needs to be heard. At the same time, some attachment history can be gleaned unobtrusively if it is not spontaneously shared, For example, the therapist can embed questions such as, "Did anybody really know you as a child?" "Who did you turn to when you needed help?" "What happened when you got into trouble?" Of course, divorce, separation from a parent for a long time, traumatic events, high-conflict marriages between parents, and high-conflict relationships or lack of engagement and/or contact with either or both parents and stepparents are factors that should be noted along with the ages they occurred.

Tuning into both the client's verbal and nonverbal presentation, the therapist can begin to hypothesize about internal working models of self and others. For example, children of alcoholic parents commonly have an internal working model of others as "I have to control my world and be in charge every minute. If I'm not, everything will fall apart and catastrophe will strike—no one else will prevent it," and of self as "I am a person who no one wants to take care of. I don't really count to anyone except for what I can do for them."

It strikes us that because most therapy clients are naturally inclined to view therapy as a relationship and a collaboration, there can frequently be something slightly off-putting, and perhaps even a little rejecting, in even the gentlest directive to pause, self-reflect, and direct attention inward, especially if what we're asking them to "be with" is at all unpleasant. So we frequently find ourselves using the word "let's," as in, "let's stay with that for a moment..." The stance we adopt is "you and I will both go "meet" what has been unrecognized or avoided within." In Fosha's words, it is "unbearable aloneness" (Fosha 2003) to deal with an overwhelming unpleasant stimulus without the help of a stronger, older, and wiser "other" to help regulate and process it that causes dysregulation to get frozen in place. Combining attachment therapy and FOT, we believe it is the ability to share what could not be shared with someone who is attentive, responsive, and engaged, and to be able to fully *experience* that sharing, that frees it and allows it to carry forward.

Once tuned into "attachment language," it becomes clear how many of the felt senses that are touched upon by therapy clients are related to attachment issues. "It feels dark," "lost," "lonely," "like it's afraid of what will happen if it came out" are common themes. The situation-specific images and memories are idiosyncratic to the person, but the basic feelings are shared across humanity. We believe it's important for FOT therapists to pick up on them and understand them. For example, when a man who came to therapy recently for anxiety got in touch with "an old feeling" that "if I ever get angry, it will destroy everything," he was not talking about causing buildings to fall to the ground. As FOT therapists, we honor unfolding meanings and are aware of the danger of overlaying a construct on the felt sense. Yet we have found an attachment framework to be valuable in understanding probable core themes and meanings and their possible origins.

Felt senses can even hint at the age of an attachment injury. "J," a very intelligent and talented writer of a high-level government briefing report, came to therapy because she could never write anything under her own byline even though major publications were seeking her out. She had talked in therapy about her distant and critical father, but she was even more disturbed by her mother. "She never punished me, she almost never got angry at me, but talking to her was like talking to a pillow. It's hard to explain. It was like nothing I said ever seemed to penetrate."

In one session, she got in touch with a felt sense that "the moment I'm writing something with my name on it, all my words, all my thoughts—they get sucked away. They're gone." Staying with it, she noticed something inside her that was protecting her from writing her thoughts.

> "Because if I write it and nobody notices, I will be..."
>
> This wordsmith suddenly could not find any word, and something about her manner made the therapist say, "Obliterated?"
>
> "Yes, exactly! I will be erased, I'll disappear. I'll cease to exist."

In attachment relationships, non-response is the worst response of all. To a baby, a non-response, whether from an absent caregiver or one who is physically there but emotionally absent, is so disorganizing to its immature nervous system it must feel as though it is no longer "existing." To the adult mind, a fear of obliteration doesn't make sense, but an experience of that feeling and the need to defend against it can be formed as an implicit memory during infancy.

For clients with the capacity and desire to stay with a felt sense for a sufficient time in session, Inner Relationship Focusing developed by Ann Weiser Cornell offers ways for the client's own psyche to provide a healing, self-regulating, and self-soothing attachment, even if the original trauma may have been preverbal. In the example above, the therapist said, "Oh! So that's what it's afraid of. Let that part know that you hear that it's afraid it will be obliterated." This regulating behavior, of acknowledging and "naming" the "part's" fear, calmed it. It wasn't alone anymore; it "had company."

But as in any dyad, regulation comes from a contingent interaction. "J" was invited to notice how the "part" responded to being understood like that, and to reflect that back to it. In this session, through several back-and-forth interactions, integration occurred whereby her block became less mysterious, intense and overwhelming, though it was not yet gone.

It should be noted that for those clients whose emotional injuries are severe, it may take months or even years of the therapist providing almost all the listening and empathy before the client is capable of providing it to herself.

We used to feel that people who had major felt shifts in a session, and who reported that sense of newness, completion and congruence that comes with that experience, needed only a little affirmation and encouragement—the work of change was done. Over time, however, we noticed that felt shifts occurring in therapy frequently were evanescent if only an intrapsychic process was completed.

So we began following up these tender new shoots of change with some version of the question, "What does it feel like to be sharing this with me?" Frequently it turned out that not every part of the self was fully on board when it came time to claim the change with a regulating other. More processing of the new beginning was needed. But, when the carrying-forward motion is fully ready, we have found that such interactions usually first elicit a small fear of not being accepted by the therapist, and then when fully met and affirmed by the therapist, bring a sense of both pleasurable feeling and tentativeness. We have adopted another technique from AEDP, meta-therapeutic processing, which is "the focus on, and the affirmation of, the experience of transformation itself, particularly the experience of the transformation of the self in the context of a healing dyadic relationship" (Fosha 2008, p.138). As we bring the felt shift into the dyadic here-and-now-between-us, we "draw out" the new state of being through a series of recursive questions about the client's emerging inner state. In the authentic space that emerges, open-client meeting open-therapist, tentativeness leads eventually to joy for both client and therapist, and to what Diana Fosha calls "core state," an "altered state of openness and contact" (Fosha 2000). We have found that transformative felt shifts are far more salient when followed by meta-therapeutic processing. Indeed, they are frequently experienced and remembered as major turning points.

Conclusion

This chapter is the beginning of the development of a model for a Focusing-Oriented Therapy that is explicitly attachment oriented. A definitive sense of when to work dyadically and when to work intrapsychically has not yet been formulated. We have already found that having an understanding of the emotional dynamics of attachment, and the powerful ways in which attachment styles, longings and injuries affect our clients, has been invaluable to the work we do as focusing-oriented therapists. And we are finding that bringing awareness and expression to the felt-sense experience of our clients and ourselves that arises in moment-to-moment dyadic therapeutic contact is adding a rich new dimension to our work. It offers both a tremendous wealth of information about how the client perceives and interacts with himself, others and the world, and provides an extremely useful vector for therapeutic change.

References

Ainsworth, M.D.S., Blehar, M.C., Waters, E. and Wall, S. (1978) *Patterns of Attachment: A Psychological Study of the Strange Situation.* Hillsdale, NJ: Erlbaum.

Bowlby, J. (1969) *Attachment and Loss, Vol. 1: Attachment.* New York: Basic Books and Hogarth Press.

Bowlby, J. (1973) *Attachment and Loss, Vol. 2: Separation: Anxiety & Anger.* New York: Basic Books.

Bowlby, J. (1980) *Attachment and Loss, Vol. 3: Loss: Sadness & Depression.* New York: Basic Books.

Bowlby, J. (1988) *A Secure Base: Clinical Applications of Attachment Theory.* London: Routledge.

Brenner, H. and Letich, L. (2003) *I Know I'm in There Somewhere: A Woman's Guide to Finding Her Inner Voice and Living a Life of Authenticity.* New York: Gotham Books.

Bretherton, I. (1991) "The Roots and Growing Points of Attachment Theory." In C.M. Parkes, J. Stevenson-Hinde and P. Marris (eds) *Attachment Across the Life Cycle.* London: Routledge.

Fosha, D. (2000) *The Transforming Power of Affect: A Model for Accelerated Change.* New York: Basic Books.

Fosha, D. (2003) "Dyadic Regulation and Experiential Work with Emotion and Relatedness in Trauma and Disordered Attachment." In M.F. Solomon and D.J. Siegel (eds) *Healing Trauma: Attachment, Mind, Body, and Brain.* New York: Norton.

Fosha, D. (2008) "Transformance, Recognition of Self by Self, and Effective Action." In K.J. Schneider (ed.) *Existential-Integrative Psychotherapy: Guideposts to the Core of Practice.* New York: Routledge.

Gendlin, E.T. (1996) *Focusing Oriented Psychotherapy.* New York: Guilford Press.

Johnson, S.M. (2009) "Extravagant Emotion: Understanding and Transforming Love Relationships in Emotionally Focused Therapy." In D. Fosha, D. Siegel and M. Solomon (eds) *The Healing Power of Emotion: Neurobiological Understandings & Therapeutic Perspectives.* New York: Norton.

Kohut, H. (1977) *The Restoration of the Self.* New York: International Universities Press.

Kohut, H. (1981) "On Empathy." In P. Ornstein (ed.) *The Search for the Self, Vol. 4.* New York: International Universities Press.

Main, M. and Goldwyn, R. (1984) "Adult attachment scoring and classification system." Unpublished manuscript. University of California, Berkeley.

Main, M. and Solomon, J. (1986) "Discovery of an Insecure-Disorganized/Disoriented Attachment Pattern." In T.B. Brazelton and M.W. Yogman (eds) *Affective Development in Infancy.* Norwood, NJ: Ablex Publishing.

Munro-Davies, H.G. (1949) "Visits to Children in Hospital." *Spectator,* March 18.

Porges, S. (2011) *The Polyvagal Theory: Neurophysiological Foundations of Emotions, Attachment, Communication and Self-Regulation.* New York: W.W. Norton.

Robertson, J. and Bowlby, J. (1952) "Responses of young children to separation from their mothers." *Courrier of the International Children's Center, Paris 2,* 131–140.

Schore, A. (1994) *Affect Regulation and the Origin of the Self: The Neurobiology of Emotional Development.* Hillsdale, NJ: Erlbaum.

Schore, A. (2003a) *Affect Dysregulation and Disorders of the Self.* New York: W.W. Norton.

Schore, A. (2003b) *Affect Regulation and the Repair of the Self.* New York: W.W. Norton.

Siegel, D.J. (1999) *The Developing Mind: How Relationships and the Brain Interact to Shape Who We Are.* New York: Guilford Press.

Sroufe, L.A. (1995) *Emotional Development: The Organization of Emotional Life in the Early Years.* New York: Cambridge University Press.

Stern, D. (1985) *The Interpersonal World of the Infant.* New York: Basic Books.

Tronick, E. (1989) "Emotions and emotional communication in infants." *American Psychologist 44,* 112–119.

van Ijzendoorn, M. (1995) "Adult attachment representations, parental responsiveness, and infant attachment: A meta-analysis on the predictive validity of the Adult Attachment Interview." *Psychological Bulletin, 117,* 3, 387–403.

Wampold, B.E. (1997) "Methodological problems in identifying efficacious psychotherapies." *Psychotherapy Research 7,* 21–43.

Wampold, B.E. (2000) "Outcomes of Individual Counselling and Psychotherapy: Empirical Evidence Addressing Two Fundamental Questions." In S.D. Brown and R.W. Lent (eds) *Handbook of Counselling Psychology,* 4th edition. New York: Wiley.

Wampold, B.E. (2001) *The Great Psychotherapy Debate: Models, Methods, and Findings.* Mahwah, NJ: Erlbaum.

CHAPTER 6

The Relational Heart of Focusing-Oriented Psychotherapy

Lynn Preston

Introduction

There are many focusing-oriented psychotherapies emerging all over the world from different traditions with which Focusing has intersected, each with its own emphasis and style. What they all have in common is a careful attention to the processes of experience itself, the accessing of what is right beneath the surface of thoughts and words. Focusing is often thought of as an "inward" process, pointing to the essentially bodily nature of experience. A Focusing orientation shows us how each micro-moment of experience has within it the potential for forward movement.

What is less well known and appreciated, however, is the radically *relational heart* of both the Focusing process in psychotherapy and the underpinnings of its philosophy. I have always been fascinated theoretically and clinically by the indissoluble unity of the person and his relational context.

I first met Gendlin in the early 1970s when I was a young therapist. I was immediately entranced by his unique combination of broad, encompassing philosophical thinking, and his acutely astute down to earth clinical teaching. I was struck by the originality of his zooming out to the nature of life, coupled with the precision and detail of his zooming in to the therapeutic moment. I knew his approach offered me a home base for both the theory and practice of psychotherapy. I have studied, taught and written about his work and its interface with relational psychoanalysis since that time—

dialoguing, collaborating and debating with him through the years. There is always more to learn, more to say, more of the implicit vastness to tease out and my experiences with Gendlin guide and inspire me along the way.

In this chapter I want to give an overview of the fundamentally relational nature of Focusing-Oriented Therapy and its clinical implications, and to suggest some expansions of my own about the workings of the therapeutic relationship.

Interaction first

Gendlin's concept of Interaction First is the cornerstone of his philosophy. It speaks to the nature of living as inherently interactive. If we look at an individual as a *process* rather than an *entity*, it changes everything we think about and do in our work.

> I think living bodies are interactions with the air and the ground and food and other species members... If you're looking at me, you can see that I'm interaction... And not just on the physical level. I'm interaction with other people... If I think of a person as being interaction, then, of course it makes sense that in interacting with a new person, they're going to be different. *So, my job then as a therapist is to be the kind of interaction that will make the person better.* Even if the person says all the same words that they've said to themselves alone in their room, it's different to say them to *you*. It's a different living process. *And that's where the possibility of change exists.* (Gendlin 2005)

The crucial question then for us as clinicians is: *What is the kind of interaction that makes the client better and how can we be that?*

Making a relationship with "The Client's Client"—"The One in There"

My neighbor, Teddy, confided in me. "I'm so lonely! My wife of 30 years walked out on me. She said she was leaving—get this—because she had to 'find herself.' What the hell does that mean?" he bellowed. I imagined myself as Teddy's wife's therapist, my job now being to help her 'find herself.' What would I be looking for? Where would I find it? As therapists we are always helping people to find lost selves. But what do we actually mean by this *self* and by this *finding*?

Gendlin gave this self the catchy name "The Client's Client" or "The One in There" (Gendlin 1984, p.76). It's the self that the patient is struggling with. This is the one speaking through the cracks of the conversation. She is the unheard voice of protest, hope or longing. Gendlin keeps the distinction between the self and The One in There indeterminate. He is talking about a level of felt-sense experience, not about internal "things." At one moment it is a child, the next a wise inspiring voice. Gendlin doesn't want to reify this voice—to shove it into a pre-cut box where it won't have air to breathe. He doesn't want to assign this self a static identity or a singular function. Instead, he wants to tease out and engage the immediacy of its strivings, needs, and offerings. The One in There must be invited, welcomed, and brought into the family of therapeutic interaction. When I share Gendlin's article "The Client's Client" with colleagues and students, they often identify with his description of the problematic ways we can relate to ourselves. He says:

> The felt sense is the client inside us. Our usual conscious self is the therapist, often a crudely directive one who gets in the way of our inward client all the time. That therapist frequently attacks in a hostile way, or at least wants to use all the old information, claims to be smarter than the client, talks all the time, interrupts, takes up time with distant inferences and interpretations, and hardly notices that "the client" is prevented from speaking. (Gendlin 1984, p.83)

He goes on to say that the growth process necessitates becoming the kind of therapist to oneself that listens respectfully and puts aside his agendas, values, and interpretations. These inner therapists are receptive, willing to wait and follow what The One In There is saying or trying to say. These inner good "therapists" have what is sometimes referred to as a "Focusing attitude." Even when they disapprove of or oppose what The One in There is coming up with, they can be curious and willing to listen to the opposition. Such openness is the primary goal of therapy and is also the precondition for the ability to tap into the vast implicit dimension of oneself that we associate with the carrying forward of Focusing. The focusing-oriented therapist wants to help the client to be a better "therapist" to her inner self, to have a Focusing attitude, but this can be easier said than done. Although Focusing guidelines give us clear and helpful ways to conceptualize optimal self-responding, we know that self-alienation is not easily overcome. It is not often vanquished through just learning the skills of Focusing. All too often The One in There cannot be found, or, the self and the inner client are in a life and death battle, or even worse, they are not on speaking terms.

It is here that Gendlin's concept of Interaction First comes to the rescue. We are faced with a conundrum: what needs to be healed is self-alienation, but we need receptive self-responding for such a healing process. The resolution of this conundrum is the understanding that since we *are* interaction, a new kind of relating with another person will constitute a new living, a new system, a new self.

This understanding is freeing and empowering for me as a therapist because I no longer feel it is my job to "get" the client to change, to focus, to do or be some different way. Instead, I can find that new way in myself and bring it into the interaction. I can wholeheartedly take on the challenge of being the "New Other," the "Partner," the "One" with whom The One in There can confide, find solace, take risks, and fight.

Although it is empowering to know that I, myself, can *be* a new living instead of teaching, convincing and interpreting the client into being different, it is also a hefty responsibility! You, the reader, may say: *You mean it is up to* me *to change the dynamic? To be the one to whom The One in There must be able to bring all the unmet needs, longings and primal protest?* Yes, it is the therapist's job to make a new interaction, a new beginning. You may continue: *How can I bring something new when the client sits silently scowling in the corner, contradicts everything I say, rants and raves at me or cancels session after session and then demands to be seen when I don't have time? Can we still be a new interaction?* Perhaps it is just the perspective of Interaction First that can help us in this daunting task.

Quotes that have guided me in making a relationship with "The One in There"

1. Calling forth

> An individual is an entirely unique and particular substance which is his own…an essence which can be recognized and *called forth in the encounter*…the person feels his feelings…he is more fully alive…and is just thereby and just in that way changed from how he was before! (Gendlin 1966)

When we therapists deeply take in the unique particularity of the client, the mystery of this "one" and the special quality of the moment of meeting, there can be recognition of The One in There that is an invocation, calling her forth. It is a reaching for The One in There. We want that inner self to hear our voice and recognize that we are looking for *him*!

2. A new and different life experience

Change:

> comes from making this now ongoing relationship into a new and different concrete life experience, a kind of experiencing he could not be, and was not, until now, thus, the effects of a personal relationship must be understood as the new and different experiential process that a genuine relationship makes possible. (Gendlin 1966)

It is not *what* we are talking about, but how we are relating, that makes the difference. Whatever brings the interaction alive—laughing, telling a story, sharing food tips. The quality of contact we are making is the relating.

3. Putting nothing between

> Because I keep nothing between, the client can look into my eyes and find me… I won't hide. (Gendlin 1996, p.286)

This bare, undefended "being with" requires a letting go of role consciousness and expectations. It is a radical allowing that comes with giving oneself fully to the supreme priority of this particular relational.

4. Being a real other

> However, far most powerful in this regard is a real other person who responds not merely like a tape recorder, but who is himself still another dimension along which the client's incipient reactions are carried further into lived-out interaction with an environment. (Gendlin 1968, p.220)

We therapists are, first and foremost, real particular people with our own longings and needs, our dreams and dashed hopes, our inspirations and prejudices, our wounds and vulnerabilities. We don't want to hide behind our role as therapist, nor pretend to ourselves or the client that we are "healthier" and "above all." We are part of the human predicament. We can be most open and connected if we can shamelessly accept our own foibles.

5. Allowing your reactions to be visible

> The therapist must be a person whose actual reactions are visible so that the client's experiencing can be carried further by them, so the client can react to them. Only a responsive and real human can provide that. (Gendlin 1968, p.221)

Our real feelings, thoughts, intentions, and reactions are the stuff of the new interaction that is needed. They are the blood running through the veins of this interaction. The One in There is often exquisitely attuned to every nuance of what is occurring in us and how we are reacting to every moment of interaction; not just what we are saying, but what we are implicitly hoping, fearing, hiding, meaning. The most vital and powerful moments in therapy are often the ones in which the therapist's heartfelt reactions are openly shared.

6. The positive intentionality of the negative

> The behaviors are negative. But here, in this interaction, the therapist's aim is to enable the positive tendencies to succeed

> nevertheless... There is always a positive tendency which we can "read" in the negative behavior. (Gendlin 1968, p.224)

Some theories see aggression and destructiveness as basic to human nature. From a Focusing perspective, destructiveness is never the bottom line. We therapists want to seek what is trying to come through. (My suicidal client wants his mother to miss him and mourn his loss.) We can evoke and interact with that positive underbelly.

7. Looking at the trouble as stuck interactions

> We can look at the present therapeutic interaction as an instance of what is stuck in the person and needs carrying forward...If we conceptualize psychological contents (issues) as originally bits of stopped and incomplete interactions, we can easily explain how relating with a therapist might carry it further beyond the old stoppage... (Gendlin 2010, personal communication)

The stuck interactions imply needed healing interactions. They are needs for very specific kinds of relating in order to live the stuck interaction forward. These may include primary needs such as the need for a sense of belonging—a feeling of being deeply understood, known and appreciated. The therapist can sense and reflect on what kind of interaction the therapy is calling for.

8. Finding how I am always part of the difficulties

> What the client stirs in me is always partly me. (Gendlin 1968, p.224)

Even if the client is "always this way" (angry, depressed, oppositional, lifeless, self-destructive) she is this way now with me and my way of being is part of the mix. The good news about knowing this, is that if I sense into what is most troubling for *me* and focus on the very personal meanings it has for me, the knot often loosens and something new can emerge between us.

9. Carrying our own reactions forward

> I turn toward any discomfort and make it a *something* and carry it further before stating it… I carry my incipient responses further past the defensive covering reactions. (Gendlin 1968, p.220)

The issue of how we can make a healing interaction when we get caught in our own vulnerabilities and problem areas is one of the greatest challenges we face. We may feel like only our *positive* feelings should be shown, but when we try to hide what we deem un-therapeutic, we create an atmosphere of mistrust and carefulness. One of the lessons I learned early on from Gendlin is that I don't have to *identify* with my defensive reactions. I can be on the side of The One in There as well as being empathic to my own inner struggles. Gendlin told a story about his working in the returns department of a store when he was a college student. He went home exhausted each day after defending the store against the accusations of angry customers. He finally realized that he didn't even like many of the store's products. He then commiserated with the complainers and went home energetic. "Even if I am the store," he said, "I don't have to spend my energy defending it" (personal communication). This story reminds me of the bumper sticker: "I don't believe everything I think!" In the spirit of this guideline, I try to find something deeper and more precise than my judgments or reactivity to share. I try to stay connected to my client and to his meanings as well as to myself.

10. It is the doing in the saying

> Everything we do in therapy is interaction…the therapist reflects back, "Talking feels useless." But the implicit interaction experiences by the client's body is that the client has just affected someone (the exact opposite of the verbal statement). (Gendlin 1996, p.284)

Sam, a member of my group supervision, talked about confronting his client: "I think it was inappropriate for you to send such a Valentine's Day card to your daughter." I commented on the judgmental word "inappropriate." "Can't a judgment be *right*?" he challenged. Without a pause to take in our interaction, I retorted, "*Maybe* a judgment can be *right* but it can't be *helpful* therapeutically!" Was my judgment of Sam's judgmental language helpful? I intended to sensitize the group to authoritarian language. But what was I doing telling him that *I* am the one, not *he*, who knows what is helpful?

The New Us

Looking at the therapy process through the lens of Interaction First, we can focus on either the "you" of the client, as we usually do, or the "I" of the therapist, who is just as essential to the process. Or we can look through the window of the *interaction itself*, the "we," the unfolding relatedness that must be the vehicle of change. We can look at one interaction from three different sides. I find it incredibly helpful in therapy to be able to use all three lenses and to shift gracefully from one to another.

We have explored features of the therapist's relating, but what about the nature of the relatedness itself? Through this lens we see the therapeutic couple, each with her own unique personality, core struggles, emotional needs and longings, bringing her own experiential world into the mix. The New Us is my way of talking about the evolving developing interaction that we are, and are becoming. The therapist/client bond that creates a new living context, new air to breathe; The New Us is the birthplace of the new "I." We want to develop an "us" that is open, trusting, resilient, permeable, and attentive to the feeling level. We want it to be able to engage, welcome, and carry forward the new emergent self.

Cultivating a felt sense of implicit relational intricacy

The sense of the "us" is a vital dimension of experience. We are all subliminally aware of more strands of implicit relational intricacy than we can consciously process. Somewhere we register, for example, the imperceptible shrinking away, or breath of release, or slight tone of disappointment in the other, as well as our own tinge of defensiveness, pleasure, concern, anxiety. As a therapist I want to cultivate the *accessibility* of my felt sense of the interaction. I want to "feel in my bones" the micro-movements of the partnership in its striving to connect, to grow and to be free. When I have the impulse to say something to my client and I don't know if it will be helpful or distracting, or even hurtful, I can look to this under-the-surface awareness for guidance. When I do say what is on my mind, I pay close attention to the reaction of my client and also to the quality of "us-ness" registering in me.

An improvisational spirit

Improvisation is a skillful, spontaneous interaction—one that comes directly from the implicit realm, unmediated by conscious deliberation. Gendlin talks about it as an experience of coming freshly from underneath. As a therapist I want to cultivate an improvisational spirit in my interactions, an ambiance of lively, unguarded, playful interchange. My willingness to respond in a spontaneous, perhaps surprising, manner can be an invitation to the client to join me in a freer, less careful engagement that draws from the well of the implicit.

Carrying the relationship forward

The power of a Focusing approach is the premise that *every bit of human experience has a forward movement inherent in it.* I am continually amazed at the clinical power of this perspective! It is not only that the developmental thrust of life is the fuel that motors psychotherapy in the large scheme of things, but that each moment, *every bit of experience,* no matter how dark it is, has within it an implied *way ahead.* Working with the natural inherent tendency toward development guides the path of the therapist step by tiny step. Each moment of interaction anticipates a "more" in the next moment. Therapists can look for *what is trying to happen here.*

This same awareness can be brought to the step-by-step development of the therapeutic relationship. The unique life of the particular connectedness of these two people needs to be carefully carried forward. We can ask ourselves: *What does this relationship need? What are* we *up against now, together? What are we implicitly trying to do? What are we hiding from? How are we missing each other? Are we trying to keep our balance or find common ground? Are we pulling in different directions? Are we awkward and careful with each other? Are we trying to negotiate issues of closeness and distance?* These Focusing questions will bring intricate connections different than the ones we ask about the client or ourselves. The language of *we* can be very helpful in exploring sensitive or volatile issues, such as: *We seem to have trouble ending our sessions. Our discussions about money are difficult for us. Talking this way seems new for us.*

Talking about you and me

There are times when the workings of the relationship are not in the foreground and are a living forward, not a verbal exploration. Talking about it can detract from its natural, spontaneous, unselfconscious unfolding. And there are times when putting the detail of our relating into thinkable, shareable words is one of the most vital aspects of building the "new us." Therapy can be thought of as a process, of *making the unsayable sayable.* Of going to the edge where what is unpackaged and untested can be sent forth to be witnessed. The intimate edge of finding words for our direct experience of each other builds relational strength, trust and resiliency. What we are allowed to know and to share about how we experience each other delimits the horizons of our sense of belonging. Talking about you and me is a delicate and *care-full* process—not careful meaning unspontaneous, but caring.

Case example: meeting Dee

My buzzer rang. I answered, expecting my client Pat. Much to my surprise, a stranger stood at the door. She handed me an envelope and said, "I'm Dee. My friend Pat gave me her session. There's a check in the envelope."

I sputtered, "She didn't mention this to me."

"It happened quite last minute," Dee explained. "Is it okay?"

I paused for moment, thinking, "What does this mean?" Then I felt a little letting go, like finally surrendering to the rain in a downpour. "Well, let's see what happens."

I invited the stranger in. She smiled and began to tell me how she had a meltdown over the weekend and was uncharacteristically at her wit's end. Dee said that she had always done well in her career and had wonderful jobs until the recession hit and she was laid off. She'd been sending out hundreds of resumes but getting no response. She said that she had always been a "push-through" person," but now she'd come to the end of the line and there was nowhere to push through. Although Dee had always been the person that others relied on for her resourcefulness and stability, she now felt invisible, resource-less. She had poured out her heart to Pat and said that she felt like nobody knew how much trouble she was in, so Pat had given her the session. I was engaged and impressed with the way she was speaking—right from the feeling level. Dee was what I call a natural focuser.

L: How is it to be a "push-through" person with no place to push through?

D: It's demoralizing, confusing, disorienting. It's like the world has turned upside down and everything is different. I've always been able to go after what I want and now I can't.

L: The world is different—not responding to you in the same way—and you feel different. [Inviting a focus on how The One in There is different]

D: Nobody is reaching out to me maybe because everyone always has seen me as the one who has it all together. The one who is blessed.

L: [Sigh] Yes, I see. Maybe they can't conceive of "the one who has it all together" needing something from them. [Carrying her sense of it a little further]

D: [Shrill] WHAT AM I SUPPOSED TO DO? I've always been the responsible one. How can I be responsible? How can I push through when I get no response?

L: What a question! [I say emphatically, matching her intensity] Maybe *we* can pause here and see what might come from that question. Let's listen and see if something shows up. [Focusing invitation]

D: I...I think I'm supposed to ask.

L: Ask? [A checking and marking]

D: Yes. [She looks down again as if to find what is there] I never had to ask for anything. Even as a child, I didn't ask my parents for anything. They saw me as the strong one in the family and somehow I think that I need to learn how to ask.

L: Ask for help? To be a new way? [I am chewing this over with her]

D: It's hard for me.

L: Hard in what way?

D: It feels weak and ungrateful to ask. It's not appreciating all I have, all I've been given.

L: Asking doesn't fit with who you feel you are in the world. It doesn't seem right for you, just for other people. [Reflecting the point she is trying to make]

D: Yes, that's right. *I'm* not the one who asks.

Pause. Dee looks up, appearing stuck.

L: Did it feel like asking when you turned to Pat and she gave you her session? [Asking her to check inside to see how the inner self actually experienced what she did, helping to make it acknowledgeable]

D: [Looking surprised] I guess I was asking, then, wasn't I? I cried. I told her everything. I was even angry at her for not noticing how distraught I've been.

L: How did it *actually feel* to ask? [Inviting her to check with her felt sense]

D: [Smiling] It actually felt strong and direct. It felt like it took courage and I had it. It felt good. It didn't feel weak or ungrateful. It felt straightforward.

L: Straightforward! Strong! Courageous! What a recognition that is! The actual experience was so different from how you thought about it. [Reflecting and validating]

D: It really was different! [Resonating, both of us taking this in as if we were savoring the taste of a new food]

L: And is this coming to me, a stranger, a kind of asking? Are you somehow asking me for something? [Carrying the theme further]

D: [Laughing] Yes! That took a lot of courage—was really a risk. I've never done anything as difficult as that.

L: How is it? [Smiling, inviting a further articulation]

D: It feels very good. You know, *I am the kind of person who can say what is really going on. I am someone who can take risks.*

L: You were a push-through person about being able to ask. [Helping to name the new living]

D: Yes, I am that person, even though I've never done it before. This is truly who I am.

Discussion: a few comments about the relational dimension

The One in There that Dee was struggling with was one that felt demoralized, confused and alone. We made an interaction of company, welcome, and acceptance. When she demanded advice, I offered her *guidance* and companionship to facilitate letting something come. That moment was a negotiation of what she wanted and what I offered. We both took a risk of trying something new together and stretching toward each other to encompass the other's way. We both felt that wonderful sense of opening when something surprising did come. It was also a step of forward movement in our partnership, a successful coordination. I was asking to speak directly to The One in There in the Focusing and also when I asked how it actually *felt* to *ask*. This was a moment when she seemed stuck and was implicitly asking me for help. We were making a relatedness in which the needs and the *strengths* could both be embraced. We were both delighted to find the new self emerging from the new interaction; a push-through person asking for help.

Conclusion

Gendlin's radical idea that *our job as therapists is to be a new interaction from which a new self emerges* puts therapeutic relatedness at the heart of all that goes into Focusing-Oriented Psychotherapy.

As the "felt sense self" is evoked, heard, welcomed and carried forward, a unique quality of therapeutic relationship evolves; a most intimate, delicate, and powerful interactional dance from which the client is able to find a *new*, more alive, more trusting, open and resilient self.

In this chapter we have discussed a framework for the relational dimension of FOT and have begun to outline some of the principles of *being* a healing interaction. There is a vast territory to be explored here and we need input from clinicians from many different cultures to carry this subject forward.

References

Gendlin, E.T. (1966) "Existentialism and Experiential Psychotherapy." In C. Moustakas (ed.) *Existential Child Therapy.* New York: Basic Books. Available at www.focusing.org/gendlin/docs/gol_2146.html, accessed November 14, 2013.

Gendlin, E.T. (1968) "The Experiential Response." In E. Hammer (ed.) *Use of Interpretation in Treatment.* New York: Grune & Stratton. Available at www.focusing.org/gendlin/docs/gol_2156.html, accessed November 14, 2013.

Gendlin, E.T. (1984) "The Client's Client: The Edge of Awareness." In R.L. Levant and J.M. Shlien (eds) *Client-Centered Therapy and the Person-Centered Approach. New Directions in Theory, Research and Practice.* New York: Praeger.

Gendlin, E.T. (1996) *Focusing-Oriented Psychotherapy: A Manual of the Experiential Method.* New York: Guilford Press.

Gendlin, E.T. (2005) *The Theory of Focusing-Oriented Psychotherapy,* Video 5, New York: RelayTherapyMedia.com.

CHAPTER 7

Exhilarating Pessimism

Focusing-Oriented Existential Therapy

Greg Madison

No more talk about hitching your wagon to that star.
Few of us have wagons and there are no stars.

(James Matthew Barrie 1930)

Introduction

Intuitively we know that every therapist *is* his or her own "integration." Our whole living process, much more than we could ever say about life, is the foundation out of which we understand people and practice therapy. In this sense there is no such thing as a "Focusing" therapist, an "existential" therapist, a "person-centered" or "psychoanalytic" therapist, as if knowledge of a particular theory could wipe out our living experience and become a new foundation for being. *Every* moment shapes us by evoking a response; the world rouses and elaborates us, affecting how we live in the next instant and how we respond to the world as it further affects us.

Theory, culture, hope, and despair, and much more than we could distinguish conceptually, is doing its work in each moment. When I sit across from my client, I am *all that*, forming freshly; a therapist who tries to be "professional" in the sense of reducing the impact of their unique life experiences, their confusion, fear, biases and questions, bereaves their clients, leaves them with gaps where another real person should be. We need to be thoughtful, not absent. First I am a person. Thinking as a psychologist or psychotherapist, though it consumes most of my daily activity, remains a small strand of who I am.

In this chapter I want to show how these attempts to be "experientially inclusive" impact upon the practice of Focusing-Oriented Therapy (FOT). Who and what I am existentially, including the events of my life *and the facts of life itself,* are the foundation into which professional "knowledge," skill, and sensitivity integrate.

I also need to confess how often I fail; fail to achieve the openness I value, fail to live from the subtle awareness that I am, and fail my clients by backing into theory or homily when I am confused and at a loss. This is not a chapter about achievement, but rather a humble attempt to return to an existentially inclusive awareness of life.

Three decades of Focusing (Gendlin 2003) have not made me perfect or even good, but they have honed an embodied awareness for those frequent moments when I back away from what feels true. Practicing Focusing has imbued my living with the potential of experiential process and the pessimism of sometimes finding no way forward. This lived integration of *potential* and *pessimism* resonates through my life and my work as a focusing-oriented existential psychotherapist. However, it is "pessimism" which I feel is neglected in Focusing therapy, hindering its promise to be profoundly inclusive of all human experience.

A positive bias

As I see it, part of the issue is that in our understanding of Focusing we "read in" cultural assumptions, exemplified in words such as "positive" and "life-affirming," which then hinder existential insight. In order to uncover these assumptions it helps to focus on the felt meaning of terms such as 'positive,' "life-affirming," "carrying-forward," each time we use them. These concepts cannot just be adopted; Focusing is meant to open up concepts experientially. Each term must be *continually* unpacked.

Focusing and Focusing-Oriented Therapy grew out of Gendlin's work at the University of Chicago in the early 1960s. As a movement, method, and philosophy, Focusing has roots in the particularities of its American origin. Although Focusing and FOT are now international, elements of that original culture remain within Focusing writing and practice. In *Smile or Die: How Positive Thinking Fooled America and the World* (2009) Barbara Ehrenreich reminds us of the diversity of cultural orientations. "Some cultures, like [America], value the positive affect that seems to signal internal happiness; others are more impressed by seriousness, self-sacrifice, or a quiet willingness to cooperate" (p.3). Ehrenreich differentiates between the culture of positivity and the values of what she calls "existential courage." "The truly self-confident, or those who have in some way made their peace with the world and their destiny within it, do not need to expend effort censoring or otherwise controlling their thoughts" (p.6). While we cannot assume that the "positive" experience is a censored, controlled, or less true event, the cultural reinforcement of "positive" demands that each insight gets a pink bow before it can be accepted as true.

What I am referring to is described in the book, *The Positive Power of Negative Thinking* (Norem 2001): "Precisely because the positivity zeitgeist is so strong and compelling, we need to work to reframe the oversimplified picture that equates optimism with all that is good and pessimism with all that is evil" (p.13). Norem believes that to propose a positive attribute to negative thinking "sounds almost heretical in American society, bastion of full glasses, silver linings, and the ubiquitous yellow smiley face" (p.1). However, "positive thinking" requires a selective perception that does not resonate for everyone. For some of us, holding a "pessimistic" insight *is* "positive" when its impact is expansive, connecting us to the experiential depth of an "existential truth."

It may be true that "positive psychology's approval of 'positive illusions' [offer us] a means to happiness and well-being" (Ehrenreich 2009, p.158), but for some of us at least, this insistence on happiness feels claustrophobic and flat. The *truth that resonates*, even in its unpalatable forms, feels more expansive and "life-affirming." It is exhilarating to stand in the space that is created by symbolizing one's deepest truths. But, according to Ehrenreich, "We've gone so far down this yellow brick road that 'positive' seems to us not only normal but normative—the way you should be" (p.195). Later I will argue that Focusing and FOT, rather than another instance of this subtle norm, could in fact become a way through it.

Exhilarating pessimism

Gendlin is clear that we don't want sloppy optimism, "With so much suffering and destructiveness all around us, optimism is an insult to those who suffer" (1996, p.23). However, he believes that "pessimism is an insult to life" because such an attitude could defeat life's forward direction and "To follow or encourage a growth direction is very different from promoting a set of values…good and bad must be rethought just as all notions of content must be rethought" (ibid).

Gendlin is careful to protect an unfolding experience from being dumped upon by something "positive" in the sense critiqued above. He does not want a pre-defined "good" or "bad" label applied to what is still in process. The process changes its description and therefore what "good," "bad," "positive," "negative," optimism," and "pessimism" even mean. But his use of "pessimism" above seems normative; equivalent to "defeat of the forward direction" and this is what I am trying to avoid with the term "*exhilarating* pessimism."

Gendlin and his colleagues clarify that the energy of the forward movement "is not optimism or preference for the positive" (Gendlin, Grindler, and McGuire 1984, p.272). "It comes, in fact, as one is both separate from *and in touch with* one's negatives" (ibid). The life energy that is released from "being-with" *any* experience is what is valued, not some preference for "positive" and "optimism." So a description that sounds pessimistic is no less valid if it resonates with life experiencing. Resonating, that flow of energy is the key.

But what kind of "pessimism" is also life affirming? This points to the *exhilarating* in exhilarating pessimism: the expansive feeling of bodily resonance even when the content looks negative, even hopeless. The "life energy" is released by acknowledging how things *really* are, without any spin that they are moving towards something sunnier. "Exhilarating pessimism" is a re-thinking of pessimism that in fact prioritizes the bodily experience above cultural norms, even the contemporary demand to find the positive in everything.

Explicit statements that come from this "exhilarating pessimism" may *sound* negative. Even the term "exhilarating *pessimism*" sounds like a contradiction: a life-enhancing negativity? Really? But here "pessimism" is not negative, but an antidote, a corrective, to the claustrophobic insistence of 'positive.' It is the attempt to connect with what *actually exists* without any spin, the valuing of truth rather than convention, happiness, or even health. You can sense that from this view the meaning of the concept "life-affirming" changes.

Exhilarating pessimism is the act of staying close to embodied life and not assuming the outcome should be called "positive" just because there is a moment of relief or expansiveness. The body knows that many of its longings have been defeated and unfulfilled, that it will die; perhaps that each body is a pawn in the survival of the species (of course the body knows its limitations pre-conceptually, not like the suppositions I list here).

Is this life worth living? How could we know? We are taught that our goals are achievable but not to question what the purpose of achieving them would be, given the whole context of a human life. Pessimism is both ontological and epistemological. We don't know if human existence is worthwhile and we don't know *how* we can ever answer that. Yet, we live.

Pessimists are often seen simply as dissenters and cranks, but "we must learn to avoid thinking of pessimism as a psychological disposition somehow linked to depression or contrariness" (Dienstag 2006, p.17). It is not mere complaint or defeat. In fact it has been argued "it is optimism, rather than pessimism, which is best understood as a negative emotion or disposition (resentment of the present or of time itself)" (p.42). The pessimist reminds us that life is fleeting and not under our control. All striving is in some sense futile, all claims to "knowledge" in some sense arrogance. Perhaps it is the desperate denial of what our bodies most deeply know that makes us import "light" and "angels" before our eyes can adjust to the dark?

The *existential* in Focusing-Oriented Existential Therapy

Exhilarating pessimism develops from wanting to realistically confront our human condition. Existentialism values this intention and uses phenomenology to bracket our assumptions in order to confront existence as clearly as we can, given our capabilities at any given time. It is an attempt to value what is "true" over what is "life affirming" in conventional terms of happy, adjusted, and comfortable. The existentialists do not share the "cynical hopelessness" of the misanthropic strand of pessimistic philosophy (e.g. Schopenhauer), but instead try to maintain an inclusive description of human existence that rings true for the whole spectrum of what we actually live.

Existential philosophy depicts us as homeless, thrown into a world that cannot meet the claims of the human spirit. "Our natural and social environment oppresses us with its foreignness, its unsuitability as a home for all that is specifically human about us as individuals" (Gray 1951, p.114). This sensitivity to the human condition means we remain cut adrift without an omnipotent anchor, wagon or star, to manage the undercurrents of everyday life. The only "anchor" is the ever-shifting experiential process.

However, awareness ignites the body and when we pay attention to our experience of homelessness, something already expands. Heidegger says that "rightly considered" and "kept well in mind," "it is the sole summons that calls mortals into their dwelling" (Heidegger 1964, p.363). Without any positive spin, openness to the *question* of how to dwell, can result in an "exhilarating pessimism" which is not an answer to the question but it is an experiential "home" for those who are not convinced by what is proffered in the marketplace of answers. This is a home of flow, not substance. As I have suggested elsewhere (Madison 2009) we are homeless not because we have been exiled *from* home, but rather because we have been exiled *by* home from the flow of the self. The coziness of the tranquilized "substantial" distances us from the self that calls to be known as the elusive and ungraspable.

Through its ability to "unpack" concepts, Focusing offers a method of inquiry that transports us from the explicitly substantial back to implicit process. However, we must be willing to focus on our most closely held assumptions, including positivity, otherwise Focusing cannot break through to the vast expanse.

In the expanse we may feel a deep sense of unease that the existentialists believe has metaphysical origins and which experientially is a doorway to unfolding insight, "we, human creatures, perceive dimly in the experience of the uncanny, that the world rests on nothing. It has no basis or ground" (Gray 1951, p.116). Or, as the philosopher Karl Jaspers says it, "The bottomless character of the world must become revealed to us, if we are to win through to the truth of the world" (Jaspers 1932, p.469; cf. Gray 1951, p.117).

The *therapy* in Focusing-Oriented Existential Therapy

Existential-phenomenological *philosophy* offers a relentless questioning of what we take for granted in human existence and does not flinch from the so-called "pessimistic" side of life. Existential *therapy* is consistent with this attitude and so also implies a deconstruction of therapeutic orthodoxy; the "received wisdom" of psychological theory, therapeutic frames, therapist neutrality, etc. Existential therapy offers no prescribed theoretical canons to hold onto, no practice manuals for reference when things get rough. Typically there is no pre-set goal and no prescribed outcome to measure. Received meanings fall away so that the uniqueness of the client's way of being can shine through. Therapy without wagon or star. However, the "pessimistic" inclusion by the existential therapist often gives Focusing-Oriented Existential Therapy (FOET) a demeanor that differentiates the practice from more "positive" versions of FOT.

Elsewhere I have described how FOT can be a form of existential therapy (Madison 2010). The common values include:

- unfinished process and open questioning is prioritized over conclusive answers
- non-objectifying dialogue takes the place of expert diagnostician with specialist knowledge
- overall appreciation for the unpredictability of an unfolding engagement rather than the clipboard agendas of protocol therapies
- Gendlin's philosophy (evidenced in these two volumes), rather than just the Focusing method, is increasingly the practice base for FOT. The existential-phenomenological psychotherapy tradition has always been primarily philosophical.

Likewise, Gendlin's distinctive philosophy has practice implications for all psychotherapists (Madison 2010), for example:

- the conception of "lived body" as ongoing, unfinished process
- the potential of therapy as social emancipation
- the principle of "interaction first" and the palpable therapeutic relationship
- the implication that cognitive analysis alone is not a reliable guide to change.

If we converge the experiential and existential we create a practice within which the *whole perspective* of human life, not just our current dilemmas, are welcome; the unavoidable tragedies, mortality, as well as the inexpressible beauty of existing, address the client and therapist through their moment-by-moment embodied connection. Existence and experience can be taken as one. Anything existential that is not experientially given remains theoretical conjecture (including what I've said here), no different from any other dogma or therapeutic creed.

Specific illustrations of FOET

I would like to suggest that it is through exposure to the unfinished experiencing of human dialogue that we can respond meaningfully to the absurdity of human existence, including its exhilarating pessimism and sublime tragedy as much as its moments of optimism, joy, and clarity. We open up to continual discovery of what it means to be human in the presence of other beings like ourselves. We have "truthing" but not the truth, questions that temporarily elicit answers that only shift the questions...

Understanding is "interaction first" and "cognition last." Therapist interventions arise from the therapist's "internal" felt sense of what is alive experientially in the moment, not from theoretical postulates of what is important or even explicit indications from the client. When an intervention occurs to the therapist it can sometimes be a good idea to pause and rehearse the intervention to oneself to see if the therapist's body resonates with the words before sharing them with the client. Such an intervention can make explicit something that was, until then, inchoate "in the flow"; we speak in a way that expands the whole feeling of the session. But it is not exactly the feeling that we pay attention to, but the "knowing" that is implied within the feeling. So, a "negative" feeling can feel good when it is acknowledged not because we are affirming the "negative" but because we are acknowledging the deeper "truth" implied in the feeling. It is that embodied connection to a true moment that is our guide in FOET.

At any moment in therapy we can ask into either side of the same living event: "How is the person living their personal situation, including any stuckness?" and "What is life's view of this current moment?" When a word or image comes that resonates, the therapist does not make this happen, nor does the client, except in as much as both abstain from all the usual assumptions that obstruct its happening.

Sometimes I feel my deep continuity with a universe that accepts me *as* I am *but* is indifferent to that fact *that* I am. Such experiences feel exhilarating, expansive, but not carrying forward. Strictly speaking there is no "carrying" and there is no "forward." Gendlin's other term for how the body shifts, "self-propelled" (1964), is a more neutral description. And the body propels itself towards what? Increasing expansiveness, as well as aging, and death.

The cross-cultural example

In *A Process Model* (1997, p.55) Gendlin offers the example of how a person who lives across cultures acquires an implicit understanding of people's complexity that makes coming to know the next new person easier. This is a positive account of the abilities that generate in a person who has been exposed to cultural difference, but it avoids the other side. From research I have done with this population (Madison 2009), I can say that such a person is also less likely to fit into any one place anymore. The person has developed more intricately than any one culture—no one place can hold the interactions their body implies. No place feels like home anymore, except in temporary moments.

S: There is a lot of...sadness really. I don't mean regret, I've loved my life so far, at least compared to the lives I see around me, it's been good. It's just... What will happen to me? [Becomes emotional] I've lost so much by not staying anywhere. Who will

> know me when I'm old? So, this is my life? Why didn't anyone warn me? I don't belong anywhere anymore... [Crying]

The client is acknowledging that her lifestyle has been "good" *and* it has left her feeling sad, alone, and worried about her future. This feeling can continue to shift for Sally, and learning to live with her sadness and loss may become valuable to her. But every decision she has made and each shift that comes not only brings new potential but also forecloses other possibilities. Exhilarating pessimism is the stance of wanting to be inclusive about the facts of life, doors open and doors close. A therapist who is willing to stand there alongside the client, without reframing or spin, can share a "between" that to some extent redeems both. Focusing and FOT have spread around the world into diverse cultures because these practices offer a way to connect through to the living source that usually gets censored. More on this in the next illustration.

Co-presencing our givens

Our common humanity is palpable. It is not based upon shared knowledge or collected information. Our commonality is the living process "between." We understand each other because we are the same process "source." Connection, surely, is something we are all concerned with. Our relatedness is an aspect of our existential condition—it is unavoidable that we move towards and away from others. We do not need to assume that this is something that needs to "shift" or be "focused away" into something "adaptable" and "positive."

In FOET, clients learn to bring their awareness to what was labeled "not-me," or driven into oblivion because it was "negative" or "pessimistic" and made others feel uncomfortable. It is deeply healing when the therapist celebrates the return of what culture said could only be repugnant to others. It is even more healing when the therapist says "me too" implicitly, "through this we belong with each other."

> Rick was trying to sense into a decision about his career path but quickly realized something else was underneath his indecision. In the session he looked me in the eyes and said "I just don't think either job will make any difference. There's still something

about me..." He took a deep breath and said "sometimes I think everyone feels this way. Maybe everyone feels there is something wrong with them, they aren't good enough or something." Rick pauses, looks down and says, "Maybe it's about being adopted, like I can't ever get over that." We had spoken a lot about Rick's early life and adoption. I wanted to catch the other statement too, it was new, so I said "yes, and maybe we all have something like that feeling, that there's something wrong with us and we aren't quite good enough?" Rick was silent, then he asked, "Well, does everyone? [Pause] Do you?" I smiled. I liked the question, though I had to stop to feel into an honest response, "I try to ignore it and tell myself it's silly or too clichéd, but in the background I do wonder if I'm good enough and if there is something wrong with me." Maybe we keep it secret from each other because we make it personal. But maybe it's just part of being human. Does it make a difference to you to know I feel the same, and maybe we all do?" This was a challenge to Rick; to reconceive his "personal frailty" as an indication that he qualifies as human. He relaxed and breathed deeply, hardly speaking for the rest of the session.

Human frailty

Human being is a carrying forward to death, a "being-unto-death" as Heidegger (1964) proclaimed. So although experiential carrying-forward has a feeling of "rightness" or a sense of "truthing," it need not be a kind of Pollyanna optimism or a yellow brick road. What we find may not make us happy, unless truth makes us happy.

The hospital physiotherapists asked me to visit Julie, a young mother who had collapsed a week before from a rare neurological event. They had reassured Julie that she would make a full recovery and be no more likely than anyone else to suffer a repeat of this episode. However, Julie stayed in bed and refused to engage in exercises despite the encouragement of her loving husband or the pressure to "think of your little boys, they need their mother." Julie could not imagine being able to live while knowing this kind of collapse was a possibility. She could not put it to the back of her mind and just assume life would be ok again. As I listened I felt the urge to contradict her bleak outlook with something positive but nothing came to me. What happened to her could just as likely happen to me—this is the truth. I left our initial meeting feeling anxious and vulnerable. The body is a fragile machine as well as much more. Would I make it back to my office? I felt haunted by Julie's realization that every moment is uncertain. Two days later as I approached the ward the physiotherapist stopped me and asked what I had done to Julie. I assumed she must be much worse, but instead I was told that she was engaging in her rehabilitation and talking about returning home where she was determined to make a full recovery. When I asked Julie about the change in her she said she had needed someone to really hear how devastating it was, without minimizing it or trying to convince her that she was being silly or worse, a bad mother. She felt better because I had listened openly to her deep experience of devastation without any attempt to resolve it or to look for a "forward direction." I had allowed myself to be affected, and by both of us facing the truth of our human vulnerability, sharing it in that hospital room, she had found she could in fact live again.

Existential insights

Therapy is one place where we should be able to enter into explorations about life and death as far as we dare. Of course, this requires therapists who are willing to accompany their clients into deep territory. Those rare sessions that become "existential" throw us into a world of death and anxiety, where we are exposed, vulnerable, and on unfamiliar ground. Usually our way of conceiving of mystery falls into quotidian euphemisms, for example, "Of course everyone dies, what's the big deal?" We flee death by falling into the everyday, into cultural formalities and rituals surrounding death, thereby avoiding an experiential confrontation with our palpable existence. The existential does not override the experiential; they go back and forth between grounding and symbolizing, informing and refining each other. In experiential-existential therapy the point is that the therapist must be willing to enter this realm when/if it appears in the session. As moments of existential insight they are valid for client *and* therapist.

Years ago I participated in research into the possibility that Focusing can facilitate "existential insight" into the deeper personal meanings of one's own mortality (Kuiken and Madison 1987). We invited young university students to engage in an age-progression fantasy right up to the moment of imagining their own death. Then half the participants filled out scales and questionnaires about their experience while the other half were guided through a 30-minute Focusing experience on the feelings aroused by the guided fantasy. The focusers seemed more likely to temporarily see through the camouflage of life. They cared significantly less about conventional success, career, money, etc. but cared significantly more about personal growth and spiritual understanding. I remember one young woman who emerged from her session in tears. She assured me that she was not sad or distressed. Until that day she had thought of herself as career-driven; relationships were not a priority. The tears indicated a new understanding of how much she wanted to have her own child and to express love to another human being.

Concluding thoughts

At moments the interaction of therapy goes all the way in, from individual significance, to deeper existential/transpersonal levels, inviting exploration of the therapist in their professional role, both the therapist and clients as unique persons, and therapist and client as examples of human existence generally to which both parties may have meaningful responses.

In discussions about optimisim and pessimism with Gendlin, he suggested, "It wouldn't be so sad if it weren't so beautiful. The latter is wider and explains the first" (personal communication). In response, I said, "it wouldn't be so beautiful [or exhilarating] if it wasn't so sad."

I say both "optimism" and "pessimism" are culturally corrupt. But for me *exhilarating* pessimism gives me a balance, something full of vivid life without it taking on the soft tones of spiritual niceness or sunny cheerfulness that I find so stultifying. For me exhilarating pessimism is the larger space that holds moments of optimism, moments that feel wonderful but make no difference. It is the lack of any source of redemption that redeems most deeply.

We do not only need to learn how to die, we also need to learn to be born. We are not born all at once. We spend our lives trying to midwife the aspects of self still stuck nascent, waiting to see the light of day.

This chapter is a fragment of what is emerging as a model of therapy: experiential, existential, and focusing-oriented. Of course, none of what I say should be concretized and imposed upon the reader's experience. What I say about exhilarating pessimism, existential insight, truth, and death, should be held up to one's experience to expand it, if indeed it resonates at all. Perhaps most succinctly I could say in response to Barrie, *we* are both wagon and star. And that is our mixed blessing...

> To continue on the pilgrimage into the unknown was nothing heroic; it was the only real option—to keep walking away from the familiar, the patterns and processes that affirmed my identity. ...such journeys are known as "going tudong," from the Pali word dhutanga meaning "that which shakes off"—"shakes off" the protective skin of your normality, because whatever is habitual becomes dead tissue, dressed up as "me," "myself." Realising you can't shake off your own skin, you take on a practice that does it for you. Maybe undertaking that jolting and confusion was a kind of heroism after all. And it might even entail being kind to yourself. (Sucitto and Scott 2010)

References

Barrie, J.M. (1930) *The Entrancing Life.* London: Hodder and Stoughton.

Dienstag, J.F. (2006) *Pessimism: Philosophy Ethic, Spirit.* Princeton, NJ: Princeton University Press.

Ehrenreich, B. (2009) *Smile or Die: How Positive Thinking Fooled America and the World.* New York: Granta Publishing.

Gendlin, E.T. (1964) "A Theory of Personality Change." In P. Worchel and D. Byrne (eds) *Personality Change.* New York: John Wiley & Sons. Available at www.focusing.org/gendlin/docs/gol_2145.html, accessed November 14, 2013.

Gendlin, E.T., Grindler, D. and McGuire, M. (1984) "Imagery, Body, and Space in Focusing." In A.A. Sheikh (ed.) *Imagination and Healing.* Farmingdale, NY: Baywood. Available at www.focusing.org/gendlin/docs/gol_2226.html, accessed November 14, 2013.

Gendlin, E.T. (1996) *Focusing-Oriented Psychotherapy: A Manual of the Experiential Method.* New York: Guilford. Available at www.focusing.org/gendlin/docs/gol_2144.html, accessed November 14, 2013.

Gendlin, E.T. (1997) "A Process Model." Unpublished manuscript available from The Focusing Institute: www.focusing.org/process.html, accessed January 27, 2014

Gendlin, E.T. (2003) *Focusing: How to Gain Direct Access to Your Body's Knowledge.* London: Rider.

Gray, G.J. (1951) "The idea of death in existentialism." *Journal of Philosophy 48*, 5, 113–127.

Heidegger, M. (1964) *Being and Time,* trans. J. Stambaugh, 1996. New York: SUNY Press.

Jaspers, K. (1932) *Philosophie,* volumes II and III. Berlin: Verlag von Julius Springer.

Kuiken, D. and Madison, G. (1987) "The effects of death contemplation on meaning and purpose in life." *Omega. Journal of Death and Dying 18,* 99–108.

Madison, G. (2009) *The End of Belonging: Untold Stories of Leaving Home and the Psychology of Globalization.* Charleston, SC: Createspace.

Madison, G. (2010) "Focusing on existence: Five facets of an experiential-existential model." *Person-Centred and Experiential Psychotherapies 9,* 3, 189–204.

Norem, J. (2001) *The Positive Power of Negative Thinking.* New York: Basic Books.

Sucitto, A. and Scott, N. (2010) *Where Are You Going?* Chithurst, UK: Cittaviveka Monastery. Available at www.buddhistteachings.org/tudong--%C2%A0a-journey-into-the-unknown, accessed November 14, 2013.

PART III

Modes of Clinical Practice

The FOT Way

Part III presents various modes of practice, including working with children and infants, group work, art therapy, and working with couples. The first chapter, however, is an innovative discussion of the concept "structure-bound" process. In it, Christiane Geiser and Judy Moore continue to flesh out fundamentals of working as an FOT while developing a model that addresses and depathologizes some of our most change-resistant patterns.

Next we have five chapters covering all the most common modes of therapeutic practice. René Veugelers presents a very accessible description of his work with young school children while Zack Boukydis dips into his experience of developing parent–infant interventions to cast light on how a Focusing and listening sensitivity can enhance this powerful bond.

John Amodeo and Annmarie Early illustrate how it is possible to integrate Focusing moments into Emotionally Focused Therapy (EFT) with couples, increasing the level of communication and connection in the relationship. Calliope Callias and Charlotte Howorth write about their experiences of integrating Focusing skills into their work with groups and Part III winds up with Laury Rappaport's presentation of her development of Focusing-Oriented Art Therapy. Each chapter in this part exemplifies how these authors have developed FOT into unique models of therapeutic delivery.

CHAPTER 8

New Ways of Processing Experience

How to Work with Structure-Bound Processes

Christiane Geiser and Judy Moore

Introduction

> It is obvious...that a therapist, in order to be effective, must respond to the present experience of the patient and not to the structure-bound aspects of his behavior. (Pollio *et al.* 1977, p.125)
>
> No one is greatly changed by responses and analyses of how he does not function. (Gendlin 1964, Section 20)

Our aim in this chapter is to demonstrate some ways in which the process of experiencing (or parts of it) can become structure-bound, so that we can no longer access its intricacy and work with it therapeutically. In order to move beyond these stopped places in ourselves, in our clients, and in the interactional field between us, we think that it is important to identify patterns of structure-boundness and work with them directly as "present experience." Addressing these stuck patterns can release life and energy that has previously been trapped in familiar yet often destructive ways of being.

For the past 30 years, Christiane Geiser and Ernst Juchli, founders of the GFK Institute in Zurich, have worked with colleagues' to engage in a detailed and systematic consideration of personality difference, acknowledging the fact that we are all limited by collective and individual "structure-bound" patterns of thinking, feeling, behaving and embodiment.

A project to translate this work from its original German into English, so that it can be developed and presented further, is currently under way at the University of East Anglia (UEA), Norwich, UK, with Judy Moore and a group of colleagues. This project arose through dialogue between Judy and Christiane over a number of years as Christiane brought insights from her experience to bear on their various discussions. Realizing that the model was both insightful and potentially extremely useful both for personal understanding and therapeutic work, Judy invited Christiane to present her and her colleagues' work to an invited group at UEA.

This was not only a matter of translation and presenting a "model" to a new group. As the original model had been experientially co-created, it now needed to be re-experienced before it could be fully understood, developed further or even changed. Without an embodied felt sensing of lived examples the material could be misperceived as prescriptive rather than descriptive and process-oriented.

The co-writing of this chapter has involved a similar process of going backwards and forwards between finding the right words and experiencing. We hope that the reader will be able to continue this process by going back and forth between reading and experiencing to get something of the "feel" of why this material has such potential.

Beginnings: why a model is helpful

Although personal and cultural patterns are ubiquitous, in clinical practice we often meet some "always the same" patterns which cause suffering. They impact heavily upon the therapeutic relationship so that we end up going round in circles together whenever we reach these stuck places. It was in recognition of this phenomenon that the GFK group developed a specific interest in the formation and recurrence of these so-called "structure-bound" patterns (Gendlin 1964) and tried to understand and describe them during professional reflection and supervision. This reflective process functioned both as a "carrying forward" in itself and also served as the foundation for the next phase in the generation of what came to be an ever-evolving model. Generations of therapists have found this fluent, relational process knowledge extremely useful and many have also contributed to its further development.

This knowledge helps:

- to realize how our own patterns as therapists function and how they colour our working with clients and have an impact on it
- to look at similar patterns in clients and those that differ from our own
- to realize how we and our clients are interconnected
- to understand what happens in our relationship during therapy if we both get stuck.

A "model" in this sense is not an ontological one; it only "points" to something. It is not in itself "true," but the product of an ever-changing dynamic.

The theoretical background: structure-bound processes, frozen wholes and stopped processes

> I want to put forward the theory that those very processes that mark out psychopathologies which seem on the surface to be difficult, even bizarre, are also to be found in normal-range clients, not to mention normal-range therapists. (Worsley 2009, p.189)

Instead of using the term "psychopathology" the GFK group chose instead Gendlin's early term "structure-bound." In difficult processes the *manner* of process changes. Gendlin observed:

> ...my experience is a "frozen whole" and will not give up its structure...the structure is not modified by the present. Hence, it remains the same, it repeats itself in many situations without ever changing. ...structure-bound aspects are not in process. (Gendlin 1964)

The term "structure-bound" is a neutral one; it is about form rather than content. It says nothing about illness or disorder, but something about one-sidedness, about not being in process.

The great advantage of the GFK approach is that, rather than searching for external diagnoses, we can discover and name these life-preserving and life-preventing patterns and habits of thought, feelings and behavior through precise and patient questioning and exploration *with* our clients.

In *A Process Model* (1997) Gendlin writes about "stopped processes" and we could also look at our patterns in terms of this concept. Grindler-Katonah explains it in this way:

> When the usual way a process that is carried forward is stopped, the organism remains sensitized, and has the potential to find new possibilities for carrying this forward that would not have been discovered if this particular process was not stopped. (Grindler-Katonah 2007, p.107)

The term "sensitized" is interesting. The GFK group in the early days chose a similar term to describe different versions of this "potential', describing them as "sensitivities" (in German: *Sensibilitäten*).

This "potential" in a stopped process is double-edged, as we will see later in this chapter. As long as the implying continues to stay there "the body carries the stoppage": there can be fresh new possibilities, little repetitive trials (termed "leafings" in *A Process Model*) or an immediately formed new occurrence, through the impact of an "intervening event" (Gendlin 1997, pp.76–79). But there can also be stereotypical patterns, where there is no carrying-forward, and then the stopped process stays the same and will not be resumed. Gendlin has modified his observation more recently in a letter to the Japanese philosopher Yasuhiro Suetake:

> I would argue today that each repetition *is* a little different but when we are structure-bound we do not move on from the little different. Instead, we go on from the same, and again from the same, and again from the same. So it may require interaction to stop the structure-bound repetition. (Gendlin 2008)

This is important. Within the therapeutic relationship there are many possibilities for such interactions, each of which can potentially bring about change.

The general dynamic

The GFK model recognizes that there is a general dynamic to the frozen patterns of structure-bound repetition. First of all we will show what constitutes this dynamic.

We all have a tendency to respond to the world assuming that people around us respond in the same way that we do. We often do not realize the specific impact we have. We each have a tendency to foreground particular issues, topics, themes and ways of acting and feeling and thinking.

For example: when a close friend is late and we don't know where he is:

- Someone with a tendency to foreground issues of anxiety will immediately think that there has been a catastrophe—or, at the first pulsations of anxiety, she will immediately compensate with a soothing thought like "It'll all be fine..."
- Someone with a tendency to foreground issues of rules and agreements will either be relieved because he himself is always late—or he will be outraged because he is on time and expects the same from other people.

When our lives become more stressful we are potentially up against life situations that are beyond our capacity to process effectively, whether through complexity in or around us or simply through overload or tiredness. Then our sensitive areas begin to "vibrate": we are even more inclined to foreground them, and other issues go to the background or to the periphery of our awareness.

A narrowing process then begins: our overall feeling changes. Atmosphere, bodily sensations, feeling, thinking become more and more overtaken by the issues and questions of our particular pattern. We look at the world through these lenses and lose the bigger picture; our movement inside ceases to be the back-and-forth process between implicit experiencing and explicit symbolizing of that experiencing. It changes. Often it becomes a downward spiral or a circling around in a very narrow space, uncomfortable, sometimes very intense and painful, but something that we are nevertheless inexplicably drawn to.

Because all life is inherently interactional, people around us realize that there is something "in the air." Typically their responses do not help to resume the process, to stop the pattern, which will be an interesting point to look at later on. We fall out of a meaningful shared field. We feel lonely and misunderstood and either withdraw or try to connect with others over and over again from our "stopped" place. But this only makes things worse.

When there is no change in the interactional field around us or in us, our normal complexity breaks down. We enter the structure-bound pattern completely. Repetition and stereotypical reactions occur in many different areas. The stopped parts of us cannot respond to fresh and new inputs any more, symbols do not accurately cover the intricacy of the situation, and we are cut off from felt sensing and new meaning.

When this process continues, and the narrowing is complete, there is a tendency to split into two poles within our sensitivity pattern. The poles are both very simple and very extreme. Nothing falls in between: everything is either "good" or "bad," "yes" or "no." We can end up "landing" on one or other of these poles and stay there, stuck in a place where we might find ourselves having thoughts like "the whole world is against me," "everything is always my fault" or that "this will never end."

Usually this stuck state loosens after some time, because we are exhausted or can go back to "business as usual." But then nothing has really changed: there has been no carrying forward of the process, and there is always a risk of falling into this familiar narrow place again. We are inclined to embed it into our private (and shared) narrative ("It is always like this and always will be") and so through this reinforcement it becomes even more frozen.

But *why* do we go to these places? If we sense into them carefully and slowly, we may perceive a kind of "attractor," a pull or suck we can hardly resist. Something in us *wants to* go there, and another part knows that we should not. The advantage of this odd kind of "home" is that we feel secure and stable, because it is so well known: there is no complexity; there is no need to change our view of the world. At the same time, the disadvantage is immense: we lose our flexibility. We feel bad, people around us feel bad; there seems no possibility of change and we lose the ability to take a larger perspective on "all this" any more. And normally we have no idea how to avoid falling into these traps again.

But through extensive self-scrutiny we can begin to understand more about these dynamics. We come to realize that each of us has patterns of behavior that permit us to disengage from a "shared" reality. These interior, familiar places of comfort and suffering are not places of process. It is incumbent on us to monitor our own "stuck" patterns and see how they might impede us not only in our professional helping role but in all of our relationships.

The specific patterns

The general dynamic described above applies to *all* specific sensitivities listed below. To date the sensitivities identified relate to the foregrounding of:

- anxiety (see Table 8.1)
- rules and agreements (see Table 8.1)
- worth (see Table 8.2)
- trust
- control, planning
- awareness of symptoms
- intensity
- attention
- shame
- guilt
- problems and difficulties.

To learn more about the dynamic of each pattern we have to become aware of the *specific* ways in which the narrowing process takes place. The generating of a structure-bound pattern is, in part, an *activity*, even if it doesn't feel like this. Much detective work is needed to find out all the little signs with which any specific pattern starts to form. You might ask yourself where the beginning and the ending of your own inner spirals are, whether there is a place where you might be able to stop or deal with a particular spiral if it begins to take you over. On which poles do you tend to land, and what do you say to yourself and others when you are there? What would be helpful? Can you notice not only the shortcomings of your pattern and the impact on others, but also the strength and even the gift that is a part of it?

Table 8.1 Sensitivities of "anxiety" and "rules and agreements"

As response to the world, a tendency to foreground:	**The two poles**	**Shortcomings (if unbalanced)**	**Strengths (if balanced)**	**Impact on others**	**What helps**
Feelings of anxiety	A disaster is about to happen, everything feeds the anxiety *or* everything is fine, all is idyllic, no fear at all.	From 0 to 60 catastrophic thinking, high bodily arousal *or* immediate soothing, glossing over, sometimes foolhardy risk-taking.	Antennae for frightening situations, making provision against emergencies *or* boldness, zest for life.	'Infected" by the anxiety or denying it *or* slightly suspicious of the idyllic touch or the assumed fearlessness.	Recognizing when danger is real and then acting appropriately. Learning to recognize and name different arousals of energy.
Handling of rules and agreements	Deliberate or compulsive rule-breaking *or* inflexible conformity, anticipatory obedience.	Not abiding by the rules (and inventing own rules) in a subversive or rebellious way *or* unthinking obedience, not regulating their own life.	Questioning of meaningless conventions, fighting for freedom *or* will keep with rules and commitments that are thoroughly considered together.	Others might experience embarrassment, frustration, anger *or* admire them because they sometimes live an unconventional lifestyle.	Sharing the field with others and thinking about rules collectively. Learning about the balance between maintaining agreements and expanding freedom.

It is possible to capture a shorthand version of all of these sensitivities in diagrammatic form. The danger with a diagram, however, is that the sense of process gets lost and only the summaries, the "little boxes," are visible. In supervision or self-reflection with colleagues we might speak in shorthand about "anxiety people" or "rule patterns," as if these were pathologies. But we have to remember that symbols have to retain a living quality in order to have metaphoric resonance, in order to accurately point towards process.

In the "waiting" example given above we outlined two possible responses and in Table 8.1 we present a snapshot of some of the characteristics observed in these patterns.

Implications for therapy: the "me with you"

It goes without saying that our work with clients is lighter and sometimes easier if we can go directly with the fresh air, with the life-forward energy. It helps when we can rely on a stable and fluid interaction between us and when both of us can easily refer to our felt sensing of the whole situation.

But sometimes there is no fresh air at all. Yet the GFK group has found that it is possible and even desirable to work with clients directly from their—and our own!—stuck places, to identify them and proceed from there.

The intersubjective element in the creation and removal of stoppages is important. All of these patterns are about relationship, about our mutual being-with, about interaction. We are never literally "individuals." We happen together, we share an experiential space. All that is "in us" is always part of a relational situation and always has been. Even if we are not aware that we are in a narrowing process, the other person reacts to us in a specific way and can draw our attention to the narrowing that is taking place.

In the therapy session we live in a kind of "shared body," in a "new us" (Preston 2005). Sometimes a therapeutic relationship, like any other, can go around in circles, becoming frozen so that there is no carrying forward any more. But this "new us" also has the capacity to move in a new way, and carry the whole intricacy of the process forward. Our clients, struggling with painfully stuck states, urgently need an experiential response instead of structure-bound answers in order not to repeat their well-known patterns. Gendlin (1968) asks:

"If this newly different interaction process won't happen here and now—where and when will it?"

What this means in a practical way for client work

It is important to understand in a bodily way two inner movements. The first of these is a forward direction and a real carrying forward that offers a "felt shift," which changes the situation. You cannot "make" this movement: a felt shift "comes," and it is only in retrospect that you may recognize what it "was" (Gendlin 1997, p.251).

The other inner movement is a structure-bound "wanting," a "hunger" for a response, an occurring which seems to carry something forward, but, in reality, doesn't. It remains in the same well-known spiral, the "wanting" is always for the same response in the other. But this response doesn't really satisfy, does not resume the stopped process. The movement *seems* to be right; it is so appealing, and the emotions seem to be so clear and compelling that it is not easy to realize that you should not follow this pull. This applies to both client and therapist—and for the shared "body" of the therapeutic relationship (Geiser 2010, p.98).

So, during therapy sessions the therapist has to listen and look, to find a bodily resonance in relation to the client. The therapist may realize: *something is going on here.* There is a "something more," but the resonance differs from a "something more" which comes out of a Focusing process. Something is in the air: maybe a background feeling, a subtext. It is important to stay with this felt sensing. Then, over time, other signs might manifest: sentences or feelings of the client become repetitive, the tone of voice, the breathing, the body language changes or stays the same in a frozen way. The danger is that the therapist's responses will make the narrowing more complete. Then the process cannot be challenged or questioned any more. There will be no more distance, no more self-reflection, no more meta-level.

When the therapist also starts to react with a particular bodily resonance, she has to sense into herself. She might well lose the ability to step back, to access the felt sense, to empathize. She is likely to react out of her own narrow place, her own structure-bound spiral. It is important for her to realize what is going on and to recognize the process.

Case example: Structure-bound interaction in therapy

A client has for many weeks been lamenting his past, present and future life. At first his therapist was full of empathy. Such a difficult life, indeed. So many problems to manage. But over time the therapist starts to get impatient, even angry. In her own world (in her structure-bound pattern) there is no helplessness, no lamenting, but only doing and planning and bringing tasks to an end without thinking about all the consequences. After a long time of exploring and empathic reflections she starts to give advice ("Couldn't you try this? Or that? This would be a good strategy") only to realize that her client will immediately answer with new problematic ways of thinking and analyzing. All this makes the mutually frozen situation worse.

This example shows the encounter between a structure-bound pattern of dwelling on problems and foregrounding difficulties "in" the client with a pattern of controlling, foregrounding strategies and plans for each and every situation "in" the therapist—very different styles of thinking and living. If they trigger each other it can become a really stuck place. It is incumbent on the therapist to recognize her pattern first, to work out what is happening and find the way back to a full-bodied listening from where she can allow a felt sensing of the whole situation to emerge again.

So, in our interactional dynamic we have to learn that:

- a narrow place is pulling at a narrow place in the other person and vice versa. We have to be aware of it and step out of the spiral
- there is also a tendency to pull into the opposite pole if someone is stuck in one pole (e.g., saying "But there is nothing to be anxious about!" when someone is frozen with anxiety). Do not try to work "against" the spiral. This tendency takes us away from person-centered working and does not meet the client where he/she is.

When these patterns are very strong it is important to remember what *not* to do:

- Do not work on major issues or try to decide something important during this time.

- Do not believe that the intense feelings that are surfacing in the session are the ones you should follow.
- Do not decide something important from this place.
- Do not follow the spiralling thought patterns of your client for too long.

Instead: Stay there. Hold on, even if the narrowing is complete and you really have to struggle to stay upright and focused yourself. Stay accepting and empathic and slow down. Try to get back to your own felt sensing of "all this." What is going on here? In which way exactly *is* the whole of your "being together" stopped right now?

How to get back into process

Returning to acceptance and empathy is *always* the first step. There is no way of leaving it out. When you as therapist *really* are able to accept a pattern, however tedious and wearisome it may be, when you are able to find the way back to real empathy, this will make considerable difference. This "Ah, I see, *this* is how it is for you," the contrasting experience of having a well-trodden pattern interrupted by acceptance and understanding is often groundbreaking for the relationship and both client and therapist can start from a new place again.

When and how to address a structure-bound pattern between you depends on how long you have been working together, on the "maturity" of the client (and therapist?), on his/her ability to self-reflect and on the quality of your relationship.

These patterns are unknown at first and it is painful and often even shameful to learn about them. So it takes time and trust and, over and over again, empathy and acceptance. It is good to question these patterns at times when both your client and yourself (and your relationship) are relatively free from being narrowed. If your client can stand back and acknowledge that this pattern exists in his/her life, realize how it has an impact on his/her relationships and how it, together with the therapist's own patterns, colours your being-together, he/she can, over time, learn that he/she has a choice.

Case example: the client who devalues herself

Lorraine, a 50-year-old woman, and a very experienced secretary, had worked for 25 years in a business company and came to talk about her difficulties at work. Whenever we explored them, we ended up in a stuck place. Lorraine thought about leaving her workplace, but on the other hand she liked it, and at that point we ended up in a "running around in a circle" place. I started becoming detached and losing our relationship, because I had the feeling that nothing reached her.

Then, one day, she said a little sentence, "Why do I still have this uneasy feeling, after all these years?"—and suddenly I realized the undertone. This was not a "real" question, one asked with curiosity and a wanting to know. There was a sense of self-blame in it, and she looked at me as if I would blame her, criticize her too.

It took me some time not to automatically work against the spiral ("But you are so experienced and you are so much appreciated by your colleagues and your boss!"). And it took her some time to come to a place where she could believe that I really did not blame her. She realized, with much sadness, the place in herself where she always, automatically, evaluated and devalued herself and others. Accepting that this was true she began to conduct a kind of detective work, noticing that, for example, every morning after waking up, she would register all the things that she had to do, thinking that others would do them better and so she would be devalued.

We agreed that in future I would be permitted to intervene every time when this typical silence occurred, this look on her face or in her eyes, or when this typical little resonance in my body appeared, indicating a subtext, a background feeling.

I could then say: "Now it is happening again. Did you realize it? What exactly is going on in your private world? What do you expect me to think, to do? Am I allowed to tell you what it does to me? Can I tell you about my resonance? Could you believe me? Can we (both) accept 'all this' and feel empathy towards it?"

Over time, Lorraine could have a glimpse of a world where comparing herself to others is not the most important mode of living. And we could even have a look at the strengths and gifts of her sensitivity, which she had not been aware of until now.

Table 8.2 gives some aspects of the foregrounding of issues of value and worth.

When we have explored a pattern long enough and then it appears in the therapeutic relationship again, we can sometimes say "No. Don't go there." Suetake (2010) calls this a "therapeutic stoppage" (p.125). It is a "saying no" to this kind of processing, to this vicious circle, but not to the person herself.

When we say "no" in this way we can create room for a pause, an opportunity to look at what is happening, to change direction, to say "yes" to something different. It can be frightening to leave a familiar place without a sense of where to go next and so it needs some exploring and the discovery of a new "movement," a different and more life-enhancing way forward that will need to be "trained" by trying it out over and over again before it feels like a real alternative.

Over time, within the therapeutic relationship, it becomes increasingly possible to stay in places without frozenness or repeating circles and clients find themselves, even on their own, in a different mode of relating to themselves.

Table 8.2 Sensitivity of "worth"

As response to the world, a tendency to foreground:	**The two poles**	**Shortcomings (if unbalanced)**	**Strengths (if balanced)**	**Impact on others**	**What helps**
Issues of worth and values	Feeling completely worthless as a person, unrealistic overrating of others *or* devaluing others and overrating themselves.	Always making comparisons: who is better, who is worse? Feeling completely negated by criticism, easily hurt *or* criticizing others openly or clandestinely.	Experts on the worth of something or someone. Putting themselves forward can be easy *or* holding back, encouraging others to come to the foreground.	Others feel devalued or overestimated, which creates the same uneasy feeling. It becomes difficult to discuss things, because issues of worth always get in the way.	Learning to leave the comparing mode. Learning that something is different, not better or worse!

Conclusion

It can be extremely helpful to use an experiential model such as the one outlined here, for our work with clients and for our self-reflection in supervision. Needless to say, the map is not the territory. But the ability to name patterns as patterns, as well as an understanding of how to work with those patterns, can be helpful in carrying forward the process of change.

There is, even in a structure-bound pattern, a felt potential for development, a possibility of something new and different to come. Compassionate awareness of these patterns—our own and our clients'—seems to be the key to unlocking our stuckness and the gifts it might contain. We have a choice. This choice can be accessed through a clear experiencing of the pattern itself, which can lead to new understanding and ultimately to a significant feeling of freedom and to different qualities of relationship.

References

Geiser, C. (2010) "Moments of movement: Carrying forward structure-bound processes in work with clients suffering from chronic pain." *Person-Centered and Experiential Psychotherapies 9*, 2, 95–106.

Gendlin, E.T. (1964) "A Theory of Personality Change." In P. Worchel and D. Byrne (eds) *Personality Change.* New York: Wiley. Available at www.focusing.org/personality_change.html, accessed 17 November, 2013.

Gendlin, E.T. (1968) "The Experiential Response." In E. Hammer (ed.) *Use of Interpretation in Treatment.* New York: Grune & Stratton. Available at www.focusing.org/gendlin/docs/gol_2156.html, accessed 17 November 2013.

Gendlin, E.T. (1997) *A Process Model.* New York: The Focusing Institute.

Gendlin, E.T. (2008) Personal letter quoted in Y. Suetake. "Some odd concepts in Gendlin's Process Model and their clinical implications." Unpublished paper presented at Philosophy of Psychotherapy Conference, UEA, Norwich, UK, 2011.

Grindler-Katonah, D. (2007) "Cross-cultural communication: A model for a new pattern of relating." *The Folio,* 104–109. Available at www.focusing.org/folio/Vol20No12007/13_CrossCultural.pdf, accessed 17 November 2013.

Pollio, H.R., Barlow, J.M., Fine, H.J. and Pollio, M.R. (1977) *Psychology and the Poetics of Growth: Figurative Language in Psychology, Psychotherapy and Education.* Mahwah, NJ: Lawrence Erlbaum Associates.

Preston, L. (2005) "Two interwoven miracles: The relational dimension of focusing oriented psychotherapy." Available at www.focusing.org/fot/2_interwoven.pdf, accessed 17 November 2013.

Suetake, Y. (2010) "Some odd concepts in Gendlin's Process Model and their clinical implications." *Person-Centered and Experiential Psychotherapies 9*, 2, 118–127.

Worsley, R. (2009) *Process Work in Person-Centred Therapy,* 2nd edn. London: Palgrave Macmillan.

CHAPTER 9

"I Can See You, You Can't See Me"

Focusing-Oriented Therapy with Children: A Fresh Approach

René Veugelers

Those were the words of a 12-year-old boy called Bram, after he wrapped himself in toilet paper and pretended to be a mummy. I mirrored his words as he laid himself on a table and lay still...for more than 15 minutes. I occasionally let him know that I saw his chest rising and falling and invited him to sense inside when there was any inner movement and to just follow it. Then I simply waited. Eventually he began to move slowly and shuffled towards me a bit stiffly. He was really walking like a zombie. As he reached me he said: "I can see you and you can't see me." I mirrored these words back and invited him to sense inside if they had a quality or if there was an inner place where they were coming from. Smiling, he said: "Yes, this is about me" and started to unwrap himself, throwing the paper into the room with lots of energy. Before this session Bram had not looked me in the eyes—afterwards he always made eye contact. When his father came to pick him up we shared this story. He was very touched, realizing that these words and descriptions exactly fitted their way of being. In this article I will describe my working process with Bram, who is diagnosed with Asperger syndrome. He experiences panic attacks and has lots of anger. He had several different therapies, none of which really worked or were attuned to him enough to make any discernible difference. Our way of being and working together evolved as a step by step process of moving forward with a lighthearted sense of spontaneity.

Attitude

A child can form and hold strong connections with their implicit knowing, their own self-governing, with what can be sensed in the body and with their felt sense (FS) of life experiences. Sometimes this is implicit, just waiting for the right moment and quality of attention to bring it to light and sometimes it asks for and needs a bit more exploration. The mirroring and pausing aspects of reflection are essential for me and remain at the core of my basic attitude. This is a never-ending process of development requiring the therapist to stay in close connection with her/himself, through their FS.

In essence, as a therapist, I am mostly with my own felt sense—checking how and when to respond and when not to intervene. I am careful with process questions; listening to what may be behind words, attitudes, and behavior, as a way of quietly intensifying and deepening my empathic capability. I must stay with the "tension-field" between structuring and following, always returning freshly to ask inside: "In this moment…am I contributing to the developmental process of the child's personality?" and/or "Am I where the child is? … Am I connected with the child?" The attitude I carry is crucial, pointing to the essence of Focusing with children and how it differs from the way we may work with adults.

I aim to maintain an awareness of the four main areas of connection to a FS: bodily awareness, symbols or imagery, connection with your life or story, and the emotional quality. Working with children I am always looking for a fresh entry point to the aliveness of the moment, through any one of these. It is this commitment to check in freshly with both the connection and the ongoing contract being formed and reformed with the child that sets it apart from other approaches that may be used with adults.

As a therapist, I ask myself again and again: "Are my thoughts, speech or actions against…to…for…about…the child?" This enquiring attitude supports me to be *near* and to be *with* a child. I constantly ask: "Is this unfolding more from 'the outside to the inside' of the child, or from 'the inside to the outside'?" Trusting and being connected to the implicit wisdom of any child in front of me and the wider arc of the process itself, allows me to work confidently. I want to share some important elements of my way of working with children that facilitate the step by step development of a child's inner process.

First contact

I use body language as a constant reference point and offer open questions about any distressing situations in a child's life that may often be tangled. I keep one eye on facial expressions and gestures and if I notice something happen that may point to some emotion being active, then I mirror it, like when his eyes change, his hands tighten, or if his feet start moving quickly. These elements all come from inside with no interpreting...just mirroring. All kinds of feelings become clearer. It's like looking through a microscope to give all our senses some attention. Then children are both seen and heard within the safety and creative center of their own way of being.

Contact–contract

Initially Bram said that he was upset and afraid he couldn't handle situations. He was very angry with his sister and sometimes his parents. We agreed to give these feelings attention and to find ways together, from the inside out, for how these feelings may want to be expressed, to unfold and to discover what they needed or wanted. Bram really wanted to be "happy," so this was our contract and our direction.

I am aware that this is always his direction during each step forward that we make together, whether that is full of newness or whenever we retread old ground. When there are new elements of emotion forming, I check in with Bram about whether it is ok that we give these new things some attention. The purpose of this is always to allow Bram to stay in control of the process. He guides himself, supported by my containment and I keep renewing a fresh, open connection with him, making the direction and the forward steps explicit. I am letting the child know my intention (I am transparent and congruent) and when the child doesn't want or can't follow the next step...then I move back and pause...returning to the previous step of the process instead of always trying to offer something "new" that may not be wanted or needed.

Working with the body

Children need to make a bodily connection and ground themselves solidly. The first few times we worked together, Bram clearly had a lot of energy. Immediately I attuned to this and so there was no "sitting down and inviting the attention to go inward." Instead, we used his bodily sense of this energy to make a more grounded connection.

Working with children who have Asperger syndrome draws you to find ways of describing their FS of the whole inner energy, because it is often harder for them to connect with separate feelings or some body parts. For example: their energy level can often be like "a tornado, my inner volcano, a lion or...a whushhhhhh!" It is much easier for them to relate through metaphorical language as it can articulate the energy of things altogether and may also imply the direction they want to move in or point to whatever aspect in them needs some attention.

On one occasion I saw that Bram's feet were restless, so we invited them to start to move more. He stamped his feet, jumped up and down, and moved around using his arms and his whole body. I invited him to sense the difference between moving faster or more slowly and I also had a body map available to him, made on the computer, on which he could draw where and what he was sensing inside. This became evident as Bram expressed: "I want to concentrate better. I can't relax and focus enough." "I want to be more slow. I feel like a madman." And also, "How can I end my activities more gentle? It's hard, I cannot do many activities at once, so I get frustrated, how can I do that better?" So, we also agreed that each time we worked together we would start with bodily movement. This would become our contract and his structure to give him a feeling of safety.

Bram I

What followed the invitation to "draw his body a little" was a good example of Bram more fully inhabiting his body. After we did some movement together he stayed with his attention in his feet, one foot was on a new piece of paper and the other foot on a separate sheet. He drew all kinds of colored lines inside his initial outline. Then he grabbed a fresh piece of paper to draw his head and then another, drawing other body parts. We then looked at all these separate elements lying on the floor together. Suddenly, he remarked that: "It seems like a puzzle, all kind of loose things and loose elements." I asked him which part needs attention. He said "my feet." He looked at his feet, looked back at the drawings and drew something more of how it was inside his feet. He shared that his feet were old with a lot of "happenings" and that "they had experienced difficulties but they were still happy." Then it finished naturally. We agreed that some other time we could look at other body parts.

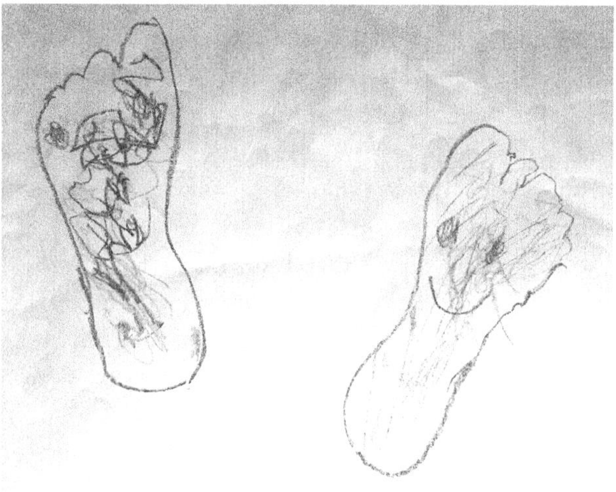

Over the following weeks I invited Bram to check his inner body in the same way. Some more body parts got attention and their inner stories emerged from out of this new way of working.

Listening in three directions

Listening to your own FS, reflecting the FS of the child, and inviting the child to be more attuned to their own felt senses: those are the three directions. It seems simple though it is not easy at all. It is an organic process of consistently finding the right balance between mirroring, reflecting, pausing, and also allowing the right description or expression to emerge from the felt sense form of "just summarize how it all is now."

Trusting the process is a particularly important aspect of FOT with children. The more you are able to stay connected with your own FS the more you can sense what the quality could be of the child's FS. This is always speculation. (Even when we may have a clear, strong FS we are always have to check this with the reality of the child's senses and their responses.)

Mostly a child will not have any immediate words. Offering small attuned pieces of reflections and choices of a possible FS allows the child the elbow room inside to sense deeper into what "suits" them. As a guide I use my own FS as a kind of compass. Only after my own inner pausing and balancing of all these elements can I really offer an attuned intervention to a child.

Bram II

Another moment in the therapy, when Bram was very angry, showed the delicacy of the interaction and relating between me, as a guide, and the child. His mother brought him that morning to therapy with the words "just solve it please." Bram was enraged, shouting at his mother. When she left the room, he visibly settled down. His eyes were almost closed and he ignored me. Without warning, he walked to a large closet in the corner of the room and remained quietly inside. I did nothing to disturb this activity, only mirroring what he did, that he was entering the room and moving to the closet.

While he was inside I resisted the urge to look in the closet and just waited. Every so often I invited him to bring his attention back to check how it was inside right now. I carried no expectation of a reply. I reflected: "There was some emotion when you entered the room and maybe you could check inside how this emotion is right now, or if it wanted to do something?" Bram kept quiet for more than 35 minutes.

The whole time I was waiting I could not see or hear him, apart from catching the sound of his breathing. Suddenly I saw his little finger around the door, then his arm, then his face, then his huge smile, and his wanting to have a pillow fight like we had done at other times. I just mirrored his whole behavior and we fought with the pillows. At the end I invited his hands to express something of how it was inside right then, but he could not. When his mother came back she saw another son altogether. When I asked him if he wanted to share any of the stories he replied: "I stayed in the closet and I was able to start to really move from out of myself instead of other people asking me. I really needed this time." I mirrored this back, invited him to check where he could find this starting point again. He just held his hand on his belly and smiled. Both Bram and his mother left with a smile.

Boundaries and safety

When working with children it is particularly important to be aware of your own boundaries. More clarity within yourself about this will improve the level of safe containment that you can confidently offer to a child or a group. It is important to be as congruent as possible and there are some specifics of language that support us in that intention. For example: using the word *and* instead of but. "I see your feet running through the room *and* that's not allowed right now," "I see your fists want to smash the window *and* it's not safe to do that here. Let's find a safer place for you, your hands, and for us both." Bram tended to hold energy in his body. The more time he spent with me the freer he felt. He always liked to move and walk though sometimes he became a little too enthusiastic. Then he wanted pillow fights. There was always some anger connected with this so I was very aware of safety aspects and offering him clear boundaries at the time. Structure is important here and so instead of just letting him fight for an hour I would make a contract for five minutes" pillow fighting and then we would check inside how it is (offering a chance to pause the situation between us) and then another five minutes and then finding a step to a more personal issue. I would always repeat these structures to maintain consistency for any child.

Bram III

An example of boundaries and safety was a moment in therapy when Bram was becoming more and more liberated in his movements. As a consequence his anger was more available for him. Mostly this was internal and we did some more pillow fighting to support him to be more connected in his body. There was a visible, discernible change here. Bram was more and more into hitting the pillow as if the anger took over his whole body. I mirrored this process back and invited him to make some smaller steps with me so that he could stay more in control instead of the anger taking over his whole body. He looked at me and we both agreed that we would first make ourselves aware of our whole body by stamping our feet and then letting our hands follow the invitation to express any anger that was perhaps still inside.

Bram drew his inner anger here:

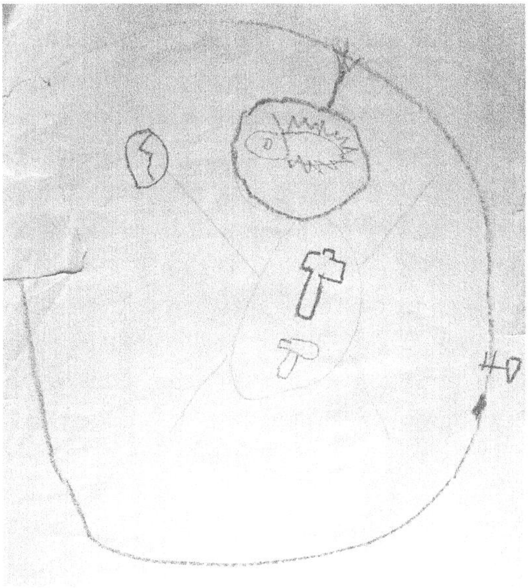

Afterwards, he was much more able to hold his inner anger. He described it as if there was a hammer banging on the inside of his body and the pressure was growing step by step. It was a little animal in his head that got wilder and angrier and the only thing that helped this animal was...to explode! After he drew this picture we had a pillow fight with a new awareness of what this little animal needed. He told me the animal felt much softer, less angry, and that the anger did not get hold of him as it had done when we started.

Mirroring and suggestions

These are necessary elements of the basic attitude in Focusing with children, though they are more subtle and delicate in nature, than at first glance. Children are often quite capable of "talking" about something: the more you reflect, the more this will encourage them to "talk" instead of sensing inside. So it is important to find a balance of mirroring the qualified words and supportive senses in their language instead of just mirroring everything. There are characteristics to mirroring when being with children that are well worth noting. A good way of mirroring builds more depth of inner connection, trust, courage, safety in the child, and can carry forward the inner process of discerning different possibilities. You can mirror what a child says or shares, particularly something "special," and also what the child does and shows with its body. The emotional quality and tone of bodily felt feeling matters greatly in discerning what is sensed behind words and behavior: a discovery, a visual change, or the indication that something positive or new has come.

How the therapist expresses their hypothesis about what they think is going on within the child's world can have a positive impact on the unfolding process. The expressions are tentative and respectful. These are some examples: "Would you like to hear what I'm feeling inside about what we're doing?" "It seems like...." "Sometimes there are children who..." "Maybe something in you..." Always make clear to a child that he can always disagree with whatever you suggest or reflect back. The child can check inside if it feels all right, or if their body disagrees somehow with anything. Encourage children to say "no" when something does not fit. Keep checking, regularly, with the child for any quiet "no," both verbal and nonverbal or in any other way. Active mirroring, in contrast to asking questions, gives more space to children to explore themselves. Sense the difference for yourself between "Was this an exciting play?" and the open quality and curiosity embedded in the quite different statement "Well...this was an exciting play..." followed by simply waiting for what comes now, freshly, from the child, into this open and welcoming space. Timing is crucial to these interventions as well as intonation of the voice and the subtle quality of our own state of mind and intention. I make choices and take decisions constantly when mirroring which can lead to felt shifts, if we greet whatever comes without judgment in the inner body of the child. Again, simply said, though often not so easily done. The relationship between therapist and child depends on the quality of our connection to our own felt senses (see "Listening in three directions," above).

Symbolization

Children are already able to symbolize from their FS at a young age, though they may not easily find words. Symbolization using creative expression is easier for children and therefore the most accessible way for them to express their experience.

Words and language can arise from the inside out, instead of learning from the outside in. Children may have no solid language for their feelings yet so you can offer them a possibility of expressing how "it" feels inside, in their own way. When you allow them a creative pathway to symbolize their feelings and senses through movement, sound, or art making, they can find it easier to freely express and explore themselves and their inner senses. I always say: "Let your hand choose the colour," "Invite your hand to start moving from the inside out," or "Your hands know what they are doing." I do not ask for any words of explanation once a child is symbolizing. When children are allowed to develop their own rhythm and experiencing process, something is generated. The specific mirroring/reflecting of the guide makes space for sensing behind words and behavior, perhaps for a subtle emotional quality or new symbolization arriving, without any clear meaning yet. In general my intention is always to maintain connection with my felt sensing while I am expressing anything relating to them.

Symbolization through play, drawing, clay, and storytelling is like a continuous "finding a handle" and "resonating" (two of the steps from Gendlin's *Focusing*, 1981) allowing "something inside" to be heard and move forward. Sometimes a child is accompanying its expressing with words. The therapist can invite words to come after the expression: "Does the drawing have anything to tell us?" or "Which part of the drawing could use some attention from you?" Or you both can look at the colours, direction, and weight of lines, mark making, and both the place inside where the child drew from and the place where they choose to draw. My attitude and invitations are not in any way about analyzing or judging. Instead, I support children to find their own words for what is expressed and to discover and explore what is going on in their body through drawing. Other things to note include; what is the child's wish, their desire or need, and what supports the process to move forward in small, incremental steps.

I want to share an example now of symbolization in Bram's creative process. Earlier I described how he expressed his inner anger. This example is about how I supported him to express anxiety.

Bram IV

Bram told me that he had a nightmare and was really scared. He did not feel heard or understood by his parents; this made him even angrier. I invited him to sense inside for how and where his feelings were. He was not able to and became even more frightened. He could not make a bodily connection and was overwhelmed by images. I explained that I saw his need and that something seemed to be holding everything inside. I suggested that maybe he was able to describe it to me, so my hands could draw his image. It was immediately clear to me that this would support his process. Step by step his inner FS showed itself on the paper through my drawing. I kept checking that he was in control. I saw that his whole body was involved and that his attention was fully concentrated. I also saw his body relax more as the expression became clearer. At the end I invited him to check inside, if this drawing was a good representation of his feelings and if he wanted to add something more (maybe with his own hands). He clearly and directly said "No, this is really my nightmare. It's inside my chest. It wants to come out, with his axe."

We looked at it together and step-by-step his inner story began to unfold. This figure was a dwarf that always haunted him while he was sleeping and that scared him. Seeing and facing him now, on the sheet of paper, brought relief and Bram wasn't so afraid anymore. We both looked at the expression and found that the crux of this all was that the dwarf was not able to move. He just stood still on his silly feet. Bram became really relieved and said that his hands wanted to tear the drawing apart. I invited him to do this, while I invited him to check with his feelings inside. So he did. With each tear of the paper, he became more alive. His chest was not painful anymore. At the end he was very glad. It invited him even more to be involved in the process. I asked him to check if his hands could, right now, draw how it was inside—Bram was happy to do that.

After drawing his anxiety as a whole like this, his hands then wanted to draw his inner self. He felt really FREEEEEEEE, happy, and empty. So far he has never had this nightmare again.

Endings

Bram and I have worked through his issues for 18 months and I still work with him. At first we met weekly and after 20 sessions we agreed to meet fortnightly. Both Bram and his parents have witnessed many changes: he has found more inner peace, his confidence has grown, and he is much more able to share and express his thoughts and feelings. He has become more playful, is making real friends at school, and has developed more trust in himself. We agreed together that at the end of this year we would stop therapy. The issues that still need some attention relate to finding ways to identify when he has a problem and finding possible action steps that he can take to really "do" something about it or when he needs to ask for help and support from other people. We always decide together about any next step that should happen.

Summary

It's not possible for me to capture the essence of Bram's process here or to relate the whole story of an approach to Focusing with children. It's about a unique relationship that emerges over time and a consistent way of being with a child, using the Focusing steps and process as a guideline. Regardless of the age of the child, when a parent, teacher, or therapist has the basic attitude and makes space for a child, felt sensing can be simple and direct. In this approach children learn to trust their deepest inner sense of rightness and to trust their bodily feeling with all the truth and meaning to be found there. They will come to involve their bodily felt sensing in their everyday life just by getting more used to listening to it and knowing that this feeling carries meaning under the story that helps us all to relate to and deal with problems in daily life. Rather than deny our difficulties, sorrows, and troubles, or drown in them, we can allow ourselves (whether adults or children) to feel the difficult, sorrowful, scary, or angry feelings without another layer of anxiety, judgment, or criticism. Children can clear space inside by learning to see the value of briefly placing problems outside themselves, through lighthearted, creative play and self-expression, for example drawing, painting, or sculpting the whole problem or their bodily sense of "it." In this way any problem becomes more visible for a child and solutions can emerge from the expression itself or a difficulty may even become quite resolved from the expression alone. As a consequence, children remain more firmly at the center of their understanding of thoughts, feelings, emotions, situations, and their whole lived experience. They can learn to concentrate, listen more empathically to other children, and also to resolve conflicts within themselves and with others.

In this chapter I have mentioned several elements worth bringing to the attention of anyone working with children using a Focusing attitude, including:

- Maintaining consistent contact and making fresh contracts about next steps and a fluid awareness of the main entry points into a FS: bodily expression, symbols, or imagery, something around the story or life connection and the emotional quality present.

- The importance of consistent mirroring and inviting things back to the body, where our implicit knowledge of things is carried. For example: "May I ask, where do you notice it in your body? How does it feel? And how does 'it' want to be expressed...?"
- Always being aware of our own boundaries first, our level of congruency, and the resulting knock-on effects in corresponding levels of safety and confidence for the child.
- The benefits of metaphorical language, creative play, symbolization, repetition, and consistency of structure during the ongoing process and how these behaviors build trust. Together, all this supports children to discover the next right step for them, to make in their developmental process.
- Also be aware of how it is possible to repeat each Focusing step, over and over again, so that they form the foundation of the structure and spirit of being together.

Acknowledgment

Thank you to Tom Binns for his editorial help in preparing this chapter.

References

Gendlin, E.T. (1981) *Focusing*. New York: Bantam.

CHAPTER 10

Principles and Practice of Focusing-Oriented Parent–Infant Consultation and Therapy

Zack Boukydis

Introduction

This chapter describes a training program called focusing-oriented parent–infant consultation and therapy. The chapter describes this approach and the basis for bringing Focusing and listening into prevention, intervention, and clinical work with parents, infants, and families.

What is parent–infant therapy?

Parent–infant consultation and therapy has evolved in an interdisciplinary field called infant mental health (IMH; Heffron 2000; Zeanah and Smyke 2009). IMH involves supporting the developing mother (father, family)–infant relationship in clinic and community contexts. Professionals from many disciplines that touch on the lives of parents and infants contribute to IMH practice. My professional work has involved bringing mental health practice into professions that work with parents and infants (Boukydis 2006, 2008, 2012). Central to this work is training which has at its core learning about empathizing with parents and infants in a dual process which includes practitioners learning about empathizing with and listening to themselves. Alicia Lieberman, an IMH leader said: "1. IMH practitioners make an effort to understand how behaviors feel from the inside, not just how they look from the outside; and 2.

The intervener's own feelings and behaviors have a major impact on the intervention" (Lieberman 1998, p.11). This is where Focusing is relevant. This chapter offers a response to how someone can understand how behaviors feel from the inside:

1. by attending in one's body to the common interpersonal space that is shared by adult and infant (Boukydis and Gendlin 2004)
2. by learning how attention to the "intervenor's" own felt sense can help them know how to respond to complex events in parent-infant interactions and relationships.

Because this work occurs at the beginning of the life cycle there is an emphasis on prevention of potential concerns and strengthening mental health and health practices with parents and infants. Professionals may also be involved with parents and their babies where there are identified risk factors with: 1) parent; 2) infant; and/or 3) the developing relationship (Lickliter 2008; Zeanah and Smyke 2009).

Effective and helpful consultation in infancy prevents chronic dysfunctional patterns in the later parent–child relationship (O'Connor and Parfitt 2009). Parent–infant consultation involves: 1) the parent–infant dyad and problems that arise in daily interactions; and 2) the parent–infant dyad when viewed and supported in the context of every important relationship in the family. The work involves attentive support and collaboration with parent and infant in order to improve the developing relationship; redefining parental misperceptions of infant behavior; articulating parental understanding and response to differences in infant temperamental or emotional style; discovering and changing influences from the parent's own history of being parented; and improving parental competence and self esteem (Zeanah and Smyke 2009).

What is the focusing-oriented approach to parent–infant consultation and therapy?

The focusing-oriented approach is based on: 1) a history of work with parents and infants in the client-centered/experiential realm (Guerney, Guerney and Andronico 1976; Mahrer, Levinson and Fine 1976; Bowers 2008; Stapert and Verliefde 2008; Armstrong 2010);

2) extensive research on parent–infant interaction and the meaning system which develops between parents and infants (Papousek and Papousek 1987; Preston and Shumsky 1998; Tronick 2010); 3) 35 years of clinical work and consultation on the parent–infant relationship (Boukydis 1990, 2012); and 4) a redefinition of enduring concepts in the field of IMH (reflective function; mother–infant attachment; representations) into a framework which provides a theoretical and practical understanding of change in the ongoing parent–infant relationship. This last point could be understood as drawing from Gendlin's Theory of Personality Change (Gendlin 1964) to provide the foundation for trainings called Seeing and Supporting Change in Parent–Infant Relationships (Boukydis 2010b).

The approach is based on a philosophical model of empathic relations between parents and infants (Boukydis 1985, 1990, 2012; Boukydis and Gendlin 2004) including parents" direct reference to their "felt sense" or bodily felt intuition in interactions with their infants; strengthening or recovering the capacity to use bodily felt meaning in the relationship; the importance of preverbal sensory and emotional communication between infant and parent; and an understanding of how mother and baby are relating to, and affecting, *one* process (Boukydis and Gendlin 2004).

A whole method of practice for the focusing-oriented approach has been developed (Boukydis 1990); and my recent book, *Consultation with Parents and Infants in the Perinatal Period* (Boukydis 2012), outlines the theoretical underpinning and practice specifics in this approach. While this chapter focuses on focusing-oriented parent–infant consultation and therapy, there is another body of work bringing Focusing into work with parents and infants in hospital and community settings (Boukydis 2006, 2008) and in preventive services (Boukydis 2010a, 2010b).

Key elements of the focusing-oriented parent–infant approach

Listening and attending to felt experience of self and self in relationship to one's infant

The baseline for this approach is active resonant listening and developing a trusting relationship with a parent and baby. Of course, this includes the practice of experiential listening (Friedman 2007; McGuire 2007) and a special concentration on listening/resonating in an interpersonal context where the bodily felt presence of the listener can sometimes resonate with, or subtly enliven, the felt experience of the parent in an interaction with their baby (Boukydis 2012). Much of the training experience in this approach also involves consultants attending thoughtfully to ways of providing a quiet interpersonal space where mothers and fathers can notice their own experience of themselves, and their felt experience with their babies. One simple poignant example of this "providing a quiet space" occurred recently in our Close Collaboration with Parents training program (Boukydis, Ahlqvist-Bjorkroth and Lehtonen 2011), based in a neonatal intensive care unit (NICU). A nurse in our program sat down beside a mother whose preterm baby was lying on her chest having skin-to-skin contact. Even in the busy NICU environment, the nurse had regular contact with the mother, "watching her baby together"—nurse and mother. This time the nurse commented: "She seems to be not just touching you; but moving her fingers—maybe to explore you…?" The mother, paused, then said: "She does this a lot, I call it her, 'playing the piano.'" Both nurse and mother smiled. Then the mother said, with tears in her eyes, "She is playing my heart strings." This story highlights the importance of a caring relationship that allows for listening, for the mother to be more conscious of her own experience.

The baby's gesture, moving her fingers on her mother's skin, had a unique relationship to the mother's evolving felt sense of the interaction—evident from the movement in mother's words from "playing the piano" to "playing my heart strings." In the context of parent–baby relationships, this is called the metaphorizing process (Boukydis 1990, 2012; Gendlin 1964, 1997), where gestures, touch, tastes, etc. can have this unique enlivening relationship to the parent's felt sense. The metaphorizing process will be elaborated on in Part IV.

In relationships with babies it is essential to notice, and interact with, immediate bodily felt experience. Babies evoke salient, sometimes strong, visceral responses in parents, adults, and children. Work on intuitive parenting (Papousek and Papousek 1987) provides an understanding of the neurobiological basis for how babies' ways of communicating and parents' ways of responding are highly adaptive to insure the infant's survival and socio-emotional growth. There is an extensive body of research on parent–infant interaction which provides an understanding of how infant's signal or express their needs and how parents, through different kinds of caregiving and play, help infants "regulate" their internal states of arousal, a process called mutual regulation (Papousek and Papousek 1987; Tronick 2010). While this work provides a useful framework, most of the research has been done on auditory and visual modes of communication using video recording and different technologies for coding infant–parent behavior in interactive exchanges. Where the focusing-oriented approach intersects with this work is to explicate the role of bodily felt experience in these exchanges between parents and infants and bodily felt experience as the source of "meaning making." While babies "behaving" is compelling, there are many variations to the theme, and there are times when parents overreact, underreact, or misread what is happening for their baby. In all these situations, being able to attend to, and then interact with, immediate felt experience is very important (Boukydis 2012, pp.187–205).

Tronick (2010) has highlighted the importance of mismatches in everyday parent–infant communicative exchanges as a necessary part of learning and nurturing a relationship. Such disruptions to the implicit natural back and forth exchanges cause the parent to become more conscious of what is going on, and both partners thereby learn how to repair or "get back in sync." However, there are times when these exchanges can lead to a cycle of reactivity between parent and baby. The interaction can become "structure bound" (Gendlin 1964), repetitive, and at times can even challenge the development of the baby and the parent–baby relationship (Anders 1989). For instance, a mother came to our clinic with her three-month-old son, saying, "I'm afraid he doesn't like me." While beginning our work together, we asked if she would be willing to show us what playing was like with her son; if we could videotape their playing and later look at the tape together. We also asked her if she would play for several minutes; then hold her face "still" for two minutes before returning to a playful exchange. We explained that when she held her face still we might notice what her baby does to get her to interact with him. What we saw initially was an interaction that couldn't have felt very good for either mother or baby. As the mother began talking and playing, her son looked pensive and almost sideways at her. The intensity of her touching and talking increased, and he turned away. As this turning away occurred, she looked worried and her activity level increased. However, when the mother held her face still, her son didn't turn away, and quietly looked into his mother's face. Later, the mother looked at this play sequence with us on videotape, saying, "I'm not giving him a chance." When she looked at the "still face" part she cried and said, "He really likes me." Participating in a change process related to her interaction and relationship with her baby could not necessarily alter all that was going on for this mother, but it helped her rally. She received support for herself through therapy. She had suffered a loss during her pregnancy and an extreme lack of support for being a new mother, which left her vulnerable and anxious that she could not take care of her baby. There were some intermittent mother–baby sessions to support the "mutuality" and quietly validate that her baby not only liked her but that they were "in love."

Understanding the metaphorizing process related to evolving felt experience between babies and parents

In the same way that words and images can have a unique relationship with the felt sense, so can other sensory phenomena such as taste, smell, touch, and in addition, with infants—gestures and postures. In relationships with babies, there are times where any or all of these senses are engaged. Below are some important considerations:

1. *Experiencing and meaning-creation (Gendlin 1997) can be extended from words and images to include tastes, smells, and so on.* An "experienced" smell between a parent and their baby can resonate with the parent's felt sense. This metaphorizing process, under the right conditions, can carry forward (from the initial awareness of the smell *and* the felt sense related to that smell) to a felt shift and sometimes a more conscious awareness and a subtle or noticeable change in the parent–infant relationship. Much of this "interacting" on all sensory levels goes on without conscious attention by the parent, and is part of experiencing in everyday life. Understanding the metaphorizing process is important in

the focusing-oriented parent–infant approach. The consultant can learn to become aware of times when the infant's presence carries forward the parent's experiencing process (see Case example 1); relates to a confused and unnamable feeling in the parent's body (Case example 1); or points towards "stuck" feelings in the parent and in the dynamics of the interacting (for example the mother who said, "I'm afraid my baby doesn't like me").

The parent's actions, including just their physical presence, can also metaphorize the infant's process and can carry forward stressful or problematic functioning for the infant (Boukydis 2012, pp.187–205). The section on methods includes several ways that parents can reflect their infant's behavior and the felt experience in the interaction.

Case example 1: Rosa

One day Aliz, mother of Rosa, was making lunch in the kitchen. Rosa, two months old, was lying on a blanket on the floor playing with a rattle. Rosa began to fuss and Aliz said, "Just a minute, I'll be there, I have to finish mixing this ..." Rosa put her fingers to her mouth, began to suck, and stopped fussing. Aliz turned from the counter to Rosa, and said, "Wow, you can do that?" An hour later Aliz described this event to a pediatric office nurse, "You know, I was touched, surprised... I didn't expect that. It's the first time." "First time?" the nurse asked. Aliz said, "Well, I've seen her do that before (put her fingers in her mouth while fussing) but...but, it's the first time...I felt she can do something to...help herself and...doesn't need me so intensely every moment of the day." There were tears in Aliz's eyes when she said this. A later discussion with Aliz highlighted what had happened. When Rosa put her fingers to her mouth, Aliz had a feeling in her body, which she noticed but didn't have words for. Later when she talked to the nurse about Rosa putting her fingers in her mouth, she noticed that feeling, then the words "the first time" came, and then "she can do something for herself" and "doesn't need me so intensely every moment of the day." Aliz said, "I didn't know all I was feeling. My pride in her doing something for herself, I noticed that, but that feeling (she doesn't need me so intensely every moment of the day) was a surprise, and there's a lot to that." Aliz went on to explore "all that was there" in her felt sense related to "she doesn't need me so intensely every moment of the day."

One key emphasis from this example involves Rosa's gesture—putting her fingers in her mouth (and her change from fussing to calm). In this situation, Aliz could have what was soon recognized as a felt sense in relation to that gesture. There were aspects to this felt sense that she could articulate (pride for Rosa sucking her finger and soothing her fussiness) as well as other felt, but not yet definable, aspects. These aspects became more conscious to Aliz in interaction with people who were able to listen to her.

2. *The importance of listening to self during sessions with parents and infants.* Work with parents and infants is often compelling. Learning to focus as part of this work helps consultants attend to and learn about their own life issues as they are activated. In addition, while a focusing-oriented therapist learns to attend to their own felt sense during sessions, it becomes even more important to learn to attend to one's felt sense while being present during sessions which include interactions between parents and babies.

   Much of the general training in parent–infant psychotherapy emphasizes the importance of reflective supervision (Shamoon-Shanok 2009). This supervision typically occurs apart from the immediacy of being present during parent–infant interactions. Training often involves watching videotapes, undertaking observations, and speculating about the experience of parent and baby, but it does not necessarily include how to attend to, and use, the felt sense of the therapist as a fundamental touchstone (Boukydis 2010a, 2012).

   The consultant or therapist must develop the capacity to attend to their felt sense of themselves in the immediate situation of being present in the interaction and interpersonal feeling space of infant and parent. As this capacity develops, the consultant must continue to be able to match or compare their felt sense with what they observe in the interactions between parent and infant.

The consultant must wonder about the infant's and parents" experience of the same interaction and engage in the "working through" of empathic response. Empathic understanding arises in the consultant being able to engage their own felt sense of these interactions with thoughtful discernment. This includes open-ended questions of their own felt experience, and sometimes thoughtful, "wondering" questions to the participants in the experienced interaction. Through this process of attention to the felt sense, the consultant gains information that may be insightful in understanding the parents' and infant's experience.

Case example 2: struggling to get it

In my book (Boukydis 2012) I describe a situation where a parent–infant consultant is having a session with a mother and her three-month-old infant. The consultant had learned Focusing contributed to a training program. As the consultant talks with the mother, the mother begins to look out the window and doesn't seem to notice her daughter on a blanket on the floor struggling to get a rattle just beyond her reach. The consultant briefly focuses, notices her felt sense of the situation and the words "struggling to get it" arise. At first, she notices an urge to speak and says (taking the place of the infant), "Oh, you really want that rattle." However, the consultant repeats "struggling to get it" several times to herself and notices that both mother and baby seem to be "struggling to get it." If she had spoken at that moment, she might have said, "You're both yearning to get it?" Somehow, in attending to her own experience, she felt a subtle rightness about saying to the mother, "Are you trying to find the words for something you are feeling?" (Boukydis 2012, p.168). The mother looked back at the consultant, moved the rattle so her daughter could reach it, and told the consultant that she was trying to find a way to tell her that she had spoken to her daughter's father that morning and he wanted to "get back together." He had left the mother while she was pregnant. The vignette highlights a common demand in parent–infant dyadic work—attending to one's own feelings, plus the feelings of parent, infant, and the "interpersonal space" of the dyad, in order to sense how to support "change" (Boukydis 2010b).

3. *Refinement of inner child work with perspectives from focusing-oriented parent–infant consultation.* When considering Focusing and the inner infant (compared with the inner child) it is important to consider that those phenomena which come to awareness may not just be words or images but could be tastes, smells, sounds, gestures, and so on. Training in focusing-oriented parent–infant consultation sensitizes consultants to notice all phenomena and then find ways to resonate those that potentially relate to the parent's felt sense.

   Some consultants and clients work with Focusing and the inner child. Many of these attitudes and perspectives could include the inner infant. In introducing "inner infant" however, it brings up the important issue of becoming more differentiated: What is the developmental level of the child? What are his/her capabilities and what are his/her preferred modes of revealing inner experience and communicating to an empathic adult?

   Work in focusing-oriented parent–infant consultation and therapy includes times for "dyadic" sessions and individual sessions with parents. During individual sessions some therapists may facilitate parents to do inner child/inner infant work. It is recognized that, especially during the process of becoming a parent, inner child issues including a parent's own feelings and memories of being parented become activated and potentially available for therapeutic attention.

Some main emphases in "inner child/inner infant" work

1. *Empathy with the felt sense as an infant/child.* For many people the inner infant/child perspective helps them to have empathy for their felt sense, as they would in attending to an infant/child who is feeling what they are feeling. Often they can recapture the child's sense of wonder and adventure. They are concurrently developing the capacity to be an attentive parent for the wounded and scared child feelings that they process. With some parents, the process of developing self-empathy this

way is paralleled with the ability to expand and differentiate their ability to empathize with their infant.

2. *Relating to developmental level.* Relating to the inner infant or child also can be understood as attending to an important phase of early development where certain important events or constellations of experience are waiting to be attended to, transformed and healed. In Focusing it is thought that the felt sense can present to us what needs to be attended to or healed. With clients in therapy, I sometimes sense that what they are feeling might relate to a particular developmental phase. One can also address one's felt sense directly to specific developmental issues. For example, one can clear a space (respecting and setting to one side what one already knows about an issue) and then ask in an open-ended way: "My birth…?" Some of my clients have taken up the practice of asking open-ended questions related to each phase of their developmental history, and then tracking the responses/discoveries that they make. The resultant inner infant symbolization process may be a taste, a smell, and so on.

3. *Finding the right relationship: "being with" versus "being in or away from."* This perspective enables one to get the right distance—not falling into their feeling, or getting too far from what they are feeling, but "being with," in the same manner one would want to be with a child who is feeling hurt or confused. It is essentially the same when one can just be with one's felt sense. As one is able to be with one's felt sense in a friendly, attentive manner, then the felt sense can speak and be part of a moving forward process. From the perspective of attachment theory, some people learn to be a "secure base" (Lickliter 2008) while attending to their felt sense. Those who are unable to keep the right connection provide either anxiously attached connection (unable to listen openly to their felt sense) or avoidantly attached connection (unable to maintain connection with their felt sense). This relationship between patterns of attachment in the parent–infant relationship and patterns and challenges in being with the felt sense in individual Focusing is currently the basis for ongoing research.

4. *What are the methods of focusing-oriented parent–infant consultation?* (A full listing of methods is included in Boukydis 2012, pp.187–205.) In addition to listening, some of the fundamentals of focusing-oriented parent–infant consultation and therapy include:

    a. *Providing quiet attentive times,* where parents can notice their felt sense in relation to their infant. A lot of early training involves trainees learning to notice tensions about remaining silent and watching for early indications that parents might be attending to their own feeling state.

    b. *Learning ways to invite a mother to notice her bodily felt sense during events or interactions with her infant.* In some work, parents may explicitly learn Focusing both for themselves and for their baby. During supervision, a colleague discussed asking a mother, who had learned Focusing, to focus while her infant was fussing. The colleague sat beside the baby, and the mother was able to notice the feeling in her body. After being quiet for some moments, the mother said: "... its so hard for me to hear you cry...no, to sense you are uncomfortable...yes, that's it...so hard to sense you being uncomfortable...it's been there since you were born... umm...during your birth...[mother has tears]...I'm afraid you got hurt during the time when you were breech and I was bearing down on you...yes, that's it... I am afraid you are still hurt and...I caused it!" This was a moment that the mother later identified as a felt shift, and she put her daughter on her shoulder and said, "I just never knew that (fear and guilt of hurting her baby during the 'breech time') was in me when I listened to you crying...both of us feeling uncomfortable."

    c. *Attend to felt sense, or actively Focusing while watching videotaped interaction.* Video replay involves inviting a mother to notice her experience while watching a video of herself and her baby playing, feeding, etc. There are several methodologies for video replay. The practice of focusing-oriented parent–infant consultation and therapy is most productively combined with interaction guidance (McDonough 2004).

Consultants learn to choose several "attentive" segments of interaction between parent and infant and then segments which are either challenging or illustrative of a concern that a parent has voiced about their relationship with their infant. Video replay often permits the right distance and connection allowing a parent to attend to their felt sense while being essentially one step removed from the immediacy of an interaction which they may be "too" immersed in.

Conclusion

This chapter explains how the long history of work with people in Focusing and Focusing-Oriented Psychotherapy has been extended into work with parents and infants. Of particular importance is how the practice of Focusing and listening, including the importance of human presence and the metaphorizing process, deepens work with the parent–infant dyad. The new field of focusing-oriented parent–infant consultation and therapy involves: 1) training those who work with parents and infants in clinical and community settings to learn Focusing and integrate focusing-listening into their work, and 2) training therapists in the methods, especially dyadic consultation, of focusing-oriented parent–infant psychotherapy.

References

Anders, T. (1989) "Clinical Syndromes, Relationship Disturbances and Their Assessment." In A. Sameroff and R. Emde (eds) *Relationship Disturbances in Early Childhood.* New York: Basic Books.

Armstrong, M. (2010) "Focusing listening with babies." *The Focusing Connection 29*, 4, 3.

Boukydis, C.F.Z. (1985) "A theory of empathic relations between parents and infants." *Focusing Folio.* Focusing Institute, University of Chicago.

Boukydis, C.F.Z. (1990) "Client-Centered/Experiential Practice with Parents and Infants." In G. Lietaer, J. Rombauts and R. Van Balen (eds) *Client-Centered/Experiential Psychotherapy toward the Nineties.* Leuven: Van Hooten.

Boukydis, C.F.Z. (2006) "Ultrasound consultation during pregnancy: Imaging and imagining the world of the fetus." *IMPrint 26*, 19–21.

Boukydis, C.F.Z. (2008) "Working with parents and their infants in NICU settings: Use of joint observations and neurobehavioral assessment." *Early Childhood Services 2*, 1, 43–58.

Boukydis, C.F.Z. (2010a) "New directions in reflective practice: What can we reflect on?" *Infant Mental Health Journal (WAIMH conference abstracts) 31*, 6, 698.

Boukydis, C.F.Z. (2010b) "Seeing and supporting change in parent–infant relationships." *Infant Mental Health Journal (WAIMH conference abstracts) 31*, 6, 712.

Boukydis, Z. (2012) *Collaborative Consultation with Parents and Infants in the Perinatal Period.* Baltimore, MD: Brookes Publishing Company.

Boukydis, C.F.Z., Ahlqvist-Bjorkroth, S. and Lehtonen, L. (2011) "Family centered care based on infant observations in the NICU: Development and evaluation of a training program." *Infant Mental Health Journal (WAIMH conference abstracts) 31*, 6, 698.

Boukydis, C.F.Z. and Gendlin, E. (2004) "Mothers and infants: One body process with equal initiative." *Focusing Folio 19*, 1, 86–92.

Bowers, L. (2008) "Gene Gendlin's gift for children." *The Focusing Folio*, 278–290.

Friedman, N. (2007) *Focusing Oriented Psychotherapy.* Spring Valley, NY: The Focusing Institute.

Gendlin, E.T. (1964) "A Theory of Personality Change." In P. Worchel and D. Byrne (eds) *Personality Change.* New York: John Wiley & Sons.

Gendlin, E. (1997) *Experiencing and the Creation of Meaning.* Evanston, IL: Northwestern University Press.

Guerney, B., Guerney, L. and Andronico, M. (1976) *The Therapeutic Use of Children's Play.* New York: Jason Aronson.

Heffron, M.C. (2000) "Clarifying concepts of infant mental health-promotion, relationship-based preventive intervention, and treatment." *Infants and Young Children 12*, 4, 14–21.

Lickliter, R. (2008) "Theories of attachment: The long and winding road to an integrative developmental science." *Integrative Psychological and Behavioral Science 42*, 397–405.

Lieberman, A. (1998) "A perspective on infant mental health." *The Signal 6*, 1, 11–12.

Mahrer, A., Levinson, J.R. and Fine, S. (1976) "Infant psychotherapy: Theory, research, and practice." *Psychotherapy: Theory, Research and Practice 13*, 131–140.

McDonough, S. (2004) "Interaction Guidance: Promoting and Nurturing the Caregiver Relationship." In A. Sameroff, S. McDonough and K. Rosenblum (eds) *Treating Parent–Infant Relationship Problems: Strategies for Intervention.* New York: Guilford Press.

McGuire, K. (2007) *Focusing in Community: How to Start a Listening and Focusing Support Group.* New York: Creative Edge Focusing and The Focusing Institute.

O'Connor, T. and Parfitt, D. (2009) "Applying Research Findings on Early Experience to Infant Mental Health." In C. Zeanah (ed.) *Handbook of Infant Mental Health*, 3rd edn. New York: Guilford Press.

Papousek, H. and Papousek, M. (1987) "Intuitive Parenting: A Dialectic Counterpart to the Infant's Precocity in Integrative Capacities." In J.D. Osofsky (ed.) *Handbook of Infant Development*, 2nd edn. New York: Wiley.

Preston, L. and Shumsky, E. (1998) "The Development of the Dyad: A Bidirectional Revisioning of Some Self Psychological Concepts." In A. Goldberg (ed.) *Progress in Self Psychology.* Hillsdale, NJ: Analytic Press.

Shahmoon-Shanok, R. (2009) "What is Reflective Supervision?" In S. Heller and L. Gilkerson (eds) *A Practical Guide to Reflective Supervision.* Washington, DC: Zero to Three Press.

Stapert, M. and Verliefde, E. (2008) *Focusing with Children: The Art of Communicating with Children at Home and at School.* Ross-on-Wye: PCCS Books.

Tronick, E.Z. (2010) "Infants and Mothers: Self- and Mutual Regulation and Meaning Making." In B.M. Lester and J. Sparrow (eds) *Nurturing Children and Families: Building on the Legacy of T. Berry Brazelton.* New York: Wiley-Blackwell.

Zeanah, C. and Smyke, A. (2009) "Attachment Disorders." In C. Zeanah (ed.) *Handbook of Infant Mental Health*, 3rd edn. New York: Guilford Press.

CHAPTER 11

Integrating Focusing into Couples Therapy

John Amodeo and Annmarie Early

Despite living in the age of electronic connectivity, we seem more disconnected than ever from each other and ourselves. We are in the grip of a silent epidemic of depression and anxiety that disorganizes us from the inside and impedes our ability to live a richly connected life. We may numb ourselves to alleviate the pain of isolation with an unprecedented variety of activities and mood altering substances, but this only serves to exacerbate our disconnection.

As mammals, we're wired for connection from "cradle to grave" (Bowlby 1988, p.62). Our sense of wellbeing, quality of life, and even immune functioning depend in large measure on the quality of these connections (Mikulincer and Shaver 2007). Nothing can substitute for the relational bond most basic to our nature. We pursue intimate connections as a source of the love we long for. As couples therapists, how can we help people learn how to turn toward each other more effectively? What needs to happen within and between two people who want to repair broken trust, heal old wounds, and create a fulfilling intimacy?

A key premise for using Focusing with couples is that disconnection and conflict "between" often reflects a disconnection "within"—that is, from our individual felt experience (Amodeo 2007)—creating a context where interpersonal engagement is thwarted. A climate for intimacy requires two individuals who open to, embrace, and engage with their own feelings and longings—and then from that deeply felt place engage with one another. The capacity to make contact with the full range of one's felt experience and express authentic feelings creates an environment that fosters safety and paves the way for being intimately connected with others.

Struggling couples who enter our offices typically report problems with communication. While this is a valid concern, they are often not aware that the more fundamental issue is a lack of connection with themselves and their partner. When deeper, vulnerable feelings remain hidden, couples may only notice and express reactive or secondary emotions of anger and resentment, which are typically communicated through blame, criticism, contempt, and evaluations of each other. This dissociation from what is authentic within themselves leads to John Gottman's (1999) "Four Horsemen of the Apocalypse" (criticism, contempt, stonewalling, and defensiveness), which his research has shown to be reliable predictors of marital meltdown. Authentic and effective communication requires making contact with what is most subtly alive inside of us and courageously revealing this to a person with whom we want to connect (Amodeo 2001).

Our experience as couples therapists suggests that conditions for connection between couples are created when they are able to pause, attend mindfully to their bodily felt experience (primary feelings), and reveal this to each other. Couples therapy then becomes a safe haven for each person to become aware of their deeply nuanced feelings and receive gentle guidance and encouragement to contact and convey their emotions, desires, and messages in a clear, congruent, non-blaming way.

A climate for connection

While some couples who see us are decidedly ambivalent about their relationship, others tell us that they'll do anything to make the relationship work—"whatever it takes," they often say. Unfortunately, it's not that simple. It helps to have a sincere intention to resolve things, but willpower has a limited capacity to bring people together.

Neither clients nor therapists have as much power as we might like to foster connections—at least not directly. The good news is that we have a great deal of power to build connection through a different route. Positive change happens as couples' good intentions for the partnership are directed toward becoming mindful of how they are contributing to destructive cycles and finding new ways to access and communicate their authentic feelings and longings.

Intimacy and soap bubbles have much in common. As soon as we try to grab them, they burst. We can't control the course of love. We can't manipulate our way into this most tender sanctuary. We won't draw our loved ones toward us by berating them or telling them how they need to change. These reactions, rooted in our limbic and reptilian brain, push people farther away rather than draw them closer. What we're up against—and need to work with skilfully—is our survival-oriented fight, flight, or freeze response as we experience real or imagined threats to our need for safety and connection. We have found that weaving Focusing and Emotionally Focused Therapy (EFT) for couples together offers a compelling way to help couples lay the groundwork for connection by offering a structure that enables them to engage with themselves and each other more deeply and constructively.

Focusing with couples

Moving in

The practice of Focusing grew out of research into the effectiveness of psychotherapy. Eugene Gendlin (1982) found that the clients who connected with their actual felt experience grew the most in psychotherapy, regardless of the modality of the therapist. We might say that these naturally gifted clients already had the capacity to be intimate with themselves. They slowed down their speech, dropped down into their present experience, and waited for feelings, images, or meanings to emerge from the bodily felt sense of life issues or situations. It is a short step from there to wonder what enables two people to deepen intimacy as a couple. The prospect for couples to connect more easily would appear to improve as each of them pursues a path of uncovering their deeper, bodily felt experience, and sharing that experience with each other.

Partners often seek a commitment from each other in order to feel safe in the relationship. Indeed, a context of safety allows couples to take the risks necessary to deepen love and intimacy. But what often gets overlooked is the importance of an additional kind of commitment—namely, each person's commitment to the lifelong process of cultivating mindfulness of their own inner process (Amodeo 2013). To the extent that each partner cultivates a more secure internal base—that is, the greater the capacity to draw upon inner resources and rest more comfortably in themselves, the deeper and stronger the relationship can become.

A focusing-oriented approach to couples therapy is characterized by helping clients move inward to create the foundation for moving toward each other. This includes learning to embody what has been called the Focusing attitude, which includes qualities of acceptance and gentleness toward our own experience.

Focusing offers a path toward self-acceptance so that when we reach out to our partner, we can come from a more balanced, respectful, and resourced place. This calmer self-extension allows our partner to feel less defended and more inclined to move toward us. This capacity for self-soothing is also crucial when the comforting we might seek from each other is not forthcoming.

Moving toward

We have found in our work with couples that when both individuals uncover and express their spontaneously arising feelings in a tender way, a climate for connection is created. Embracing what is alive inside and allowing their partner to touch and taste their nuanced inner world allows intimacy to incubate and thrive.

Bringing Focusing into a couples session includes selectively engaging with each partner in a way that cultivates the Focusing attitude, which allows volatile emotions to settle enough so that meaningful feelings can safely emerge and be expressed in non-blaming, non-shaming ways. For example, Ted might say to Andrea, "You're on the phone too much with your family. They're more important to you than our relationship!" We might turn to Ted, gently asking him, "Would it be ok to take a moment and sense how it feels inside when she's on the phone with her family?" If Ted is willing to pause (an essential aspect of Focusing), and sense within himself, he might notice something new. "Well, I feel lonely when she's on the phone; I'd love to take a walk with her after work or watch a movie together." Hearing his vulnerable feeling of loneliness, Andrea is more likely to soften and "let in" what he's saying and wanting.

If Ted responds to our Focusing suggestion defensively, such as by saying, "How do you think it feels? It feels infuriating!" we might try to slow him down by offering some reflective listening: "I really hear how infuriating it feels to you." We might then invite him to sense how that feels in his body—and notice if anything more might emerge. Perhaps something deeper will surface. However, if Ted has little facility for sensing inside or if this issue is particularly charged, he might not be able to slow down and turn toward himself. His nervous system might be too activated. He might even feel shame if he is not able to pause as we're suggesting, and this will render our intervention ineffective and counterproductive.

It may be best at such junctures if the therapist focuses—taking some time to stay in his or her own body and finding a way to engage with this relational moment. Ted might need to hear that we really understand what he's experiencing, even if he can't express it clearly right now. He might need us to help him find words or images that convey to Andrea how he's feeling.

Gendlin has often suggested that we learn not just Focusing but other methods too. Engaging the client during such volatile or overwhelming moments is where EFT shines and becomes a helpful complement to Focusing.

A bridge between Focusing and Emotionally Focused Therapy for couples

Connecting with our felt experience is the hallmark of Focusing. Intimacy is created as couples connect with the more vulnerable feelings within themselves and reveal them to each other. But as couples therapists well know, this is not so easy to do! While designed to protect us from danger, the fight, flight, or freeze reaction often sabotages the love we need, leading to a soul-numbing isolation.

For some couples, Focusing may help to slow down the rapid-fire ping-pong match between a couple and allow emotions to settle before destructive attacks or withdrawal occur. Couples who have learned Focusing may find a rhythm of going inside and then communicating what they are noticing without attacking or blaming. But many couples need additional guidance in order to not react so automatically when there is amygdala activation—the old part of the brain that registers threat and instantly prepares the body to escape danger. EFT is just such a method that, when integrated into focusing-oriented couples work, can accelerate and deepen therapy.

An EFT perspective

Emotionally Focused Therapy (EFT) for couples is considered the gold standard for empirically based couples therapy. It was first formulated and tested in the 1980s and has been refined over the last two decades and expanded to new areas such as the treatment of couples with trauma and the healing of relationship injuries. EFT is an experiential model that draws heavily from the pioneering work of Rogers, Gendlin, Gestalt, and Systems Theory, honoring the power of emotionally charged moments in therapy for creating change. EFT has a strong research base that demonstrates its efficacy in helping highly distressed couples reduce conflict and create a bond that strengthens their relationship over time (Johnson 2004; Johnson and Whittenborn 2012).

The research on EFT demonstrates that creating positive relational shifts requires both making contact in the here and now with primary experience and speaking from that place to one's partner, honoring what is emergent, giving voice to various parts of self, and working with bottom-up implicit processes (Johnson 2004). The EFT research suggests that a positive shift toward intimacy is facilitated as each partner contacts and conveys what is living implicitly within themselves—namely, their deeper, more vulnerable feelings and longings—and shares from that place with their partner (Johnson 2004). These findings appear quite consistent with Gendlin's research: those clients who make progress in psychotherapy are attending to an implicit process. By pausing to be mindful of their bodily felt sense of their life concerns, they experience new felt meanings, insights, and subsequent movement in their lives.

Seeing through the eyes of attachment

EFT uses attachment theory as its framework for understanding both the rigid interactional cycles that keep couples stuck and the power of the relational bond in healing and connection. Key aspects of this model derive from the pioneering work of John Bowlby (1988), who carefully observed the behavior of infants and their caretakers. This research has been expanded to include the importance of adult attachment for overall health and wellbeing, as well as the ability to sustain a satisfying relationship throughout the lifespan (Cassidy and Shaver 2008; Mikulincer and Shaver 2007).

An attachment framework guides the clinician to listen with an attentive ear for what evokes reactivity and threat, reframing reactivity in terms of attachment needs and wants. When fear is activated in the relationship, we know that there is danger and we can expect a fight, flight, or freeze response. Whether in a moment of great need or when our partner forgets to do the dishes (for the seventh time this week!), we may ask, "Will you be there for me when I really need you?" This question is the fulcrum on which our sense of safety and security hinges. When the answer to this question is "Yes," then even if the dishes pile up in the sink, we feel safe and secure and can face our daily struggles with greater ease. However, when we don't feel securely connected, our primal fear system of fight, flight, or freeze is likely to be activated, making peaceful, problem-solving engagement nearly impossible.

Gendlin's (1966) assertion that we live as interactional beings is consistent with attachment theory. According to Gendlin, living implies an ongoing interaction with the environment. As he puts it, "Being with and being in (situations, the world) are not mere 'traits' of humans. They are what it is to be human, they are human 'being'" (1966, p.228).

A framework for change

A central understanding of this movement from conflict to sharing is a framework that recognizes our deep longing for acceptance, intimacy, and love (Johnson 2008). In our view, a comprehensive foundation for a focusing-oriented approach with couples emphasizes this relational longing—and gently helps couples find their way toward contact with this longing and associated emotions and felt senses. When couples hit roadblocks, an unacknowledged process may contaminate the manifestation of that longing.

Couples often express emotions and needs indirectly and in ways that thwart their ability to achieve satisfying connections. For example, somewhere within Ted is a desire for more intimacy with Andrea. He unabashedly vents his judgments and anger, but he is split off from the felt experience of this longing for contact with her. Andrea wants a connection with her family, and presumably with Ted as well. But her fear of Ted's anger and criticism keeps her shut down and unresponsive.

Both Focusing and EFT create a space where clients can safely uncover what lives most deeply within them. However, EFT follows a map of adult love and bonding that dynamically conceptualizes relational longings in terms of attachment needs, outlines the patterns that create the dance of distress that sustains disconnection, and maps a pathway forward for creating both conflict de-escalation and relational bonding for the couple (Johnson 2004). This more active approach is especially helpful when working with high-conflict couples, where small steps forward are easily subverted upon the slightest indication of inattentiveness or criticism from a partner.

Helping the couple go deeper

Some couples are at least somewhat skilled at being gentle with their feelings and working with their reactivity. Perhaps they have a fairly secure internal base due to secure bonding in childhood; they have some reasonable capacity to self-soothe. Or perhaps they've learned Focusing, mindfulness meditation, or some other way to be present with their feelings. Focusing can reinforce an innate capacity for self-awareness and self-regulation by inviting each person to go inside at various junctures during therapy, especially when vulnerable feelings such as fear, hurt, or shame have arisen—or seem likely to arise. Inviting each of them to pause a moment, attend within, and bring gentleness to whatever they're experiencing might allow a settling of their nervous system, which sets the stage for something deeper to emerge.

Focusing-oriented therapist Greg Madison (2010) explains that "Many run over those moments where a client is teetering at the edge of a process of bodily felt sensing." He suggests that "therapists offer invitations to the client to stay with what is felt but not being paid attention to, in the client's bodily experience of their issue" (2010, p.196). This principle is perfectly applicable to couples therapy. Perhaps Ted will recognize feelings of hurt or loneliness beneath his irritation. He would then be well positioned to share these more tender feelings rather than attack Andrea. We might ask him what he notices in his body when Andrea is on the phone or invite Andrea to notice what comes up for her when Ted conveys his discontent. Inviting them to pause and experience whatever they are aware of allows time for whatever "next step" in their process might unfold.

Creating safety: connecting with the couple

Focusing-oriented work with couples and EFT emphasize that the therapist's connection with the couple is paramount. Both approaches emphasize relationship–building through attuned listening—reflecting back each person's feelings and meanings in an accurate, gentle way—as well as modulating one's voice to convey kindness and promote a softening around difficult experiences. The therapist's caring presence and ability to track each person's process is a vital resource that enables clients to feel safe and allow vulnerability to emerge, which often leads to more connection.

Feeling emotionally held and understood by the therapist through active reflection often allows the couple to uncover deeper, more vulnerable feelings and longings related to their attachment needs. Moreover, using Focusing with couples can be enhanced by applying key EFT interventions that use attachment to reframe reactive comments, evoke and heighten key experiences, and encourage couple sharing in the here and now. EFT can accelerate trust building and safety by offering words and perspectives that may not occur to the client, especially when they are flooded with overwhelming emotions triggered by their partner.

Changing the steps of the dance

As a couple's cycle of distress de-escalates, they are better able to understand and express their feelings and wants, no longer retreating behind a wall for protection (withdrawer) or using criticism (pursuer) as a way to make contact (Johnson 2004). At times the therapist is following right along, tracking the client's experience. Simply using Focusing to allow each partner to uncover what they are most deeply experiencing—and sharing this with each other—can be effective in allowing their connection to deepen and process move forward. At other junctures, especially when there is high conflict, the couple may not have ready access to what they are experiencing. The therapist may then intervene more directly, for example by reframing a response to soften it or contextualizing their fear or hurt in terms of attachment needs.

At these moments the therapist slows the process down and helps illuminate the reactive places that are showing up in the session—and the feelings and needs that underlie them. With Ted and Andrea, the therapist might help Ted to explore his anger as a possible fear reaction to not getting through to Andrea and his frustrated desire for connection. With Andrea, the therapist is alert to her shutting down, watching for non-verbal markers, and helping her to voice what triggers her retreat. The therapist helps her give voice to her strong desire to be heard and appreciated and to find safety in the relationship. As the dance steps change, the more withdrawn spouse may feel safe enough to talk more directly about what they need, while the more pursuing spouse, now feeling their partner's accessibility, can begin to share their softer feelings and longings without criticism.

Engaging with present experience

With an attachment framework for understanding the powerful emotions evoked in session and as a clear guide to the underlying longings, the therapist helps to unfurl the emerging experience of each individual. Similar to Focusing, EFT works in the here-and-now with a strong present focus. The therapist tracks the moment-to-moment processes, understanding that whatever is important from the there-and-then will show up in the here-and-now. As in Focusing, clients are supported in attending to their current experience in deeply experiential ways. The therapist works with both the felt sense of the individual and the engagement between the couple as they interact in session. As each individual explores and processes their inner experience, they articulate this rich experience to their partner. The process proceeds at a slow, measured pace to allow them to attend, track, and experience what they might not yet have language to express.

At times, both Focusing and EFT invite the couple to engage with each other directly. However, EFT is often more active in choreographing interactions. The process is a movement toward engaging with the inside and the in-between; the therapist works with the felt sense of the individual and helps them find a handle from which to turn to their partner and to speak from that engaged and vulnerable place. Working directly with the primary experience with guidance from attachment theory helps the clinician to know "what to go for" as they listen, reflect, offer containment, provide safety and assist the couple to move past their protective blocks and access the deeper experiences that awaken connection. The therapist helps the partner to hear what is being said—reframing any critical or hurtful remarks as legitimate attachment needs and wants.

When Ted and Andrea bump up against a hurt that creates a defensive reaction, the EFT practitioner (and the focusing-oriented therapist who is incorporating EFT) will recognize the potentially dangerous sparks and intervene to ward off escalation. The therapist will recognize the cycle of distress activated between the couple and normalize the response to help Ted access his underlying experience. So when Ted responds defensively, "How do you think it feels? It infuriates me!" the therapist can see that something raw has been exposed—and perhaps sense the deeper fear, hurt, or shame.

Working solely with Focusing with Ted, we might intervene as follows:

Therapist: I can really hear that you feel infuriated. Would it be ok to notice how that feels in your body right now?

Ted: [Taking some time to go inside himself] My stomach feels really tight. I'm really angry.

Therapist: Just take some time and notice that tightness and how it connects with the anger... Maybe something more wants to come as you stay with all that.

Ted: Well, I'm really angry that she doesn't spend time with me. I wonder if she really wants to be with me... There's a sadness about that.

Therapist: So there's a sadness there...not sure she wants to be with you.

Ted: Yeah, I want her to *want* to be with me. I don't want to force her to do anything. But I'm missing her.

Therapist: You feel sad that she doesn't seem to want to be with you and you're missing her. And you don't want to manipulate her or force her to spend time with you? You want it to come from her. Does that say it?

Ted: Yes, exactly.

Through Focusing—reflecting back his feelings and sometimes reframing his comments slightly—Ted engages with his anger, which leads to deeper sadness. And some meaning emerges that is related to the sadness: he's not sure she wants to be with him. There are various ways to go from there. The therapist might turn to Andrea and ask, "How does it feel to hear all this?" or "What are you noticing inside as Ted shows his sadness and how he's missing you?" Or, if the moment seems safe and they are de-escalated, the therapist might ask Ted to say this directly to Andrea.

Another possibility in this scenario is that Ted's nervous system remains very activated. He stays stuck in his anger and is not able to self-regulate. If we push him too hard to notice and be gentle with what he's feeling, he may get frustrated, feel shame around his inability to stay with his feelings, or even get angry with us. Perhaps old trauma is being stirred up and he's frozen. He may need more active help to understand what he's feeling and what it's about. This is where therapist self-focusing is useful—sensing deeply inside to get a sense of what Ted may be feeling. And this is where an EFT perspective can be helpful in moving the process forward.

Weaving EFT into the session, we might proceed as follows. Note the more active role of the therapist and how EFT might be seamlessly incorporated into a Focusing approach. Also, notice how an EFT practitioner might avail themselves of Focusing methods to help clients stay connected to their body and felt sense.

Therapist: I wonder if under that infuriated feeling is some hurt, a kind of pain there because you want to know that Andrea wants *you*, not just her family. Am I getting that right?

Ted: Yes, it is painful. And kind of scary too.

Therapist: That sounds tremendously painful to feel so scared each time Andrea gets on the phone. Would it be ok to take a moment and sense with how that fear feels in your body right now?

Using EFT, we are reaching for the underlying feelings and reframing what we're sensing using attachment language. As with Focusing, we want it to be a fit for Ted—for him to safely try this on and notice if it resonates or comes close to reflecting what is going on inside him. It might take a few rounds, but our goal is to help Ted access the fear, hurt, or whatever is there, and his underlying need.

In EFT we track the feelings and don't allow ourselves to be distracted by content that is likely to create an escalation. For example, if Ted shoots a toxic comment such as, "Why don't you live with your mother, then you can talk with her all the time!," the therapist might jump in quickly with something like, "I wonder if that's the scared place talking right now. I can imagine how hard it is to stay with that fear. Would it be ok to just notice that fear for a moment and see what happens?" Jumping in promptly is a useful EFT intervention that a focusing-oriented couples therapist might consider incorporating, which is called "catching the bullet" where the therapist attempts to block a toxic comment from landing on their partner. We are continuously monitoring our alliance with Ted by checking in with our own felt sense of connection with him in order to discern whether he feels safe with our helping him give this blurry place a voice.

After helping Ted explore and get a clear felt sense of this place—and when he feels more settled—we may support Ted in turning to his partner and saying, "It does scare me when you are on the phone with her. I get so afraid that you don't want me and I just want that pain to go away." When Ted can take the risk of sharing openly with Andrea—and if Andrea is engaged enough to stay present with Ted—they begin to enter a realm of conversation that accesses the genuine desire for connection and the natural power of bonding to repair broken trust.

Though the work of therapy is always unique and emergent, the EFT model offers a map that can assist the focusing-oriented couples therapist to stay on track, navigate tricky places in a couples interaction, and provide containment, direction, and interventions that are helpful in moving the unfolding work of connection forward. Focusing might offer a process to help the EFT practitioner go deeper with each part of the couple at strategic junctures.

Although we are just scratching the surface, there are many directions possible for a focusing-oriented couples therapist in each session. We believe that incorporating other approaches along with Focusing offers the best opportunity to help couples—especially when there is high conflict. We encourage readers to consider more training in both Focusing and EFT—and find ways to creatively weave them together—as a path toward helping couples navigate the bumpy terrain that must be traversed on their way toward a more fulfilling connection.

References

Amodeo, J. (2001) *The Authentic Heart: An Eightfold Path to Midlife Love.* Hoboken, NJ: Wiley.

Amodeo, J. (2007) "A focusing-oriented approach to couples therapy." *Journal of Person-Centered and Experiential Psychotherapies 6,* 3,192–201.

Amodeo, J. (2013) *Dancing with Fire: A Mindful Way to Loving Relationships.* Wheaton, IL: Quest Books.

Bowlby, J. (1988) *A Secure Base: Parent-Child Attachment and Healthy Human Functioning.* New York: Basic Books.

Cassidy, J. and Shaver, P.R. (eds) (2008) *Handbook of Attachment: Theory, Research, and Clinical Applications,* 2nd edn. New York: Guilford Press.

Gendlin, E.T. (1966) "Existentialism and Experiential Psychotherapy." In C. Moustakes (ed.) *Existential Child Therapy.* New York: Basic Books.

Gendlin, E. (1982) *Focusing.* New York: Bantam.

Gottman, J. (1999) *The Marriage Clinic: A Scientifically Based Marital Therapy.* New York: W.W. Norton.

Johnson, S.M. (2004) *The Practice of Emotionally Focused Therapy: Creating Connection.* New York: Routledge.

Johnson, S. (2008) *Hold Me Tight: Seven Conversations for a Lifetime of Love.* New York: Little, Brown.

Johnson, S.M. and Wittenborn, A.L. (2012) "New research findings on emotionally focused therapy: Introduction to special section." *Journal of Marital and Family Therapy 38,* 1, 18–22.

Madison, G. (2010) "Focusing on existence: Five facets of an experiential–existential model." *Person-Centered and Experiential Psychotherapies 9,* 3, 189–204.

Mikulincer, M. and Shaver, P.R. (2007) *Attachment in Adulthood: Structure, Dynamics, and Change.* New York: Guilford Press.

CHAPTER 12

A Focusing Orientation in Group Psychotherapy

Calliope Callias and Charlotte Howorth

Introduction

At the core of Gendlin's philosophy is the concept that as human "beings" we are inherently interactive. We "are" interactive processes, constantly interacting with ourselves, with each other, with our environment, and with the whole universe. Attending to the implicit dimension of these processes and supporting the creation of a new kind of interaction that moves life forward is the essence of Focusing. Traditionally, a Focusing orientation has been discussed as an orientation for individual therapy. However, psychotherapy groups by nature include multidimensional interactions which offer many more opportunities to attend to an expanded implicit dimension and to facilitate participants" growth.

It is well recognized that group psychotherapy is a very effective form of therapy. In fact, it has been extensively demonstrated that the effectiveness of group psychotherapy in providing therapeutic benefit is at least equal to individual therapy (Yalom 2005, p.1). Over the years of our training and practice both of us have been exposed to a number of group psychotherapy orientations and have applied several of them in the various groups we have worked with. It is our experience that since we started working within a Focusing orientation our group processes deepened and expanded exponentially. By accessing the experiential intricacies of an individual, a dyad, or a whole group setting, new possibilities for carrying life forward and for therapeutic change are generated.

In this chapter we will discuss how a Focusing orientation can contribute to group therapy and the reasons we believe Focusing can deepen and expand group processes. We will also describe some of the moves and skills we use in creating a group environment conducive to a Focusing orientation. Furthermore, we will give two examples of how we bring in aspects of Focusing into group interactions, and how we bring in multiple interactions to support the individual's experiential process.

About group psychotherapy

Group psychotherapy is based on the premise that we are social animals and that relationships are part of who we are and who we become. Interpersonal relatedness, bonding and belonging play a powerful role in individual survival and development (Yalom 2005, p.19). It is also widely recognized that most psychological difficulties stem from social isolation and problematic past or present relationships. Groups offer the opportunity for social connections and for the sense of belonging that is so important for our development. Also, since in groups we are interacting with a number of people, we get many opportunities to learn about our various patterns of relating. In groups we recreate the past and present relationships that we have with others. Yalom (2005) describes the group as a "social microcosm," a miniature representation of each member's social universe (pp.31–47), where a variety of interactions are possible, unlike individual psychotherapy. He describes the various factors that contribute to the effectiveness of group psychotherapy and concludes that the majority of research evidence demonstrates that "interpersonal interaction and exploration (encompassing catharsis and self-understanding) and group cohesiveness are the sine qua non of effective group therapy" (p.115).

From our experience, we believe that working in groups within a Focusing orientation invites people to get underneath catharsis to an even deeper and more powerful therapeutic process. This process supports people in creating a new kind of interaction, expanding self-and-other understanding, as well as group connectedness.

The Focusing orientation in group psychotherapy

As focusing-oriented therapists (FOTs) we look at a group as a living interaction where implicit and explicit dimensions are present together, and it is necessary to attend to both in order for members to evolve and grow. Gendlin considers personal issues to be related to stuck interactions and says that "we need a new kind of interaction, one in which the client actually lives in a new way beyond the old stoppage" (1996, p.286). He also writes that "every bit of human experience has a possible further movement implicit in it" (p.13) and says that even in "seemingly destructive contents there may well be positive life energy" (p.56). Therapeutic groups offer an environment for multiple stuck interactions and destructive contents to resurface, providing many opportunities for new relational experiences and forward movements. As FOTs we see that our most important role is to work with the implicit dimension in order to facilitate the unfolding of these stuck interactions, so that a new kind of interaction can emerge and move life forward.

FOTs facilitate new interactions by listening, pointing to, and inviting the implicit from within individual members and from within the group as a whole. We also support the creation of new interactions by responding to the group from our own implicit level. We trust that this deeper dimension contains and is connected to more wisdom than we could ever consciously know. As FOTs we do not just address surface content and reactivity within the group. We are not merely looking for catharsis or intellectual understanding of why people think and feel the way they do. Rather, emphasis and attention are given to the felt sense of something underneath the words and emotions. We know that if what's felt underneath can be acknowledged, kept company, and symbolized it will bring whole new understandings and forward shifts towards healing.

As FOTs we are paying attention not only to members" felt sensing but also to our own. Working with our own felt sense helps us connect to what is underneath the client's thoughts and emotions, and helps the client to interact in a way that is different from what she/he usually experiences. This is especially important when people criticize self or others and relate with defensive reactivity. By using our felt sense we try to guide members to what is implied underneath the criticism and to initiate interaction from that place. We also support members to engage in felt sense conversations which can carry forward a blocked interaction. These felt sense conversations are the primary agents of change because they help group members live forward what is organismically implied.

As FOTs, we also try to keep our beliefs and theories on the side and to be guided primarily by our own and by group members" bodily knowing. Working with our own felt sense helps group therapists to stay in the moment "abandoning memory and desire" which, according to the group analyst Bion, "imprisons the patient in a static, devitalized conception, one that is not alive or generative" (in Billow 2003, p.16). If we find ourselves needing to use an interpretation, based on our beliefs or expectations, we always want to check to see if the interpretation resonates with the group. Checking invites the group to sense into what is actually being experienced by them in the moment. In this way, instead of being lost in the possible interpretations or interventions of a given situation, which in a group can feel infinite, the group's felt sensing can often guide therapists to the exact move that will bring an experiential shift and personal change. Thus, attending to our own and participants' actual experience guides us to the "right" next response that will help the emergence of a widened awareness and of organic and unexpected new moves in individuals, bringing a fresh aliveness to the group as a whole.

Checking for resonance, this internal sense of "rightness," can be thought of as the juice of a focusing-oriented group. Connections are deepened and interactions get unstuck when there is resonance within ourselves and within an interaction. Our assumption is that everyone is implicitly connected. Therefore, we are not surprised when deep resonance in one member brings deep resonances in other participants who are then able to further process their experience, which in turn expands, touches, and shifts everyone in the group. Resonance fosters the all-important sense of empathic connectedness to ourselves and to others which is a vital ingredient of well being.

The therapist's empathy and the empathic understanding between group members have been emphasized in many orientations as a key therapeutic element in groups (Billow 2003; Harwood and

Pines 1998; Yalom 2005). However, a Focusing orientation has an expanded understanding of empathy. As Preston describes, "the kind of empathy we are fostering is not only an intellectual capacity to put oneself in someone else's shoes, but an ability to drop down to the implicit dimension where we can directly experience our connections to the inner world of the other" (2013, personal communication). This empathic attunement is experienced by members as a sense of being profoundly understood. It is particularly important for groups because it can help people develop a deeper appreciation of their differences, and it can provide a greater sense of group safety and cohesiveness.

In our experience, we have found that an important part of a focusing-oriented group process is the *opening attunement* experience at the beginning of each session. In this attunement, members are invited as a group to pause and check inside to connect with the felt sense of themselves individually and of the group as a whole at that moment, and then to begin to share about their experiences from that place. Similarly, each session ends with a *closing attunement* that invites the group to check inside for a bodily sense of the session's experience. These attunement practices set the tone of this orientation and they are part of the "group norms" (Yalom 2005, p.120) which, together with the therapist's embodiment of the Focusing attitude of deep listening, genuine openness, and gentle invitation, help build the culture that is necessary for this particular kind of group.

Using Focusing-Oriented Therapy skills in groups

As in individual therapy, when we use Focusing-Oriented Therapy skills in a group, we invite members to "pause," we "reflect back," we "ask into," we use the language of the "I," the "You," and the "Us," and we work with "parts." These skills are outlined below.

- *Pausing:* As FOTs we may invite an individual, or two or more people during an interaction, to *pause* and sense inside, or we may invite the whole group to sense into what may be happening in a given moment. "Can we all take a moment to pause and try to sense inside?" or "Where are we as a group right now?" are examples of such invitations. These enable everyone, including the therapist, to slow down and pause to allow her/his felt sense to form.

- *Reflecting back:* In the group format, *reflecting back* felt sense words in a resonant way helps to slow down an interaction and to point to the implicit felt meaning of something. Also, when a therapist reflects back one member's felt sense words, other members may also feel an opening to their implicit experience.
- *Asking into: Asking into* requires someone to go to that vague edge of awareness and to wait for more. Questions here are not directed to what the person thinks, but point to the felt sense of something. Some basic Focusing questions that a therapist can ask an individual in a group would be "How is that for you right now?" or "What is that like inside?" Similar questions can also be asked about the whole group: "How are we right now?" "What does the group feel like right now?" "What is this like for us?" or "What do we need right now?" Inviting members to ask into the whole sense of the group points to our interconnectedness and enhances group cohesiveness.
- *Using the "I," "You," and "Us" dimensions:* The felt sense has a holistic quality, a sense of the whole of something, and at the same time it has three different dimensions that we can tune into. In a group there can be the individuals" felt sense of themselves, their felt sense of the other participants, and their felt sense of the group as a whole. These dimensions may be referred to as the "I," the "You," and the "Us," and the facilitator can work with any of these dimensions. By tuning into her/his own felt sense of an interaction, a therapist determines which dimension feels the most in the foreground at any moment. She/he then uses the language of either the "I," "You," or "Us (we)" to point to and open the dimension that at the moment feels like it's carrying the next forward movement.

  For example, the therapist may use the "we" when she/he asks the question, "Are we feeling unsafe right now?" or "How are we now that Tony left the group?" This "we" brings the attention to the felt sense of the whole group and puts the therapist right in there with the client, or the group. It also fosters the sense of "us-ness" which enhances the sense of belonging as it brings forward interactional needs and struggles. The "You" not only reflects the group member's feeling and felt sense but also points to the person's individuality as it is lived in the world at that moment. When the therapist uses the "I," she/he is speaking from her/his own individual experience, and is showing and sharing something of herself as a person, making the intervention more direct and powerful. Gendlin talks about the healing power of being with another real person in therapy. "Most powerful...is a real other person" (1968, p.10). The usage of this language and the therapist's genuine participation strongly support group members' efforts to share openly and to engage in authentic interactions, and can be central to creating new interactions.

- *Working with parts:* An FOT also uses empathic attunement to attend to the many different parts within an individual, that is, the part that wants to change, the part that is scared of change, the part that is constantly judging, the angry part, etc. She/he holds a space for each of them, and helps members acknowledge them so that they find their voice. Similarly, the therapist sees individual members as being the various parts of the group, each with her/his own experiences needing space and acknowledgment. The therapist knows that once various parts, whether within an individual, or within members/parts of a group, feel heard and understood, the organism, whether that be the individual or the group, finds a whole new and fresh way of shifting and moving forward. In addition, when members experience resonance with different parts of another group member, the deepening of that group member's process is supported. Working with parts of an individual or parts of the group teaches participants to be in complexity and to trust that as they attend to it, it unfolds and finds a way to carry the whole group onward. This process can lead to a very maturing relational experience.

Weaving Focusing and interactions in groups

In this section we will give two examples of how we use Focusing in groups. Specifically, we will show how we bring Focusing into dynamic interactions, and how we invite other members to help an individual's Focusing.

Using Focusing moves in dynamic interactions

In this example I, Charlotte (CH), show how FOT can help members connect with their implicit meanings during a fast and conflictual interaction.

John sent me an email announcing that he was leaving the group and would let everyone know that week. He came late after I had already announced his intention to go. When he sat down everyone continued to talk, and I had a feeling members were intentionally ignoring him. In an effort to call attention to the elephant in the room, I said that John was leaving and that I wondered what had happened to the feelings they had shared earlier.

Dexter (D): [In a sharp and accusatory tone] Well I always thought John was flaky—and in fact, Charlotte, I question you for inviting him into the group—you should have seen that about him and known he wasn't suitable.

I felt stung and as if I really should have anticipated John's lack of commitment. I paused and centered myself, looking for my felt sense of what D was saying, that is, the deeper point he was trying to make. D had shared how he felt he couldn't stand any more losses and I felt his hurt and anger. I wanted to reflect this back and take on the anger myself rather than have his reactivity directed towards the group.

CH: It feels like I should have seen it—I should have been more on the ball?

D nodded in agreement and I could feel his anger and hurt.

CH: It's like I left you open to being hurt. [I tried to articulate the deeper point that I felt D was trying to get to]

D: It's your job as facilitator to choose the people to join so that we have a foundation to work from.

Mary (M): [Turning to John] Well I am not so sure about that. I don't want to go down the path of blaming Charlotte. I wouldn't want anyone to blame her for me being in the group. But I do have the feeling that you never really fully had both feet in—just being honest with you and for this to work you have to get both feet in. [M was not only protecting me but was also worrying that she is somehow defective and that the group may also blame me for letting her join]

Kate (K): This kind of work is where you get to face that stuff not just glide over it. I mean I don't care—I don't need him here—I am doing what I need to do—it's his loss really.

CH: Is it like—if he doesn't need you, then you don't need him? [I did not reflect her reactivity but the message underneath]

K: Exactly—I know where my priorities lie and that I am on the right track.

CH: Yes, I get that, but I am also sensing that there may be some hurt there. Did I get that right? [I pointed to the hurt underneath, hoping it will bring more]

K: [Paused] Yes, sure—I really started to bond with John and [sniffs a little] I feel a bit deserted by him… I feel left and it doesn't feel good.

CH: It's like you don't matter somehow.

K: It's like that feeling at school when you think someone is your friend but then they don't want to hang out with you and they go sit at the other kid's table—it's OK but kind of sad.

CH: I am noticing that apart from Mary we are talking about John as if he isn't here. [I included myself with a "we" statement as a way of not pointing my finger at the group as if they are doing something wrong. This helped the group address John directly]

Janet: [Turning to John] I think they are all being really hard on you John and if I was hearing this I'd want to leave. No one has to be here—people have their lives—what's the big deal? I think of leaving sometimes and if I want to go I want to go. [Janet has often spoken about trouble with intimacy and here she is directly addressing John and coming to his defense]

M: But this is real life in here—there are real relationships, and I take a lot of risks with you guys and open in ways I just don't else where and that is precious.

CH: When you say that I get a sense of how precious we are and how precious this process is. [A reflection and use of "I" and "we" to highlight a sense of groupness and my inclusion in that]

M: Yes, and so you just leaving like this and not even having the courtesy to come on time to give us a chance to process it feels like a slap in the face of that. [The group was now moving from reactivity to engagement]

CH: I am feeling a tension between those who are speaking up for the freedom to leave and those who are expressing anger and disappointment. Would that be a way to talk about this conflict? [I was using my own felt sense of the interaction in an "I" statement. I was also making room for different individuals to have their reactions. There is a balance between making an "Us," and individuals having space for their uniqueness. When space is made for all points of view then something new can come]

There was a silence as the tension hung in the air. We were coming to the end of group and we had not heard from John yet.

CH: It's like there is so much to sort out here and so little time and I feel that too and I am aware that John, we have not heard your voice yet. What is it like having all these strong voices directed towards you about your leaving? [I included myself so that members feel joined by me and know that I am experiencing this too. I also felt it was important for John to find his voice so that he doesn't get scape-goated]

John: I have decided to come back and process this more. I have really just been taking in everything everyone has said. I really recognize the feeling of being rejected at school and I want to digest everything and say something next group about it all. [I was touched and relieved to hear John's mature response and was aware that I would miss him too]

CH: You leaving is having a big impact on all of us and we are getting to the point where there can be a real goodbye. [I used "Us" to highlight the sense of all of us engaged in this task together and pointed to the authenticity that was starting to emerge]

In this example, I used my own felt sense to help guide me through the complexity of this fast and conflictual interaction and used "I," "We," and "Us" language to both include myself where it felt therapeutic and to enhance the experience of all of us working through this difficult task together. I also reflected the deeper points members were trying to make to help them move from defensive reactivity to engagement.

Using group interactions to support an individual's Focusing

In the following example I, Calliope (CC), invite group participation to help an individual member access her felt sense and stay with inner processing.

Linda (L) shared that during the *opening attunement* she could not slow down and access her felt sense. She kept thinking of something that happened at work.

L: I am so upset with myself. I go into my boss's office and even though I've put in all these hours of work and came up with a really good project, as soon as I try to explain it to him I lose my words and feel that I come across as this little girl that does not know what she is talking about. [Really distraught] What is wrong with me? I hate myself.

CC: It is so upsetting. Even though you know the quality of your work something interferes and you lose your words. [Reflecting and pointing to something underneath]

L: [Ignored therapist's move of pointing to something and continued with self-criticism] It feels so stupid. I don't understand myself. I will never succeed. I really feel I will always stay at the same position, I will never grow.

CC: Would it be ok with you if we take a little time with that? [Inviting her to focus]

L: Maybe, I don't know... [Hesitantly slowing down] I don't think I will like what I find.

CC: You are not sure you will like what may be in there. [Resonant response]

L: It's all so difficult. [Looking frustrated]

CC: And there is all this difficulty there. [Reflecting and pointing underneath]

L: [Pausing hesitantly] I just feel this tightness all over...my throat, my chest... I know I hate my boss [the speed in her speech picked up]...it is not only with my boss I feel like that. It is also with my colleagues. I can't speak up, I am damaged, I can't do it [she has lost access to her felt sense] I hate myself. I am such a failure. [Very frustrated]

CC: Will it be ok if we stay with this hatred? With the part that feels you are such a failure? [Inviting her again to focus and using parts]

L: Don't know... It's all black...it's so heavy.

CC: It is so heavy and black. [Reflecting, hoping to help her go deeper]

L: Oh, no, I can't do this, can't really stay with that; can't even do what you are asking me. [Looking desperate] I am such a failure... No one can help me.

CC: It feels that you are failing even in here with us, and no one can help you. [Reflection and an "Us" statement to remind her of our togetherness]

L: Yes, everyone else was able to stay with their felt sense and probably they are thinking I am taking so much time and not going anywhere with this.

CC: [I am feeling her "stuckness" and I, myself, felt like I didn't have something to offer right now. I sensed that this was a right moment to include the group] Does it feel right to invite the group to see if they have something to offer us?

L: Maybe...I guess it's ok.

CC: [Towards the group] Is there something that came to anyone and feels like you may want to say to Linda? Did anything resonate inside?

Karen: I can certainly relate to this. It is so frustrating to know you are right and you have things to say and yet you can't find the words...that feeling of being stupid creeping in and then it's like your brain freezes. [Empathically resonating with L's part that loses the words]

L: Yes, it feels exactly like my brain freezes...[slowing down—the felt sense word "freezes" begins to unfreeze Linda's process]...it is horrible to lose your thoughts.

Rob: I got this stomach knot as I was listening to you Linda. I wanted to do something to help you stop hating yourself so much... It feels so familiar to me this frustration, this hatred. I felt your difficulty stopping it...it's like it spirals and I get so hopeless when I get there... [Empathically resonating with L's part that is hating her]

L: It is so difficult to stop it...I cannot get away from it...[slowing down even more]... It is so painful.

I was planning to ask Linda if she would want to stay with that feeling now, but Mina jumped in.

Mina: I don't know what it is and how this will sound, but all along as you were talking, Linda, I had this image of a horse, a white-grayish color horse that was stuck in a mud or something. It wanted to run but could not... I kept getting the sense that the horse was not about me, but about you Linda... I don't know what to make about that...does a horse mean anything to you?

L: A horse...[pausing]... I don't know...[longer pausing, then slowing down]... Well I used to have a little wooden horse toy as a child...[slowing down further]...my father had given it to me just before he left the house... I used to love that horse and dreamed that one day I would ride on a horse and run so far from my mother, from everyone...[tearing up]...is this really about my mother again? Yes, that black, heavy feeling I had every time she would find something wrong with me... [Looked ready to go deeper]

CC: That black, heavy feeling... Would it be ok if we try to keep it company now?

L: Yes, it feels like I can stay with that now.

In this example, Linda's felt sense was blocked and I was having difficulty facilitating her process, so I turned to the group for help. In a Focusing group atmosphere, I trusted that members would share from that inner place. I also facilitated that kind of participation by particularly asking for *resonant responses*, the ways they were implicitly connecting with Linda's felt sense. Members resonated and empathically connected with her different parts which helped her slow down. Mina's resonant image of a horse was the turning point for Linda's pausing and clearly opened the road for her inner process. It came as a surprise to everyone and pointed to the connection with the transcendent dimension of the human experience that this inner process may also touch.

Conclusion

In this chapter we outlined some of the important aspects of what a Focusing orientation brings in a group and we presented two examples of ways this orientaton can be used. We showed how we bring aspects of Focusing into dynamic group interactions, and how we use group interactions to deepen the individual's experiential process.

A Focusing orientation in group psychotherapy emphasizes working with the implicit and facilitates the creation of new living interactions. Connecting to a bodily knowing brings new possibilities for deeper understandings of self and others, and moves people and relations forward in a new and fresh way. In groups there are ample opportunities for multidimensional felt sense interactions which not only deepen an individual's process by going under mere thoughts and feelings, but also expand group connectedness.

References

Billow, R.M. (2003) *Relational Group Psychotherapy: From Basic Assumptions to Passion.* London: Jessica Kingsley Publishers.

Gendlin, E.T. (1968) *The Experiential Response.* Reprinted from *Use of Interpretation in Treatment.* New York: Grune & Stratton.

Gendlin, E.T. (1996) *Focusing Oriented Psychotherapy: A Manual of the Experiential Method.* New York: Guilford Press.

Harwood, I.N.H. and Pines, M. (1998) *Self Experiences in Group: Intersubjective and Self Psychological Pathways to Human Understanding.* London: Jessica Kingsley Publishers.

Yalom, I.D. with Leszcz, M. (2005) *The Theory and Practice of Group Psychotherapy*, 5th edn. New York: Basic Books.

CHAPTER 13

Focusing-Oriented Expressive Arts Therapy

Working on the Avenues

Laury Rappaport

Focusing-Oriented Expressive Arts Therapy (FOAT) is the integration of Gendlin's original Focusing method (Gendlin 1981a) and principles and practice of Focusing-Oriented Psychotherapy with the expressive arts therapies (Rappaport 2009, 2013). The expressive arts therapies include art therapy, dance/movement therapy, music therapy, psychodrama and drama therapy, poetry therapy, and expressive arts therapy (multi-modal arts therapies approaches). Gendlin (1991) describes the significance of partnering the inner-directed process of Focusing with outward expression:

> If therapy deals only with the inner data, whether emotion or felt sense, it misses a crucial dimension of the process of change. Therapy must involve more than focusing on inner data in reflective space. There also needs to be a movement outward, into interaction. Focusing as such does not sufficiently provide the moving out. (p.267)

The expressive arts provide a complementary outward expression to Focusing—while Focusing adds numerous benefits to expressive arts.

This chapter describes the contributions from Gendlin's Focusing-Oriented Therapy (FOT) that inform the foundational principles of FOAT; the relationship between a felt sense and the expressive arts; and how Gendlin's concept of "working on the avenues" (Gendlin

1996, pp.172–178) provides an important theoretical construct with clinical application to expressive arts therapy (Halperin 2008; Knill, Barba and Fuchs 1994/2004; Knill, Levine and Levine 2005; Malchiodi 2005; McNiff 2009; Rogers 1993, 2011). Clinical examples are included to illustrate the main ideas in this chapter.

Focusing-Oriented Expressive Arts

I developed Focusing-Oriented Expressive Arts Therapy (FOAT) as a theoretical and methodological approach after integrating Focusing with the expressive arts for over 30 years with a wide variety of clinical issues and populations (Rappaport 2009). In keeping with Gendlin's approach, the foundational principles of FOAT emphasize the client's sense of safety above all interventions and the importance of "the person in there" (Gendlin 1996, p.287).

Foundational FOAT principles

Safety for the "person in there" is established through therapeutic presence, the "Focusing attitude," clinical sensitivity, and reflection of the client's process and explicit statements. "Therapeutic presence" is related to Gendlin's (1996) concept, *putting nothing between*—"In front of me the space is free, ready for the other person... To be with a client, I keep nothing in front of me" (p.286). In FOAT, the therapist helps the client to cultivate a Focusing attitude—being "friendly" and welcoming, curious, and accepting toward the felt sense and unfolding Focusing process. In addition, a quality of acceptance is nurtured toward the creative process and art product. The therapist also conveys the Focusing attitude toward the client.

It is important to be mindful of the needs of the clinical population you are working with and to adapt FOAT accordingly. For example, when working with clients who have experienced trauma or have severe mental illness, it is advisable to begin with eyes open, and not encourage closing the eyes until safety and grounding is firmly established within the client.

Experiential listening is an integral part of the Focusing process. In FOAT, reflection of the client's experience can also occur though *artistic mirroring*, where the therapist may reflect understanding through an artistic reflection—such as drawing a shape, using a color, or creating an image; or *movement mirroring*, when the therapist conveys understanding through nonverbal body movement or gesture.

Relationship between the felt sense and expressive arts

During Focusing, the client is invited to access a felt sense by taking a moment to bring their awareness inside to their body, to be "friendly" toward their inner experience (Focusing attitude)—and to see if there is a handle/symbol—a word, phrase, image, gesture, or sound, that matches the felt sense. In verbally oriented psychotherapy, the client typically describes the *handle* using words: "The felt sense is a knot in my stomach. The word that matched is 'clenched.'" Or, "The image I got was of a person kneeling down, head buried, and squeezing themselves tightly in a crouched position."

However, in FOAT, the felt sense can also be symbolized through an expressive arts form—art, movement or dance, music, writing, and action (drama therapy). Gendlin (1981b) describes the value of expression beyond words: "More powerful than letting words come from a felt sense may be letting body movement come" (p.35). The felt sense provides an easy and natural doorway to creative expression.

Symbolizing the felt sense through expressive arts

The following example demonstrates symbolizing a felt sense through an art form. In a focusing-oriented arts therapy training, I led the group in a FOAT check-in:

> Take a few deep breaths down inside to your body, being friendly to whatever is there right now. [Pause] See if there's a word, phrase, image, gesture, or sound that matches the felt sense. [Pause] Check it against your body for sense of rightness.

Annie, a student in a FOAT training shares her experience:

> During the Focusing, I got in touch with a pain in my upper back and felt sense of carrying a huge weight. The image that matched the felt sense was of a large dark shape on my back. I

also had a tightness in my belly, and the image came of a small knot. There were no words, but the image felt right.

Annie expressed this image in art as she drew a small figure with a huge black shape on her back that also radiated gray (Figure 13.1).

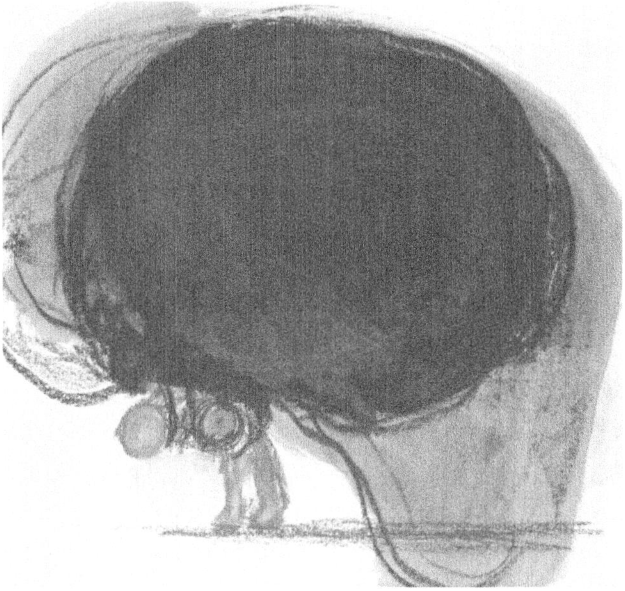

Figure 13.1 Felt sense symbolized through art

In FOAT, the client resonates or checks the symbol/handle and art expression against the felt sense. In this example, Annie shared, *At first I drew the knot outside my body but that didn't feel right. So I used water to smear that out and moved the dot to the center. That felt right.*

Art materials are used to express the felt sense. It can be as simple as a piece of yarn or a collage image. The artistic expression develops and changes through its interaction with the felt sense—as seen when Annie first created the dot outside of the figure and after resonating it during the process, moved it within the center of the figure. When teaching FOAT, I frequently say, "although the art looks like it is on the outside, it is experienced on the inside." When creating from a felt sense, there is no separation between the art and the felt sense. Meaning can be explicated further with Focusing and expressive arts methods (see the example in "Working on the avenues" below and Rappaport 2009).

The FOAT process is the same whether expressing a felt sense symbol of a gesture into movement, sound into music, or a word or phrase into writing or enactment. If, during Focusing, the client gets a gesture as a handle, I may invite the client to make the gesture. Sometimes the gesture is static, and other times it unfolds into more movement. If the client hears a sound, I may encourage the client to allow the expression of the sound. It is important that the client is never pushed to make a sound but rather invited to see if it would feel right. When the handle comes as a word or phrase, it may lead to writing a poem, creative writing, or verbalizing the word or phrase in a dramatic enactment. In expressive arts therapy, moving between arts modalities is known as intermodal expressive therapy (Knill *et al.* 1994/2004) and the creative connection (Rogers 1993, 2011).

Working on the avenues

When working with clients, expressive arts therapists—and psychotherapists working with the arts—are often faced with questions such as: Which arts modality do I use? Should I suggest moving from one art form to another with a client—art to movement to voice to writing? Should I stay with one modality? How do I decide this? Most often, the decision is made intuitively and also according to the therapist's strengths.

Gendlin's (1996) concept of *working on the avenues* provides an important theoretical and practice approach for determining which arts modality, if any, to use in a particular moment in therapy. The *avenues* are described as follows:

> Therapy can consist of totally different *kinds of experience.* I call these therapeutic "avenues." A given therapeutic event can consist of images, role play, cognitive beliefs, memories, feelings, emotional catharsis, interpersonal interactions, dreams, dance moves, muscle movement, and habitual behavior. (1996, p.170)

Gendlin explains that although psychotherapy consists of different orientations—psychoanalytic, Jungian, solution-focused, and so forth—we can find common uses of avenues across theories. For example, art therapy, guided imagery, and clinical hypnosis use an imagery avenue; dance therapy, bioenergetics, and somatic experiencing use a body avenue; and music therapy, EMDR with headphones listening to the beeps, listening to a Hakomi probe (nourishing statement, see Kurtz 1990) use the auditory avenue. Interaction between the therapist and client is also considered an avenue, such as the therapist's response to a client—such as being empathic, confrontational, or taking on a role in a dramatic enactment—and its affect on the client-therapist relationship.

The crucial felt sense

An integral aspect of working on the avenues is the felt sense. The felt sense provides the "link between the avenues" (Gendlin 1996, p.174). Being able to work on many avenues allows the therapist to work with the whole person in there—responding to the felt sense, moment-to-moment. As Gendlin states, "these avenues are already together in every person" (p.174).

Expressive arts therapists are trained and skilled to work on different avenues, such as auditory (music), visual (art), body expression (dance-movement) and so forth. "Working on the avenues" can help to inform which arts modality is most attuned to the client within the moment-to-moment unfolding of a session, and when to stay with verbal interaction. The following case study illustrates the process of listening to the client's felt sense and allowing it to inform the avenue for therapeutic interventions. In this study, the avenues of interaction, action-methods, and art are used. Notations are included to clarify the FOAT processes of how I stay attuned to the client's felt sense and how this attunement also helps to navigate between avenues.

Case example: working on the avenues

As a child, Stephanie, now a woman in her fifties, experienced trauma from medical interventions.

Interaction avenue

We begin the FOAT session with creating safety, followed by my inviting the client to check inside to see how she is feeling:

C: I notice a back and forth swaying in my body. [Felt sense]

T: A back and forth swaying...how does that feel inside?

C: There's a gentleness to it—a sense of urgency...an awareness that there's something in the trauma piece I'd like to work on. The swaying is something inside that wants to see the trauma piece and something that wants to move away.

T: Something wants to go toward it and something wants to go away. [Listening reflection] See if you can be friendly to it. [Focusing attitude]

C: Yeah—going back and forth...it's about being *in* the feelings. I've done it *that way* before but it's not how I want to do it.

T: There's a wanting to work on the trauma piece and wanting to get distance from it so you can feel it somewhat but also stand outside of it. It's like having one foot in and one foot out. Is that right?

C: Yeah—like observing it.

T: So you want to be able to look at the child's experience of the trauma but not be fully in her experience—maybe just sense her from a distance.

C: [Nods yes] For now.

T: Can you find a way of anchoring yourself in the observer...

C: I can imagine seeing her—like looking through a window—something permeable. That feels right.

This beginning phase of the session makes use of the *interaction* avenue—where I am "keeping Stephanie company" as she accesses and listens to her felt sense. My goal is to create a sense of safety for the vulnerable child-self who experienced trauma and the adult self here now. I respond with carefully attuned empathic listening for the vulnerable felt sense of the client. I am aware of trying to cultivate safety within our relationship (interaction), and also supporting the inner relationship (interaction) between the child within Stephanie and her adult awareness.

Action-methods avenue

As Stephanie continues listening to her felt experience, the memory plays like a movie. She stays rooted in the observer self while lightly sensing into the child self's experience. I continue staying present with her, offering listening responses that unfold the felt sense into a new avenue:

T: So you can see yourself as the little girl walking through the door but there's a part of her that's trying to go in the opposite way, to leave.

C: Yeah…I don't want to be here.

T: She doesn't want to be here. Can we make a friendly, holding space for her…and maybe ask her if she has something that she wants to stay. [Notice the reminder of the Focusing attitude and that there is a "we" making a friendly, holding space. This is often helpful with very vulnerable places so that the child self experiences more support and safety]

C: [Nods yes] There's fear…terror…but not showing it. It's all inside…everywhere.

T: So she's really scared and there's a sense of terror [nods yes] and the little you isn't showing it outside…but inside it's all there. [Listening reflection]

C: Yes—it's a little fuzzy. The nurse is bringing me into the examination room.

T: The scene is continuing and now there's a nurse. Can you sense how is she now?

C: She's really afraid and she's leaving her body.

T: She's afraid and she's leaving her body. Does it feel OK to be the adult you sensing her? Are you having the right balance that you wanted? [Ensuring safety]

C: Yes…I feel like there's something here [pointing to upper chest and throat]. [Felt sense] I want to *say* something to the doctor: "It's not very nice!" [Notice there are words emerging from the felt sense]

T: The adult you is choked up and wants to *say* something to the doctor...and it's not very nice! [Listening reflection]

C: Right...

T: Can you check inside...and would it be OK to hear it inside yourself and then sense if you want to *say* it aloud? [This is a careful listening to felt sense and creating safety for Stephanie to hear what she considers "not very nice" and to then see if she wants to *say* it aloud—attending to the interactions]

C: I want to take little Stephanie by the hand and take her out of the room and say to the doctor, "Leave her alone! How dare you do this to her!" There's anger right there—rubs her upper chest with two hands. [Felt sense]

T: There's anger right there. You're holding little Stephanie's hand and you want to say to the doctor, "Leave her alone!" "How dare you do this to her!" [Listening reflection]

This is where the felt sense provides a juncture to a new avenue. Words with emotion emerge from the felt sense. The words are a direct expression to the doctor. Depending on the therapist's skill, different procedures for speaking up (action-methods) can be used—such as *empty chair*: "Here's an empty chair to put the doctor in. Tell him what you want to say." After, Stephanie can reverse roles and speak as the doctor to the child self—and perhaps go back and forth a few times. This method may provide access to the doctor's caring intention (assuming that was present for the doctor), which may be healing for Stephanie. A Gestalt method can be used: "Speak directly to him," or the therapist can stay with Focusing and listening where it would be important for the therapist to reflect the strength of Stephanie's anger.

Avenue: interaction

After Stephanie expresses the anger, she shares:

C: As I talk there's a wave of sadness. Not just anger, I feel sad for her. It violated her in a really awful way. [Tears]

T: See if you can be friendly to the teary place. [Again, creating safety and acceptance; interaction]

C: So many things lost. As she got older...losses, losses, losses—that she had to go through in life.

T: You're feeling sad for the losses that little Stephanie had to go through in life. [Listening reflection]

C: [Nods]

T: Can you keep the teary place company...? [Focusing attitude]

After the release of anger, the felt sense opens to something new:

C: Another thing that just popped in is that I really want to comfort her? [Inner relationship interaction]

T: You really want to comfort her. [Listening reflection]

C: Yeah...it feels a little scary.

T: So you're noticing a part that wants to comfort her and also a place that's a little scared to. Can you sense inside what would help for it to feel safer?

C: What came is that I need to apologize to her.

T: You want to apologize to her. [Tears] [Listening reflection]

Avenue: image to art

C [To inner child] "I'm really sorry." [Tears] It's weird...there's a sadness. [Felt sense] I'm getting an *image*. There's this anger running up and down [points to torso] and in the center is sadness. [Felt sense; notice that the felt sense opens to an image]

T: There's a feeling of wanting to take care of the little you and apologize to her...and with that came an *image* and sense of anger running up and down a core place of sadness.

C: Yeah...it's there at the same time.

T: Would you like to use the art materials to express the image and felt sense? [Notice I introduce this as an option since an *image* arose from the felt sense—a juncture to a new avenue]

C: Yeah...I'm getting the colors...but there needs to be another piece, something's missing.

T: You have the colors but something is missing. Can you take a moment and check inside...and ask what's missing? See what comes. [Interspersing "asking" and "receiving" steps of Gendlin's Focusing method]

C: There's a spring, coil. Pushing here, near the heart—and then it releases.

Stephanie creates a drawing showing the lines of anger running up and down throughout the body and the sadness in the middle. She uses a pipe cleaner to create a coil-spring (Figure 13.2) to place near the heart.

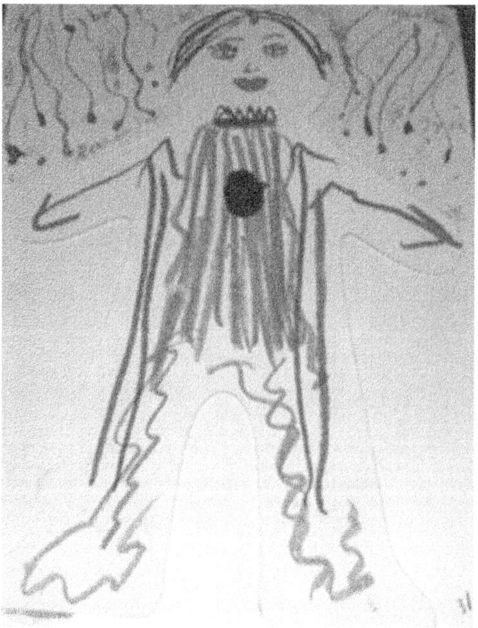

Figure 13.2 Stephanie's felt sense in art

As Stephanie glues the coil onto the drawing of the person, she presses in—and it springs! She picks up silver and gold glitter glue pens and adds wavy lines at the top and shares, "After I touched the spring, radiance and light [glitter] became released. It was under this stuff."

Therapist comments on the process of working with the avenues

Stephanie was deeply satisfied and surprised to begin with the frozen child-place of fear from the trauma, find her voice, release the anger and sadness, and uncover the radiant light. As a therapist, I stayed attuned to Stephanie's felt sense, encouraging her to stay in touch with the body process. As can be seen through this case example, the felt sense and the unfolding of the felt meaning inform which avenue is pursued throughout the process.

In the beginning, and at specific times, I attended to the safety needs of the client through careful listening and reflecting of the felt sense. When the felt sense in the chest and throat emerged, the words came of what Stephanie wanted to say to the doctor. This fostered a natural change from the interaction avenue to action-method. Gendlin (1996) describes how "role-play has the potential to change the direction of the body" (p.192), and that, before, "the energy *came* at the client; now it moves *outward* from the client" (p.193). Focusing's contribution to role-play is that the words arise out of the felt sense—carrying forward specific felt meanings that become explicit.

Next, the felt sense of sadness and anger came, symbolized as an image—changing the avenue to visual art. The movement between the avenues unfolded from one into the other organically, arising out of the felt sense. As Gendlin (1996) says,

Moving between avenues happens naturally, because...we are not trying to work with actions as such, but rather with actions that could carry a felt sense forward. These are the kind we naturally look for, because there is already a felt sense for some other avenue (p.176).

In addition, we can see that something unique occurs on each avenue. Attending to the relational dimension brings something important that is different from what speaking up does (action methods). Creating an image through art allowed for a pipe-cleaner to carry forward the felt meaning of the release in a way that nothing else could—leading to a felt shift and experience of radiance and light that had been buried. Gendlin (1991) says, "There are great advantages to be gained by using the avenues together. It allows us to discover what is essential on each avenue, what no other avenue provides" (p.177). The visual art then serves as a continual reminder of the process. Each time the client sees the image, there is an interaction between the art and the memory on a felt sense level, which continues the unfolding of its life forward direction.

Conclusion

In focusing-oriented expressive arts therapy, presence, attending to the safety of the client, experiential listening, and awareness of the felt sense help to create a secure therapeutic foundation. Once established, there is a "zigzag" (Gendlin 1981c) between the felt sense, handle/symbol (word, phrase, image, gesture, or sound), creative expression and back to felt sense. Listening is interspersed and part of the *zigzag*. The crucial aspect is attuning to the felt sense—checking back in with the felt sense as the psychotherapy and arts processes unfold. The felt sense is the home base of the client, the link among the avenues, the conduit between the different arts modalities, and an inherent source of wisdom.

Acknowledgment

I would like to thank Annie Danberg, MA, and Ellyn Herb, PhD, for their contributions to this chapter.

References

Gendlin, E.T. (1981a) *Focusing*, 2nd edn. New York: Bantam Books.

Gendlin, E.T. (1981b) "Focusing and the development of creativity." *The Focusing Folio I*, 13–16.

Gendlin, E.T. (1981c) "Movement therapy, objectification, and focusing." *The Focusing Folio 1*, 2, 3537. Available at www.focusing.org/gendlin/docs/gol_2016.html, accessed November 17, 2013.

Gendlin, E.T. (1991) "On Emotion in Therapy." In J.D. Safran and L.S. Greenberg (eds) *Emotion, Psychotherapy, and Change*. New York: Guilford Press.

Gendlin, E.T. (1996) *Focusing-Oriented Psychotherapy: A Manual of the Experiential Method*. New York: Guilford Press.

Halperin, D. (2008) *The Expressive Body in Life, Art, and Therapy: Working with Movement, Metaphor and Meaning.* London: Jessica Kingsley Publishers.

Knill, P., Barba, H. and Fuchs, M. (1994/2004) *Minstrels of Soul: Intermodal Expressive Therapy.* Toronto: EGS Press.

Knill, P., Levine, S. and Levine, E. (2005) *Principles and Practice of Expressive Therapy: Towards a Therapeutic Manual.* London: Jessica Kingsley Publishers.

Malchiodi, C. (ed.) (2005) *Expressive Therapies.* New York: Guilford Press.

McNiff, S. (2009) *Integrating the Arts in Therapy: History, Theory, and Practice.* Springfield, IL: Charles C. Thomas.

Kurtz, R. (1990) *Body-Centered Psychotherapy: The Hakomi Method.* Mendocino, CA: Life Rhythm.

Rappaport, L. (2009) *Focusing-Oriented Art Therapy: Accessing the Body's Wisdom and Creative Intelligence.* London: Jessica Kingsley Publishers.

Rappaport, L. (ed.) (2013) *Mindfulness and the Arts Therapies: Theory and Practice.* London: Jessica Kingsley Publishers.

Rogers, N. (1993) *The Creative Connection: Expressive Arts as Healing.* Palo Alto, CA: Science and Behavior Books.

Rogers, N. (2011) *The Creative Connection for Groups: Person-Centered Expressive Arts for Healing and Social Change.* Palo Alto, CA: Science and Behavior Books.

PART IV

Topics From the Focusing-Oriented Context

This final part of Volume One includes diverse contributions that offer a Focusing view on contemporary topics within the profession of psychotherapy. However, the part begins with two comments from philosophy. First, Campbell Purton draws upon Wittgenstein in order to invite us to reconsider our understanding of Gendlin's felt sense and its integral place in FOT. It is a sign of the maturity of the FOT community that we are increasingly inviting critiques and reformulations of even our most basic premises. Second, Rob Parker returns to Gendlin's philosophy with the explicit task of showing us that philosophy in general and especially the "philosophy of the implicit" has important practical implications for psychotherapists.

Next, Peter Afford presents the work he has done on bringing a neuroscience basis to what Focusing does. He reformulates many FOT terms into neuroscience language, suggesting that recent research in the field might point to Focusing as an important practice. As evidence base and "empirically validated" become ubiquitous in discussions of psychotherapy, Rob Parker offers a critique of some of these terms while giving us an overview of where FOT fits within the world of research.

The book closes, appropriately, by returning to its international cross-cultural flavour. Kevin C. Krycka, Sergio Lara and Atsmaout

Perlstein offer inspiring accounts of how aspects of FOT practice can be applied to community and social situations, promoting progressive and peaceful change in the world.

CHAPTER 14

The Myth of the Bodily Felt Sense

Campbell Purton

Introduction

Focusing and Focusing-Oriented Psychotherapy originated partly in the context of Rogers' "client-centered therapy," and partly in the context of Gendlin's "philosophy of experiencing." Throughout his professional life, Gendlin has worked both on philosophical issues related to the notion of "experiencing" and on the application of these ideas in psychotherapy. In this chapter I will be concerned both with the philosophy and with its application, but since I will be somewhat critical of the philosophy I should say at the start that I do not think of myths as entirely a bad thing, and also that I have found, and continue to find, Focusing to be a very valuable ingredient in psychotherapy. What I have come to have doubts about is not so much the practice of Focusing-Oriented Therapy but the way in which Gendlin thinks about the practice.

A typical example of what is involved in Focusing is the following (Gendlin 1996, p.40):

C: I'm mad at Tom [her new husband] for doing that. I want to push him away.

T: What does that pushing away feel like?

C: Hmmm... Like I want to shove him into that big black case my cello is in. I think I must want to shape and cut him to some mould of mine. I do that to people.

T: Well, sense it a little longer.

C: Hmm... Oh! [Surprise] It's like putting him away just now, but knowing that I will want him back later—keeping him in a safe place like a precious object.

The client begins by saying that she feels mad at her husband, and wants to push him away. The therapist responds in a way that encourages her to give more attention to her response. Then comes a pause as she attends—"Hmmm..." Following the pause her response becomes more articulated, more specific. She has the image of wanting to shove him into her cello case. Then she does something different—she begins to *analyze* what is going on—"I think I must want to shape him and cut him to some sort of mould. I do that to people." The therapist doesn't engage with her analysis, but again encourages her to attend to her response. Then comes a second pause, followed by a further change in the way she is responding to her husband, a change that surprises her. She isn't trying to cut him to some sort of mould; she is putting him safely away for a while.

The crucial places in Focusing are those where the client *pauses*, and then finds a way of (further) articulating their response to their situation. Gendlin is interested in what goes on in such pauses, and he suggests that the client is attending to what he calls the "felt sense" of the client's situation. In the extract above the felt sense would be the vague feeling that she initially labels as "being mad at" and which then becomes "wanting to push him away."

However, according to Gendlin, this is not the whole story. He holds that it is important for the client to sense the feeling in a bodily way. He regards the felt sense as "a special kind of bodily sensation" and, more specifically, as a physical sense of a situation as a whole (Gendlin 1996, pp.18–19). To illustrate this Gendlin gives the example of a student client who says that she "pulls back" in her life, especially in connection with handing in assignments and in her relationships with men. The therapist asks if she can feel the pulling back, and she says she can. Gendlin writes:

> She would not say "I pull back" if she did not actually sense it in herself. The therapist therefore instantly responds to the new feeling, and refers to it as an "it," a "something." He calls it the "pulling back." Of course it is not certain early on that she senses "the pulling back" directly as being "something there."

> The therapist need not be certain that it is. He simply invites it to be there, as a felt sense. (p.33)

The therapist responds "so as to create a 'something there'"; it is an important aspect of Gendlin's notion of the felt sense that "it is not just there, waiting" (Gendlin 1996, pp.33, 46–48), but *forms* as the client gives attention to their experiencing.[1] Once it has formed, the way is open to ask *where* it is: "If you put your attention in your body, there in the middle of your body, can you feel this?" However, in the case that he is discussing (and I think in many others) there is nothing in what the *client* says to suggest that she feels the pulling back in the middle of her body. Gendlin admits this, commenting "Is the pulling back a bodily sense? In this example there is no obvious indication of it. But how else, and where else would one sense the pulling back?" (p.34).

My point will be that if we interpret "I pull back" as a client *report* on a "something" that "is there," or is in the process of being formed "there," then it is indeed hard to see where else but in the body the "there" could be. However, it is not at all obvious that in saying "I pull back" the client is reporting on a "something"; I will suggest instead that what she says is an *expression of her response* in the situations that are difficult for her. This is very different from *analyzing* her response, as she begins to do at one point. I will suggest that what makes the interaction therapeutic is that the therapist helps her to articulate her response more fully, rather than *talk about* it. I think that Gendlin would agree with this, but he also thinks that therapeutic change results from the formation of, and interaction with, a unique kind of entity, the "felt sense," that is created in the center of the body.

Emotions and bodily location

My central question is whether it is helpful to think of the felt sense as a special kind of bodily feeling, and I will approach it by first considering what Gendlin says about how felt senses are related to emotions. Gendlin (1996, pp.57–58) writes:

1 The notion of "experiencing" needs close examination, for which I have no space here; I have discussed it elsewhere (Purton 2013).

> The first and main difference between an emotion and a felt sense is that an emotion is recognizable. We usually know just what emotion we have. When we are angry, sad, or joyful we not only feel it but we know what it is. But with a felt sense we say "I can feel it, right there, but I don't know what it is"... A felt sense is the wholistic, implicit bodily sense of a complex situation. It includes many factors, some of which have never been separated before. Some of those factors are different emotions... It is the unique sense of a whole intricacy, and so it does not fall into a familiar category.

He goes on to say (p.61):

> *Both form in something like the same bodily "place."* A felt sense seems "deeper" because it is more clearly located down in the chest or stomach, and (in another meaning of "deeper") because it is found "under" emotions. But the felt sense may also be said to be "all around" an emotion. It is a wider, more wholistic sense of more than I can say—all that is involved and goes with an emotion, or with any other content.

This is a puzzling passage, but it seems clear enough that Gendlin takes both emotions and felt senses to be located somewhere in the center of the body. Not everyone shares the view that a felt sense is always found in the *center* of the body; some hold that it can be located in any part of the body or even outside the body (Weiser Cornell 2005, pp.30–31). This is an interesting disagreement that I have discussed elsewhere (Purton 2012), and I will not examine it further here. I want to stay rather with the point that felt senses have some resemblance to emotions.

Gendlin's view is that emotions have bodily locations, and that felt senses resemble them in that respect. But *do* emotions have bodily locations? Suppose someone is angry and becomes aware of their increased heart rate and of their clenched fist. Is their anger located in their chest and fist? This seems a rather odd question, though no doubt some people may pound their chests and exclaim "I'm so angry in here!" But is the anger "in there" in the way that the heartbeat is physically in there? Suppose someone places their hand over the left side of their chest and says "I feel so sad in my heart!" We know exactly what that means, but should we say that their sadness is located *there*? *In* their *heart*? That is surely confused—to feel sad in one's heart has nothing to do with the heart that is a blood-pump, *except* that there is that gesture of placing the hand over the heart. That is something we spontaneously do, and saying "I feel sad in my heart" seems to be a linguistic version of the gesture, a linguistic way of expressing what the gesture expresses non-linguistically. When someone says they feel sad in their heart they are not reporting a feeling or sensation present on the left side of their chest; still less are they referring to anything that is happening *inside* their chest, in the heart itself.

There are *some* connections between emotions and particular bodily locations, but such connections seem to be the exception rather than the rule. If someone is feeling happy or wistful, or remorseful, it would in ordinary circumstances be very odd to ask them *where* they felt these emotions. However, it might be said that although there are no very specific locations for the emotions, they nevertheless are *felt* in the body. When one is sad there may be a physical feeling of heaviness, when one is embarrassed or ashamed one may be conscious of flushing, when one is anxious, or guilt-ridden, one's chest may feel tense, or one's mouth may feel dry. In *that* way there can be bodily locations associated with some emotions, but it doesn't seem right to say that one's flushing *is* one's embarrassment, or that the tension in the chest *is* one's guilt.

There is a good reason why we cannot make such identifications between emotions and bodily sensations: it is that we identify emotions in terms of kinds of *situation*. We speak of fear in situations where there is danger, we speak of pride in situations where the person is pleased with having done something good, we speak of embarrassment where there is social ineptitude. At least, it is in such situations that the talk of emotions *originates*; it is in connection with such situations that children begin to learn the emotion words. Later, "extra joints" may be added in the language-game: for example, the child *later* learns that there *can be* circumstances where someone is afraid yet there is no danger, but the *normal* connection between fear and danger is still there. Similarly the child later grasps that there can be situations where a person is being socially inept but *doesn't* feel embarrassed—they just don't care about their ineptitude; but that is not the normal case, that is not where the language-game *begins*.

We talk of emotions in the context of situations, and while a person needs in some way to be moved by their situation in order to count as feeling an emotion, the way in which they are moved can be various. A person who runs from a charging bull is moved in a very straightforward way, and we say they are afraid. Another person may not run, but be rooted to the spot, and tremble all over. A third may be afraid of bulls in the sense that when they see a bull their mind is filled with thoughts of being chased and gored. The emotion of fear may show in what a person does, in the physical responses they have, in the images or thoughts that come to them; the responses are variable, but the context of danger runs through all cases of fear.

If we are asked "But *where* then is the person's fear?" I think that we need to say that this is an unhappy question. There are, as I have said, cases where bodily located sensations are involved, but we can't say that those sensations *are* the emotion. The same sensations could occur in the context of a quite different emotion: for instance the flush might be of shame or of embarrassment—one can't tell which by examining *it*; the tingling feeling might be hope or anxiety, and so on. What creates the difficulty here is the assumption that an emotion is some kind of state or process with a bodily location, but emotion words, unlike sensation words, are not in fact used in that way. To say that a person is afraid, or proud, or ashamed is to draw attention to the fact that they are moved in some way through being in a particular kind of situation. The question "Where do you feel your pride?" is not a happy question because it assumes something that isn't so, that is, that "pride" is the name of a bodily locatable inner state or process. The appropriate question to ask is "In what circumstances do we say that Jones is feeling pride?" and the answer to that is something like "in circumstances where Jones is pleased that he has done something good."

Now if emotion words are not the names of inner states or processes, and a felt sense resembles an emotion (except that it is less specific), then presumably to speak of a felt sense is not to speak of an inner state or process. Or to put it another way, if emotions can't be identified with bodily sensations then it will be implausible to regard felt senses as bodily sensations. Gendlin writes of the felt sense:

> A felt sense is a bodily sensation, but it is not merely a physical sensation like a tickle or pain. Rather, it is a physical sense of something, of meaning, of implicit intricacy. It is a sense of a whole situation or problem or concern, or perhaps a point one wants to convey. It is not *just* a bodily sense, but rather a bodily sense *of*... (1996, p.63)

I think that part of the difficulty with this is that Gendlin is running together two distinct uses of the word "sense." One use is connected with the use of the sense organs, and with having bodily sensations, such as tingles or pains. The other use is connected with meaning and understanding, as when we say that we have a sense of what someone means. For Anneka to sense (correctly) what Charlie means, is for her to know what he means without yet being able to articulate her knowledge, but nothing at all follows about what bodily sensations Anneka has, if any.

If I am right that there is something awry in thinking of a felt sense as "a special kind of bodily sensation" the question arises of what, then, a felt sense is. But as in the case of emotions this question may not be a happy one. Instead of asking "What is going on in a person when they have a felt sense?" it may be better to ask "In what circumstances do we say that a person has a felt sense?"

The typical circumstances in which therapists and Focusing people speak of a person as "having a felt sense" are easy enough to describe. They are circumstances in which a person is trying to find a word, but the word does not immediately come. They then try various things: they may try simply becoming quiet and receptive, or ask themselves questions such as "Is it something to do with...?" (Gendlin 1978/2003, p.85); the poet may rotate their hand in the air as they try to find the last line for a poem (Gendlin 1991, pp.47–48). A person who is trying to find a word may also *say* "I just have this *feeling*..." and *that* may help the word to come. Then after a while they may say "Ah!...now I know what it is!" *before* they formulate what has come in words; in Gendlin's phrase the felt sense has "opened." There *is* such a thing as this "Ah!-understanding," just as there is such a thing as the original "inarticulate feeling." But the language of "things" and "feelings" can easily mislead us. When the person says "I have this *feeling*..." it is tempting to think that they are *reporting* an inner state. Yet it is not obvious that what they say is a report; it seems rather to be a linguistic version of the poet's hand-rotation: it is an expression of their searching. Similarly, the "Ah!..." is an expression of the fact that they are no longer stuck. This seems clear enough if they just say "Ah!...," but if they add "... now I know what it is!" that doesn't turn the expression into a report of something.

Äusserungen: Wittgenstein's "spontaneous utterances"

The utterances "I just have this *feeling*..." and "Ah!..." are examples of what Wittgenstein (1953/2009) called *Äusserungen*, taking the ordinary German word for "utterance" in the special sense of spontaneous utterances that *take the place of* non-linguistic responses. Typical examples of *Äusserungen* are "Ouch!" in place of a cry of pain, or "I'm afraid" in place of a cry of fear.[2] What can mislead us is that, in more sophisticated forms of language, an expression that is an *Äusserung* can look as though it is a *report* of an inner state or process. For example, if the person instead of saying "Ouch!" says spontaneously "There's a pain in my leg!" it can seem, at least if we are thinking theoretically, that they are reporting something. But what they are reporting is not something we can see; it is not like reporting that they have a bullet in their leg. So *if it is a report* it is a report of something "hidden" from others, and thus arises the notion of a pain as an inner state or process. Similarly, I suggest, when a person during Focusing says "I just have this *feeling*..." or "Ah!..." it is tempting to think that these are reports of inner states or processes, and that such inner states or processes constitute, respectively, the felt sense and its subsequent "opening."

I am suggesting that while there is nothing wrong with saying, while Focusing, "I have this *feeling*..." it is a mistake to conclude that there is "something there," perhaps in the middle of the body, that is "the feeling." The "felt sense," thought of as a feeling of this kind,

2 For more discussion of the notion of an *Äusserung* see Moyal-Sharrock (2000), Canfield (2007).

is an example of an intriguing kind of illusion that is generated by the misleading picture of the "inner object."[3] Wittgenstein writes (1953/2009, p.598):

> When we do philosophy we are inclined to hypostatise feelings where we have none. They serve to explain our thoughts to us. "*Here* the explanation of our thought requires a feeling!" It is as if our conviction answered to this demand.

For instance, we may be inclined to say that when a person expects an explosion they must have a feeling of expectation. Yet in fact they may not have *any* particular sensation; it is just that they would be surprised if there were not an explosion (Wittgenstein 1953/2009, pp.576–57). Similarly (p.607), we sometimes "have a feeling" of what time it is, but having this feeling is not a matter of noticing anything "inner": we *might* have an image of a clock face, or the words "It's three o'clock" *might* come to mind, but neither of these is a feeling. Alternatively, nothing at all might go through our mind. "In that case, *what did we go by* in saying it was three o'clock?"—"Just by a feeling"—but we could equally well say there was *nothing* we went by. "Feelings" of this kind are *fabrications* (p.609), which, nevertheless, like the creations of mythology, have a deep appeal for us. In a way this fits with what Gendlin says about the felt sense, since he regards it not as "just there" but as *created* in the interaction between the focuser and their experiencing. However, Gendlin sees the creation of the felt sense as the creation of a remarkable kind of object, and holds that it is through further interaction with this object that therapeutic change takes place. The alternative that I am suggesting is that the bodily felt sense is a creation of the imagination, like the "feeling" we "must have" when we say what time it is without looking at the clock.

3 Bennett and Hacker (2003, p.230) discuss a similar illusion in connection with some experiments by Libet and others, which allegedly show that voluntary acts are initiated in the brain some 350 msec before the person "feels the intention to act," and hence that free will is an illusion. They comment "[O]ne of the most interesting (inadvertent) results of these experiments is that people, when asked to report such bizarre things as 'a feeling of intention to move their hand,' will find such a feeling to report, even though it is more than a little doubtful whether there is any such thing as 'a feeling of intention.'"

The bodily felt sense

It may be worth emphasizing what a remarkable entity the bodily felt sense is, if Gendlin is right about it. He gives an elaborate account in Chapter VIII of *A Process Model* (1997), in which the felt sense emerges as "a perfect feedback object" existing in a new kind of space, as well as in physical space. But leaving this development aside, the felt sense still has extraordinary characteristics. Gendlin (1978/2003, p.54) writes that the felt sense:

> contains many details, just as a piece of music contains many notes. A symphony, for instance, may last an hour or more and contain thousands of separate musical tones, sounded by many diverse instruments, in a multitude of combinations and progressions. But you don't need to know all these details of its structure in order to feel it. If it is a symphony you know well, you only need hear its name mentioned and feel the aura of it instantly. That symphony: the feel of it comes to you whole, without details.

There is a picture here of a feeling-whole that has many parts or facets; it contains *within* itself many detailed tones, intervals, thoughts, emotions, and other experiences, far too many to be listed. We may imagine them in a picturesque, mythological way as cloudy masses interweaving with one another, but never really distinct. The mathematician Hadamard (1945, p.16) quotes a letter of Mozart[4] in which Mozart says that his mind seizes a whole musical composition:

> as a glance of my eye a beautiful picture or a handsome youth. It does not come to me successively, with various parts worked out in detail, as they will be later on, but in its entirety that my imagination lets me hear it.

This can seem mysterious—how *can* an extended piece of music be condensed into a momentary flash of feeling?

Bennett and Hacker (2003, p.309n) have some helpful comments on this. They write:

> [Mozart] certainly did not mean that he *heard* the whole piece in his imagination in a flash… To conceive of a solution to a complex

4 Bennett and Hacker (2003, p.309n) point out that this letter is in fact a forgery, but that is irrelevant here.

> problem, in musical composition or in any other domain, "in a flash" is no more mysterious (although no less remarkable) than being able to make a note of a complex thought by jotting down a few words or a diagram, which constitute, for the author, the epitome of his thought. What makes the jotting into an epitome of a thought is the use its author subsequently makes of it. The sudden flash of inspiration is the dawning of a capacity, not the high-speed articulation of a thought... The solution one sees in a flash is more of a pointer than a product. What we have here is a form of knowing that one *can* do something, not a mysterious form of doing something at an impossibly high speed.

Gendlin writes that one of the aims of his work is "to re-conceptualize *the body* so that we could understand how Focusing is possible, how we can feel complex situations, how the body can come up with an answer to a complex human living question we cannot figure out" (Gendlin 1997, p.181). If we accept the picture of the felt sense as a bodily feeling then there will of course be a real question about how the bodily feeling in question can possibly "contain" all that is "in" the problem.[5] It is this question that sets Gendlin off on his philosophical odyssey. However, for the reasons I have given above, I'm inclined to think that the answer to the question of how there can be such an entity as the bodily felt sense is that there *can't* be such an entity. Not in the sense that such a thing doesn't happen to exist, but in the sense that talk about a bodily felt sense is in the end incoherent. Talk of the felt sense, like talk of emotion and unlike talk of sensations, doesn't cohere with talk of bodily location.

Conclusion

As I remarked at the beginning, my criticism of Gendlin's way of thinking about the felt sense does not involve any general criticism of Focusing in practice. In the example that I started with, it seems clear that the woman benefits from the Focusing process: she is initially just "mad at Tom," but as she pauses and gives her attention

5 Gendlin is not the only thinker to have suggested a remarkable theory in order to account for our ability to grasp things "as a whole" or "in a flash"—the distinguished mathematical physicist Roger Penrose (1999, pp.568–578) thinks that what is needed is a re-thinking of the nature of time in connection with a yet-to-be-developed theory of quantum gravity.

to her situation, her response becomes more differentiated. She wants to "push him away," and then more specifically still she wants to "put him away just now, knowing that I'll want him back later." She keeps her attention on the whole situation with her husband, and the break from *analyzing* it allows her to *articulate*—to further develop—her response. She is not reporting a change in her feelings, but is finding a new *attitude* to her husband.

Also, I am not saying that we should never talk in Gendlin's picturesque "body-mythology" way. Often this way of talking does no harm, any more than does talking of "a feeling in one's heart" or "having a word on the tip of one's tongue."[6] Nevertheless, it can be misleading (Purton 2012): if we think of the felt sense as a bodily sensation we may waste time in trying to locate it (Weiser Cornell 1996, p.29), and we will be inclined, in Focusing, to give our attention to the sensations we really do feel in the body: tensions, pangs, tightnesses, tingles, etc. But while such sensations can sometimes alert us to the fact that something is up in our situation (e.g., a sudden pang can alert us to our jealousy), we will not get far by attending to our sensations in the way one might attend to them during a mindfulness "body scan," for example. What is needed is to keep our attention on our situation as a whole (through not letting ourselves be distracted by over-familiar aspects of it), and to allow our responses to become more articulated. This procedure is not well characterized as a change in how one *describes one's "feelings"*; it is a matter of a change in attitude, in how one is *living*. One finds new words, but these words are not reports of new bodily feelings, they are new *Äusserungen*—new responses, new *deeds* in the form of words. It is in that sense that we can say that Focusing-Oriented Therapy goes "beyond the talking cure."

References

Bennett, M.R. and Hacker, P. (2003) *Philosophical Foundations of Neuroscience*. Oxford: Blackwell.

Canfield, J.V. (2007) "Wittgenstein on Fear." In D. Moyal-Sharrock (ed.) *Perspicuous Presentations: Essays on Wittgenstein's Philosophy of Psychology*. Basingstoke: Palgrave.

Gendlin, E.T. (1978/2003) *Focusing*, rev. edn. London: Rider.

6 Though how should we respond to someone who says "Yes, I do have a sensation in my tongue—right *there*, where the word is!"?

Gendlin, E.T. (1991) "Thinking Beyond Patterns." In B. den Ouden and M. Moen (eds) *The Presence of Feeling in Thought.* New York: Peter Lang.

Gendlin, E.T. (1996) *Focusing Oriented Psychotherapy.* New York: Guilford Press.

Gendlin, E.T. (1997) *A Process Model.* New York: Focusing Institute.

Hadamard, J. (1945) *The Psychology of Invention in the Mathematical Field.* Princeton, NJ: Princeton University Press.

Moyal-Sharrock, D. (2000) 'Words as deeds': Wittgenstein's 'spontaneous utterances' and the dissolution of the explanatory gap." *Philosophical Psychology 13,* 3, 355–375.

Penrose, R. (1999) *The Emperor's New Mind,* rev. edn. Oxford: Oxford University Press.

Purton, C. (2012) "Focusing Oriented Therapy." In P. Sanders (ed.) *The Tribes of the Person-Centred Nation,* 2nd edn. Ross-on-Wye: PCCS Books.

Purton, C. (2013) "Incongruence and 'inner experiencing.'" *Person-Centered and Experiential Psychotherapies 12,* 3, 1–13.

Weiser Cornell, A. (1996) *The Power of Focusing.* Oakland, CA: New Harbinger.

Weiser Cornell, A. (2005) *The Radical Acceptance of Everything.* Berkeley, CA: Calluna Press.

Wittgenstein, L. (1953/2009) *Philosophical Investigations,* 4th edn. Chichester: Wiley-Blackwell.

CHAPTER 15

Two Things Therapists Should Know about Philosophy

Rob Parker

Introduction

Many people think of philosophy as empty theorizing with no supporting research. And yet philosophy is an important part of science, of psychotherapy, in fact of everything we do.

Why? Consider an historical example: Tycho Brahe (1546–1601) was one of history's greatest astronomers, the man who laid the groundwork for the later discoveries of Kepler, Galileo, and Newton. Born three years after Copernicus died, Tycho understood and appreciated the mathematical beauty of assuming the earth moves around the sun. And yet, he concluded:

> ...such a fast motion could not belong to the earth, a body very heavy and dense and opaque, but rather belongs to the sky itself whose form and subtle and constant matter are better suited to a perpetual motion, however fast. (Blair 1990, p.361)

For Tycho, the very concept of *earth* meant something heavy, opaque, and subject to continuous change and decay, in contrast to celestial objects made of *aether* that were radiant, unchanging, and moved in perpetual circles. This concept of an unmoving Earth was inherent in the medieval understanding of physics, astronomy, religion, and even social order. An earth that moved was not just a new concept; it was a new *kind* of concept, one that would force everything else to change.

Tycho was unable to think in this new way; for him, the earth was something inherently dense and difficult to move. He implicitly *assumed* what Copernicus was disputing, and he couldn't question his assumption because he didn't know any other way to think.

Philosophy can be an antidote to this problem. As the study of different *kinds* of concepts, philosophy helps us to critique our current way of thinking and gets us out of the prison of implicit assumptions. Albert Einstein described it this way:

> In the attempt to achieve a conceptual formulation of the confusingly immense body of observational data, the scientist makes use of a whole arsenal of concepts which he imbibed practically with his mothers milk; and seldom if ever is he aware of the eternally problematic character of his concepts. He uses this conceptual material…as something obviously, immutably given; something having an objective value of truth which is hardly ever, and in any case not seriously, to be doubted… *And yet in the interests of science it is necessary over and over again to engage in the critique of these fundamental concepts, in order that we may not unconsciously be ruled by them.* (1954/1994, p.xii–xiv; emphasis added)

Of course, the problem is not limited to astronomy. Consider an example from psychotherapy. Research indicates that about 20 percent of female children are sexually abused (e.g., Gorey and Leslie 1997), and the percentages are higher in clinical populations. Yet, from 1900 through the 1970s, psychotherapists almost completely ignored the existence of child sexual abuse. Between 1900 and 1970 there were only five articles in peer-reviewed journals on this topic (APA PsychNet Database, July 22, 2013). In Fenichel's *The Psychoanalytic Theory of Neurosis* (1945), the index under "Incest" reads "see Oedipus complex."

How could tens of thousands of therapists, over a period of 70 years, fail to see what is so clear to us today? Perhaps in a culture dominated by men and male perspectives, it was unthinkable that so many children could be sexually abused, and mostly by men. Whatever the reason, child sexual abuse was apparently unthinkable, because almost nobody thought it and the problem wasn't addressed.

These two examples point to a basic reason for philosophy: Conceptual understanding is both empowering and limiting. Concepts shape our approach to the world; how we make sense of it, what stands out for us, and what we overlook. Concepts thus enable us to explore the world, but also shape *how* we explore and what we learn, as the order of our concepts interacts with the more intricate order of reality (Gendlin 1997c).

In the world of psychotherapy, for example, cognitive behaviorists often use concepts related to computers, while person-centered therapists tend to use concepts related to living organisms. The choice of one kind of concept over another has deep and pervasive implications for how we do therapy:

- Computers are inanimate and made of parts (including lines of code) that can be fixed or replaced; so a cognitive therapist is like a technician who helps the client correct dysfunctional thinking.
- Organisms are animate and function holistically (they are not made of parts that can be individually fixed or replaced); so a person-centered therapist is more like a gardener who tries to create the right conditions for the client to grow.

And for how we do research:

- Cognitive behaviorists tend to prefer experimental research designs, which break problems down into separate parts (independent and dependent variables) and determine what causes what.
- Person-centered therapists, interested in how clients grow and develop during therapy, often prefer qualitative research designs, and then have trouble getting reimbursed by organizations dominated by mechanistic assumptions that don't recognize the value of qualitative research.

And what we research:

- One group might study dysfunctional thoughts, while the other studies unconditional positive regard, and neither topic would seem useful or relevant to the other group.

Thus, evidence from person-centered research might not seem useful to a cognitive behaviorist, and vice versa. One might say that this is "only" philosophy, yet philosophy is important when it affects what we do, how we do it, and whether we are reimbursed. Unexamined assumptions can have profound consequences.

The differences between cognitive behavioral and person-centered psychotherapy are relatively easy to label and discuss. Some concepts have such deep roots in our thinking that it is difficult to even identify them. For example, it seems obvious to many people today that the universe is made of separate inanimate *things*, like stars and planets or atoms and molecules. Yet it seemed obvious to many medieval Europeans that the universe is an organic whole, with various "parts" acting in harmony with each other according to a divine plan. It took the greatest minds in Europe hundreds of years to develop our current "obvious" way of thinking. Yet this, too, may be about to change. Discoveries in quantum physics and quantum biology suggest that the universe can't be completely understood in terms of separate parts after all. In short, what seems "obvious" is always changing.

Philosophy can help us be better psychotherapists by teaching us to think in different ways, and as Einstein reminds us, to over and over again critique our fundamental concepts so that they do not rule us.

Reversal of the order

By itself, the possibility of different kinds of thinking can lead to mere relativism. Gendlin's Philosophy of the Implicit (POI) takes us further, by showing how concepts are created from experiencing and have a very precise, more-than-logical relationship to experiencing (Gendlin 1997c). The key is in understanding what Gendlin (1997b) calls the *reversal of the order.*

To illustrate this, consider why things fall. Most people would say things fall because of gravity. But what is gravity? In 1400, gravity was the tendency of things containing the element earth to move to their proper place in the universe, the center of the planet Earth. By the mid-seventeenth century, gravity was an invisible force acting at a distance. By the early twentieth century, gravity was a curvature in space-time. And today, many physicists believe that gravity is a force mediated by subatomic particles called gravitons. So what is gravity? Gravity is a concept. The concept isn't arbitrary; each new version of gravity is more precise and/or more inclusive of other phenomena. But gravity is still a concept. Things don't fall because of gravity; rather, we have a concept of gravity because things fall.

In Western thinking it is common to assume the world has a predetermined order, such as fixed laws of nature, and to fit our experience into that order. POI reverses that order and sets it straight, by putting interaction with the world (i.e., experiencing) first.

How do new concepts and meaning come from experiencing?

Consider a metaphor such as "my love is like a red, red rose." In creating a metaphor, we don't make a list of my love's qualities, and then list the qualities of dozens of other things until we find a match between "my love" and "roses." Rather, we experience something we don't have words for, and we point to the nameless experience by saying, "it is like *this*." Only after the metaphor is created can we name similarities that make the metaphor work (my love is fresh, beautiful, etc.), and generalize the similarities into concepts (freshness, beauty, etc.).

Notice that myriad aspects of my love and a rose function in the metaphor, but only as they express the felt meaning. The facts that my love finished high school and the rose lives in dirt don't function in this metaphor, but might in some other. Notice also that the metaphor can surprise us; we might realize, for example, that a loving relationship needs to be cultivated so it can grow. Metaphor is an instance of the reversal of the order. Concepts about *how* my love is like a rose come from the metaphor, not vice versa. And language is also like this. Whenever we name something, we are saying it is like something else. Where, then, does metaphor come from?

Living is ongoing interaction with the world; so as embodied creatures, we know in a pre-conceptual, bodily way how to interact with the world and what is needed in different situations. We can experience this body-knowing as a "feel" for our situations that is more intricate than conceptual understanding. If we can pause and *be with* our experiencing *now*, so it becomes *this* concrete experiencing instead of an implicit background, two things happen.

1. *First, it becomes a kind of experiencing* in the sense that we could later compare it to another experiencing and say how this one is like,

and unlike, the other one. *This* experiencing becomes the first, and so far the only, instance of its kind; it is an instance of itself. Thus any experiencing we identify (any "this") is inherently a comparison, a metaphor, because it is "like this."

2. *Further, experiencing is changed (carried forward) by becoming a kind.* Instead of a nameless unnoticed background, it becomes *this* (kind of) experiencing; an instance of itself. Then, if we specify how it has changed, we repeat the process and create *another* kind. It is no longer the way it was before, it is now like *this.* This is an example of the IOFI (Instance OF Itself) principle. Any experiencing can be an instance of itself and thus a source of new meaning, and (as we saw with metaphor) the new meaning will be relevant to the situation at hand.

We can do this over and over: identifying the flow of bodily experiencing, saying what it is like, identifying how naming has changed it, saying what that is like, and so on. This process is called *Focusing.*

Thus any experiencing can be a source of new concepts, and a way out of the prison of unexamined assumptions. We can create new meaning whenever we attend directly to our experiencing, instead of using taken-for-granted labels and concepts. And, as we saw with cognitive behavioral and person-centered therapy, we discover different things when we approach the world in different ways; and each new discovery can be conceptualized in a vast number of ways. There is no final, definitive way to understand the world. There is always more than can be represented in concepts, and therefore always room for new concepts and new discoveries. That is why science progresses and our scientific concepts continuously change (Gendlin 1997a, 1997b).

It is important to distinguish concepts from reality, to question our concepts and use them as tools instead of being ruled by them. Our society has confused concepts with reality for hundreds of years, and so it is easy for us as therapists to continue this old habit. In the next sections, we will discuss some ways this can happen, and how to avoid them.

Science and therapy

It seems obvious to many people that the brain is some kind of machine; over the years the brain has been compared to almost anything that is both exciting and poorly understood: telephone switchboards, electrical circuits, holograms, computers, and now the Internet. In each case there are some similarities, but also many differences. Consider the computer analogy. The function of a mind/brain is fundamentally different from that of a computer program (Dreyfus 2009). Far from being hardwired, the brain is very adaptable, especially in children (see below), it has no wires (neurons function differently from copper wire), and the so-called brain "circuit" is actually a coordinated series of electrical and chemical actions performed by a string of neurons, more like a bucket brigade than a current flowing passively from a negative to a positive pole.

Unlike computers, our brains have remarkable capacity to change and adapt. Imagine what would happen to a computer if you sawed it in half, yet removal of an entire hemisphere is a common treatment for certain kinds of epilepsy. Children recover from this procedure remarkably well; in one pre–post study, the average change in IQ was less than five points, and many patients had higher IQs after surgery (Pulsifer *et al.* 2004). This capacity to reorganize is a characteristic of living organisms; it is hard to even think about, let alone explain, with mechanistic concepts.

Careless use of mechanistic concepts can influence clinical thinking and practice. Imagine a child who grew up in an abusive home, and withdrew from the world because it was dangerous. She didn't engage in normal activities, didn't learn to do things, didn't learn to distinguish relevant details of her environment, and didn't remember things; not because she couldn't, but because she didn't want to, for good reasons.

What would happen to her? In a few years, her lack of practice in dealing with the world would show up as severe cognitive and neurological deficits. For example, she might have poor long-term memory, and her hippocampus could well be smaller than normal, just as she would be a poor runner with atrophied leg muscles if she had never practiced walking.

A neuroscience analysis might suggest pervasive developmental disorder (PDD) with memory and other cognitive deficits caused by hippocampal damage secondary to chronic childhood trauma. The prognosis would not be hopeful. But if we can question fundamental concepts and be open to the actual experiencing, we might find more. In this case the "more" might be a resourceful child who managed to survive chronic abuse by hiding inside herself, and who now needs to learn that she is safe, that she can come out of herself, explore the world, and learn to trust people.

I worked with a child like this. The initial impression was severe autism, and the eventual diagnosis was PDD; yet, after about two years of therapy, she was earning passing grades in a mainstream classroom, developing healthy social relationships, and generally acting like a normal child. This doesn't make the neuroscience story irrelevant; years of disuse might have permanent effects on a leg or a hippocampus. The point is that as clinicians, we need to distinguish concepts from reality.

By enabling us to discover and critique the assumptions implicit in neuroscience theory, philosophy can free us from one way of thinking. Then, the Philosophy of the Implicit (Gendlin 1997a, 1997b, 1997c) enables us to create new ways of thinking. If we know the clinical situation well enough to have a felt sense for what doesn't fit our available concepts, we might use Thinking at the Edge (a way to bring into public language what we "know" implicitly, see Gendlin 2004), to create a new theory.

Therapy practice

Several years ago I worked in a children's psychiatric hospital where children and their parents were each assigned a different therapist. This led to very interesting team meetings, in which the parents' therapist would discuss how difficult the child was, and the child's therapist would discuss how difficult the parents were. These were smart, well-trained, caring therapists. The problem was that they could only understand their clients in one way, because they had only one story. Of course, this happens to all of us, and again philosophy can help in two ways.

First, if we understand the danger of having just one story, we can deliberately cultivate two stories, for example, the child as the problem, and the parents as the problem. Of course, both stories must be elaborated to incorporate each new piece of information. After a while this becomes a habit, and the result is an expanded awareness. We can feel in our bones that if there are two stories, there could be more, and we are more open to the intricacy of the actual situation.

Then, POI reminds us to be with the actual interaction. We dig beneath conceptual formulations; if a client says, "my husband is argumentative," we ask for a concrete example. We attend to the client's moment-by-moment awareness of his/her experiencing, and whether our interventions expand that awareness (Gendlin 1984). All the theories we know are useful here, the more the better; but instead of being grounded in theory, we are grounded in the interaction. This frees us from concepts in a radical way. We have a new ground to stand on: no longer concepts, but what the concepts do, moment-by-moment, in real time.

Trusting the "more"

Whether we are therapists or clients, we tell ourselves stories about ourselves and our lives. These stories can function implicitly, under our awareness, as when each life situation is about being accepted or rejected, but each situation seems to stand alone, unrelated to the other acceptance–rejection situations. Or, the stories can be explicit, as when someone is explicitly devoted to accumulating wealth and power. But whether implicit or explicit, our life stories imply explicit next steps and each next step is in the direction of an explicit goal, something that must be attained in order for us to be OK.

But life is more intricate than a story and, to the extent that we live a story, we are not living life. An explicit goal, like money or acceptance by particular people, is often a conceptual representation of something deeper, something implicit. It is a kind of idol, an image we create that stands for and eventually replaces something much richer and larger. To ignore this larger intricacy, and identify with some small conceptual version of it, is a kind of idolatry. By confusing concepts with reality, we overlook the rich intricacy of life, harming ourselves and perhaps others in the process.

Yet because this intricacy *is* our life, we can experience it in the felt sense of each situation. If we can let go of idols and be open to our felt sense of what this situation "wants" or "needs," the felt sense can open and expand, and new steps can form that were unimaginable before. This is not easy to do, for clients or therapists. It's hard to let go of our story and be open (and vulnerable) to the inchoate sense of our concrete experiencing. It takes a certain attitude; hopeful but not for any specific outcome, acknowledging that our conceptual understanding is limited, and sensing something larger that knows better.

Even to say this requires a new use of language, because words like "what the situation needs" usually refer to some idol or predetermined goal, and are meaningful only within the context of some story. But POI enables us to speak in a meaningful way without assuming a story (Gendlin 1997a, pp.251ff). Spoken from a felt sense, words like "what the situation needs" can have a very precise meaning. We can "feel" this meaning, even though we can't say it with everyday words. And the felt sense (or, more precisely, a felt shift) can open a whole new understanding of a situation. By grounding ourselves in our bodily knowing of concrete situations, we can escape the prison of specific stories, and live with greater awareness of the actual intricacy of life.

Conclusion: two things therapists should know about philosophy

As therapists we necessarily think with concepts and stories. We have shown how easy it is to confuse these with reality, and how doing so can limit our conceptual understanding, therapeutic practice, and actual experience of ourselves and our clients. We have also discussed two lessons from philosophy that can help us escape the rule of concepts and stories, and become better therapists.

1. There is no final "correct" way to conceptualize reality

Concrete interaction with the world is more intricate than concepts, and can be conceptualized in different ways, with different results. Although the world is not arbitrary and only some conceptual systems work, it is possible and often useful to know and use two or more conceptual systems. This can free us from being ruled by one way of thinking, and open us to more aspects of a problem or situation.

2. If we stay with the body's knowing of a process or interaction, it can open new steps that we couldn't have imagined before

How can we know what is needed in a situation, without clear concepts? It happens all the time. We react immediately, without thinking, if someone swerves in front of us on the highway. All the myriad aspects of the situation (speed, other traffic, road conditions, etc.) function together to form a single response. Because our bodies *are* ongoing interaction with the world, including the social world, in any situation where we have sufficient experience, our bodies know what is needed and what to do. Everyone has experienced this; it is not new.

The Philosophy of the Implicit shows how this body-knowing can open into new ways of experiencing and understanding. In many situations precise concepts are needed, but our available concepts are inadequate. If we, as therapists or as clients, can bring awareness to our bodily experiencing of the situation, it can form a single felt sense of what is needed that opens into larger understanding, and new ways forward.

References

Blair, A. (1990) "Tycho Brahe's critique of Copernicus and the Copernican system." *Journal of the History of Ideas 51*, 3, 355–377.

Dreyfus, H.L. (2009) "How Representational Cognitivism Failed and Is Being Replaced by Body/World Coupling." In K. Leidlmair (ed.) *After Cognitivism.* New York: Springer.

Einstein, A. (1954/1994) "Foreword." In M. Jammer, *Concepts of Space: The History of Theories of Space in Physics*, 3rd enlarged edn. New York: Dover Publications.

Fenichel, O. (1945) *The Psychoanalytic Theory of Neurosis.* New York: Norton.

Gendlin, E.T. (1984) "The Client's Client: The Edge of Awareness." In R.L. Levant and J.M. Shlien (eds) *Client-Centered Therapy and the Person-Centered Approach: New Directions in Theory, Research and Practice.* New York: Praeger.

Gendlin, E.T. (1997a) *A Process Model.* Spring Valley, NY: Focusing Institute.

Gendlin, E.T. (1997b) *Experiencing and the Creation of Meaning: A Philosophical and Psychological Approach to the Subjective.* Evanston, IL: Northwestern University Press.

Gendlin, E.T. (1997c) "The responsive order: A new empiricism." *Man and World 30*, 3, 383–411.

Gendlin, E.T. (2004) "Introduction to thinking at the edge." *The Folio 19*, 1, 1–8.

Gorey, K.M. and Leslie, D.R. (1997) "The prevalence of child sexual abuse: Integrative review adjustment for potential response and measurement biases." *Child Abuse & Neglect 21*, 4, 391–398.

Pulsifer, M.B., Brandt, J., Salorio, C.F., Vining, E.P.G., Carson, B.S. and Freeman, J.M. (2004) "The cognitive outcome of hemispherectomy in 71 children." *Epilepsia 45*, 3, 243–254.

CHAPTER 16

Neuroscience and Psychological Change in Focusing

Peter Afford

Looking at Focusing in the light of neuroscience can be illuminating. Focusing concerns our inner processes of feeling and thinking, and neuroscience sheds interesting light on how these processes unfold in our minds and bodies. Although Gendlin is a philosopher and frequently critical of science, he describes life processes that are intimately linked with our biology (Gendlin 1997). By rooting his thinking more in subjective experience than in psychological abstraction, he touches into the biological substrates of our inner lives—the very ground of neuroscience.

Neuroscience used to be firmly planted in cognitive territory and may have seemed irrelevant to a discussion of feeling. However, more recently it has ventured beyond cognition into our emotional lives and our relationships with our bodies (see Damasio 1994, 2000, 2010). So the time is ripe to bring a little science into our thinking about Focusing and the subtleties of Focusing-Oriented Therapy. Furthermore, familiarity with the experience of Focusing may help in understanding certain aspects of current neuroscience, in particular the startling differences between the two cerebral hemispheres.

Neuroscience and the two cerebral hemispheres

There are two striking features about the architecture of the brain. One is that underneath the wrinkly cortex (Latin for covering) lie "subcortical" areas that appeared earlier in evolution. These include the brainstem (the top of the spinal cord) and the much talked about amygdala and hippocampus. The other striking feature is that the entire brain, including the two cerebral hemispheres of the cortex, is lateralized between right and left sides.

These vertical and horizontal divisions are inter-linked because the subcortical areas have richer connections with the right hemisphere than with the left. And subcortical areas lead to the body. While motor control of limbs belongs in each contralateral hemisphere, autonomic regulation of the viscera within the body happens mainly in the right hemisphere. So this hemisphere is part of a greater whole, while the left is like an ivory castle that stands alone.

The hemispheric divide has fostered many popular assumptions that are unwarranted and from which neuroscientists distance themselves. One such assumption is the notion that some people are "left-brained" and logical, whilst others are "right-brained" and creative. But a landmark work published in 2009, Iain McGilchrist's *The Master & His Emissary*, pulled together the research findings on the subject into a thesis about neural "lateralization" that is scientifically respectable. The summary of these findings, laid out below, holds true for the majority of people (including most left-handed people).

Anatomically, only 2 percent of neurons in either hemisphere are interlinked via the corpus callosum, the band of tissue that joins the hemispheres. The corpus callosum allows each side to know what the other is doing, but it also allows the side that is more efficient at a particular task to inhibit the other and thereby become dominant for it. And the left hemisphere is more effective at inhibiting the right than vice versa.

The various regions of the right hemisphere are more interlinked (via myelinated axons or "white matter," in contrast to the "gray matter" of the cell bodies themselves) than are left hemisphere regions, which prefer greater "independence" in order to fulfil their particular function. The right hemisphere functions more as an integrated whole, the left more as a collection of specialist parts.

Anatomical differences lead to functional differences. McGilchrist (2009) believes the key difference in functionality is that the right hemisphere does broad attention, enabling us to be vigilant for changes in the environment, while the left looks after precise attention, enabling us to grasp what is in front of us—both material and conceptual. Left therefore dominates for conscious awareness of the foreground, while right dominates for what is less conscious in the background. Right notices whatever is new at the edge of awareness and spots apparent discrepancies, while left manipulates what is already known at the center of awareness. Left divides the world into categories, while right experiences its interconnectedness. Detail, therefore, falls to the left, context to the right. And the right hemisphere looks after affect regulation, somatic regulation—the body—and the implicit aspects of relating and communicating.

McGilchrist's (2009) thesis is that the right hemisphere is the "master" and the left the "emissary," but the development of Western civilization has led to the emissary betraying the master—and our state of disconnection from the natural world. Focusing is an inner activity that returns the emissary to the master by emphasizing our bodily felt experiencing. It would seem to promote integration of the hemispheres by combining broad attention (right) to what is happening in the body, with precise attention (left) for holding onto and articulating what is happening.

Attending to bodily feeling fires neural networks in the right hemisphere that link with the body. And thanks to the interconnectedness of areas within the right hemisphere, such attention can stimulate other functions of this side of the brain, including affective and somatic regulation, and bring them closer to awareness. The right hemisphere is where signals from our external senses and internal bodily senses come together. When our experience is of emotional overwhelm, trauma and dissociation, external and internal senses don't integrate.

I shall explore how the characteristic features of Focusing, as Gendlin describes them in his classic paper "A Theory of Personality Change" (1964), dovetail with this picture of hemispheric specializations.

Focusing

Gendlin (1990) describes the method of Focusing as, "to spend time, attending to that inwardly sensed edge" (p.210). Such an "edge" is what we experience when what we are *saying* (left) does not fit what we are *feeling* (right). Our precise attention (left) is called to an unexpected feeling that requires our broad attention (right). The discrepancy may make us pause to "look within" for the "right" words to articulate our experience. What we really want to say may come into "focus" if we are patient—this is why Gendlin called it "Focusing" originally. And it is this natural phenomenon that his research identified as the key to effective therapy (Gendlin 1981). A fruitful therapeutic dialogue is more likely if the client searches within for what he really wants to say instead of merely stating something logical—and if the therapist does so too.

Focusing is that deliberate turn of attention within to seek out "inwardly sensed edges." The left hemisphere turns to the right and, if we are patient, fresh things come to mind—feelings, images, memories, something more we want to say. All of these are right hemisphere biased functions. What is new comes spontaneously (right), in contrast to searching in our mental filing cabinet for explanations (left). Therapists like what arises from the right hemisphere as, whatever it is, it signals therapeutic movement. For clients, it gives them confidence in the therapy and their capacity to benefit from it.

McGilchrist (2009, p.179) says that the right hemisphere "presences," that is, is simply present with an experience, while the left "re-presents," that is, finds a named category for what has arisen in the right. Right therefore tends to be the source of whatever arises freshly in our minds, whereas left manipulates what is already there, and does not produce anything really new. But it's the co-operation of both hemispheres that is the holy grail here—we need the integration of both.

Felt sense

The bodily sense we turn to in Focusing is called a "felt sense." Gendlin (1964) points out that as well as emotions (our visible affective state, which may be biased to right or left or involve both), and our feelings (our repertoire of inner states we can think about in named categories, left), we can also "refer directly" to "an inward bodily feeling" (p.111). Attending to a felt sense brings to the foreground how we are experiencing a situation inside (right), which we seek to grasp (left) when Focusing. We can be emotional and we can talk about our feelings without necessarily being aware of an underlying felt sense.

Confusion sometimes arises around what constitutes a felt sense. Sometimes it is described as a vaguely felt knowing about something (that may lack discernible physical sensation), but generally we look for it in the middle of the body (where physical sensations abound). So is the felt sense a sensation or not? Neuroscience can clarify this point. A felt sense is the right hemisphere's take on our here and now inner experience, a subtle quality of feeling. It is holistic (raw perception, before the left hemisphere divides it into separate units), non-verbal and informed by the ongoing state of the body. The degree of bodily change, and therefore of physical sensation, varies with the person and the experience. But, with bodily attention, the right hemisphere takes over and the felt sense comes to the fore, whether or not we notice a particular sensation.

We may experience a felt sense while lacking the words to communicate its meaning. Gendlin describes this from the client's perspective:

> He may call it "this feeling," or "this whole thing," or "this is the way I am when such-and such-occurs"... Nothing is vague about the definite way he *feels* it... Only *conceptually* is it vague. (Gendlin 1964, p.116)

Focusing is the process whereby the concept that fits the felt sense becomes clear. Felt sense is a more complex phenomenon than emotion. It may be the inner "place" (body and right hemisphere) from where emotion seems to arise. Emotion, on the other hand, can be left hemisphere biased (e.g., anger), and it can involve the right hemisphere overwhelming the left with high arousal (e.g., anxiety, upset) that disrupts cognition—neither of which are Focusing experiences. The ease with which we can ignore felt senses reflects the left hemisphere's ability to inhibit the signals coming from the right. Focusing is a practice that aims to overcome this inhibition.

The body

The body where we find the felt sense is the subjective body each of us experiences from within, rather than the body observed by another person (such as a therapist) attuned to body language. Gendlin's felt sense is in reference to *my* body, with all its aches, pains, sensations and emotional goings-on—and with its capacity for resonance with other bodies.

Our awareness of relating and communicating generally steers clear of this body. Antonio Damasio (1994), a neuroscientist who writes about feeling and body, says that while the brain is continually mapping what is happening in the body, the conscious mind nevertheless throws a veil over the inner workings of the body so it can attend to the outside world. If it didn't, bodily processes might endlessly interrupt conversations.

Focusing relies on what science calls the "interoceptive" sense. Kinaesthetic sense is of the body's movement, and proprioceptive sense tells you where your limbs are in relation to each other. Interoception tells you how the insides of your body are feeling—organs and viscera. These senses generally go about their business beneath the surface of consciousness, thankfully, but when we are Focusing we pierce Damasio's veil.

Body "mapping" is involved in these senses. While each hemisphere maps the position of the contralateral arm and leg, only the right hemisphere maps the *inside* of the body. Hence the ease with which we can ignore what's happening on the inside (left inhibiting), and hence activation in the right hemisphere in Focusing and why this contemplation feels so different from a left hemisphere-biased state of mind.

Neuroscience tells us how the brain changes the body, via neural (nerve) and chemical (hormonal) signals to alter emotional states, and how the body changes the brain, via feedback (neural and chemical) about its actual emotional states and how this then changes cognitive states. In Focusing, we attend to how the body actually *is*, and the renewed integration of feeling and thinking, and therefore of right and left hemispheres, may trigger a release of tension in the body—a "felt shift" (the idea that the integration of hemispheres allows the felt shift and release of tension is speculative but consistent with current neuroscience).

Experiencing

Underlying our explicit collection of experiences, good and bad, which we can talk about endlessly (left), is our implicit ongoing experiencing in the here and now (right)—undivided and continually unfolding. Gendlin (1964) states that "experiencing is the process of concrete, bodily feeling," and "one can always refer directly to experiencing" (p.111). When we do so, we stop trying to explain our experience, and instead notice our actual experiencing—in the body.

Awareness of bodily experiencing puts the right hemisphere back into the frame; thereby fresh feelings, images and thoughts can arise. They may surprise us—in fact they usually do, because the right hemisphere's novel constellations are beyond the left's existing categories. What emerges may include painful feelings, and Gendlin (1964) points out that, paradoxically, these can feel enlivening. It can feel better when left hears what right is trying to tell it, even if tears come in the process, than when left stays isolated in its ivory tower. Something new is stirring within (right), instead of just feeling stuck and trying to explain why we're so stuck (left). Left hemisphere inhibition may spare us embarrassment, but it doesn't necessarily feel good. Letting nature take its course feels better than stopping its flow.

Implicitly functioning

Gendlin (1964) says that experiencing and most behavior is "implicitly functioning" in that we do not think it explicitly before we enact it: "quite without such direct reference to experiencing, most of life and behavior proceed on implicit meanings" (p.113). For example, although we think about what we want to say, we do not consciously construct our sentences in advance. Implicitly functioning aspects of mind dissolve the supposed boundary between "conscious" and "unconscious" minds. So does neuroscience. Although most neural activity generally lies outside awareness, much of it need not do so.

For example, the left hemisphere is associated with explicit processes of behavior and speaking, the right with implicit processes of affective and somatic regulation and non-verbal communication. Such implicit processes are not so much unconscious as beyond the normal spotlight of focused attention. When we shine the spotlight in their direction, there they are: maybe "less conscious" rather than "unconscious." Therapists get very interested in these less conscious, implicitly functioning, processes, and bringing them to the light of consciousness involves broad attention (right) and a process like Focusing.

Damasio (2010) says that "mind" is a flowing combination of actual and recalled images that do not need to be conscious to do their work. His notion of mind, like Gendlin's, is one of process, rather than a thing, a mind that lacks a sharp distinction between conscious and unconscious. The brain is like the ocean—we see the waves breaking on the surface, but there is constant movement between what is on the surface and what is below, and what we see depends on where we look.

Carrying forward

A felt sense is a doorway to implicit meaning. Attending to a felt sense allows what is implicitly functioning to come to the surface, and this gives rise to a multiplicity of explicit meanings. There is an unfolding of something new (right), rather than a rearrangement of what is already in one's mind (left). Gendlin (1964) states that "to explicate is to *carry forward* a bodily felt process" (p.114). Carrying forward relieves tension in the body as we recognise the good sense of our own feelings. The change is deeper than merely cognising something, we experience a felt shift.

Carrying forward starts in the right hemisphere and then presumably involves both hemispheres working together. On its own, the left hemisphere argues, explains and makes up stories. Nothing really changes, the client feels no different. But if left turns to right to engage the body and the felt sense of implicit meaning, something new can unfold. Right receives the ever-changing signals from the body, which, married to external sensory signals, creates new mental images (in Damasio's sense), which in turn affect the body. Left then articulates what right says is really happening.

Carrying forward feels good—it leaves us with a sense of real inner movement. Something *is* different in our organism. The whole inner landscape changes—right hemisphere networks re-organise, body and mind are different. Gendlin (1964) says that insight arises from carrying forward, but does not cause it. The neuroscientist Jaak Panksepp (2010) makes a similar point: "insight is something that emerges as a result of therapeutic transformation; insight is not the primary agent of transformation, but rather a *consequence of it*" (p.25).

According to McGilchrist (2009), explicit reasoning depends on the left hemisphere, while the implicit reasoning of problem solving and insight depends on the right. We already solve problems before we are aware of the process of doing so and before we find words to describe the solution.

In the therapy room, carrying forward means something fresh arises in the client's mind—implicit meaningfulness becomes new explicit meanings. Because right hemisphere networks are pivotal, the body changes too—heart rhythm, breathing, blood chemistry, muscle relaxation and so forth. The client no longer *feels* stuck with whatever they brought to therapy. And the therapist's resonance and attunement (right) enable her to empathise with the client's change.

Global effect

Gendlin describes the unfolding of fresh meanings in therapy as sometimes having a "global effect":

> ...it is not just this problem resolved, or that trait changed, but a change in many areas and respects... The individual is flooded by many different associations, memories, situations and circumstances. (Gendlin 1964, p.120)

Everything that comes shares the same felt meaning, and the client can only voice a little of the flood. Time for digestion and integration is needed.

There are good reasons for expecting such a global effect from a significant felt shift that starts in the right hemisphere. One is the interconnectedness of areas on this side of the brain, so that changes in one may trigger changes in others. Another is that changes in the right hemisphere can trigger corresponding changes in subcortical areas, with which it is richly linked, and therefore down in the body itself. And a changed body will send different signals back to the brain as feedback loops rearrange themselves. Finally, right will send different signals to left—which then adapts to them.

So, a significant unfolding in the therapy room may cause a cascade effect starting in the client's right hemisphere and spilling over into their body and the rest of their brain. This is in contrast to a change in a left hemisphere region that may be too independent to trigger such a cascade, so that a cognitive shift fails to translate into an affective or bodily change.

Self-propelled feeling process

If "global effect" describes the changes immediately following a felt shift, the idea of a "self-propelled feeling process" describes what comes next. Gendlin (1964) says "as the individual engages in focusing...he finds himself pulled along in a direction he neither chose nor predicted" (p.123). A larger process is set in motion which "has a very striking, concretely felt, self-propelled quality" (p.124).

It is likely, perhaps inevitable, that a cascade of changes on both sides of the brain, and in areas linking body and brain, will change the person's ongoing experience after a therapy session. Their perceptions will be different, and so their feelings will be different, and then they may think different thoughts. In contrast, changes at a purely cognitive level may be swiftly derailed as old affective patterns reassert themselves.

Gendlin (1964) suggests there is a *natural order* of unfolding to personality change. Such change cannot be deliberately engineered, and attempts to do this will backfire. Instead, our biology takes over and does what it has evolved to do. Certain things come to the surface of conscious awareness before certain other things—we have to "trust the process." In Focusing-Oriented Therapy, we let the felt sense of both client and therapist (but particularly the client's) guide us.

Neuroscience would say that the neural networks in our heads are self-organizing—"autopoietic" (Maturana and Varela 1987). So we might also expect a natural order to the process of psychological change. Neural development follows its own course. And such a course unfolds more effectively when less-conscious unfolding (right) takes the lead, rather than more-conscious rational plans (left).

Stopped processes

Gendlin thinks that Freud's theory of repression does not fit with what actually happens in therapy. Instead, Gendlin describes the deeper problems that clients bring to therapy as "stopped processes" that are "structure bound" in nature:

> Experiencing is always in process and always functions implicitly. The respects in which it is *structure bound* are not experiencing. The conceptual content *in an abstract way* can appear to be the same...*structure bound* aspects are not *in process.* (Gendlin 1964, p.129)

When there is experiencing, both hemispheres contribute. Right supplies fresh detail and emotional tone—an unfolding felt sense. Left supplies some order, articulation, arrangement of things into comprehensible categories. But when experiencing is missing, we may have some conceptual content—for example, "my mother issue"—but no immediacy of feeling that would be a basis for exploring it experientially. Left is active, right is inactive; why is this?

I believe what may be happening is that left may inhibit right to protect against painful feelings, in which case right may try to send emotional signals to left, but left stops it. There are many psychological terms for this phenomenon, including defence, resistance, suppression, avoidance and denial. Left likes to suppress signals from right so it can concentrate on the matter at hand without being diverted by the vagaries of fluctuating emotional and somatic states. And left likes to construct stories that deflect the other person's attention. This sort of story constructing is different, however, from genuinely creative story telling in which both hemispheres co-operate.

Neuroscience describes how emotionally overwhelming experiences are traumatic when the brain cannot integrate external sensory signals with internal bodily ones. This leaves what Allan Schore (2010), a therapist who writes about neuroscience, calls "dis-integration of the right brain" (p.114). If right doesn't marry external senses to internal senses, it may have no message at all to send to left—blank. The consequence is an ongoing dissociated state around the memory fragments of an experience and any reminders of it. The stopped and structure-bound processes described above are likely to involve dissociation.

In practice, most sticky psychological problems that clients bring to therapy probably involve both right hemisphere inhibition and right hemisphere dissociation. If they didn't, the client would probably be able to resolve painful feelings and experiences with their own social support.

So how can the therapist address dissociation and stopped processes where the fertile ground of experiencing is missing?

The therapeutic response

Efforts to interpret what is not implicitly functioning in the client are fruitless and, worse, shaming. According to Gendlin (1964), the therapist needs to respond to "aspects of experiencing which *are* implicitly functioning but to which the individual himself tends not to respond" (p.132). By doing so, she draws the client's attention to something that is happening in an emotional and bodily way (right) that he is not aware of (left). The principle is that carrying forward what is implicitly functioning tends to reconstitute structure-bound experiencing. If the client can engage with feelings and implicit meanings that he normally ignores; stopped processes may restart. No neural pathways are immune to the effect of other pathways, and if new constellations start firing, unconstrained by inhibition, they may wake their neighbours. This could cascade down the line, so that supposedly "repressed" feelings and impulses could then also unfold in this way.

Ideally the therapeutic relationship can tolerate feelings that are hard to understand and prone to evoking shame. This is important because when previously inhibited aspects of our emotional functioning eventually emerge into awareness, they may be met by empathic understanding for the first time. This entails a dramatic shift in the client's brain, reflected in a dramatic moment in the therapy room. The client finds himself somewhere new in his neural networks, which may be the catalyst for dissociated fragments of experience to integrate at last. Nature likes to complete processes and cycles. Gendlin's reconstituting of stopped processes may be seen as the integration of dissociated experience. Such a process of integration seems to follow a natural order, not an order planned by the therapist.

Therapeutic work that carries experiencing forward often happens without direct reference to the body, which is already implicitly functioning in emotionally charged moments anyway. But resolving trauma and dissociation requires engaging with the body if fragmented aspects of inner experience are to be integrated with the rest of the client's life in right brain (right hemisphere and subcortical areas) networks (Levine 2010).

Conclusion

Because felt senses, feelings and memories unfold in a process over time, Gendlin proposes that "the unconscious" is better thought of as "incomplete process" (1964, p.138). This makes sense from a neuroscience perspective. There are unconscious processes in the brain that will never become conscious (though their effects can), and processes beyond conscious awareness that can move within consciousness if we shift our attention towards them. The implicit processes of the right hemisphere might be described as "less conscious," the explicit processes of the left as "more conscious." There is no stark conscious–unconscious divide between the cortex and the sub-cortex. Although conscious awareness is associated with the frontal cortical lobes, Damasio (2010) is clear that "core consciousness," which provides the here and now aspect of awareness, is generated way down in the brainstem.

In therapy, overcoming left hemisphere inhibition looks like admitting to something we had previously avoided, for example a feeling the client has previously felt but never expressed. And "reconstituting stopped processes" looks like a new integration of inner and outer fragments of experience, as when a client experiences the unfolding of new, and often painful, feelings, memories and associations. The fresh material that comes into consciousness has not been sitting for years in a dark place in his brain awaiting the searchlight of therapeutic attention to be shone upon it. Rather, it is a new constellation of experiencing that forms in the moment, made possible by the unusually supportive atmosphere that client and therapist together have managed to create.

References

Damasio, A. (1994) *Descartes Error.* New York: G.P. Putnam's Sons.

Damasio, A. (2000) *The Feeling of What Happens.* London: Heinemann.

Damasio, A. (2010) *Self Comes to Mind.* London: Heinemann.

Gendlin, E.T. (1964) "A Theory of Personality Change." In P. Worchel and D. Byrne (eds) *Personality Change.* New York: John Wiley and Sons.

Gendlin, E.T. (1981) *Focusing.* New York: Bantam.

Gendlin, E.T. (1990) "The Small Steps of The Therapy Process." In G.Lietaer *et al.* (eds) *Client-Centred and Experiential Psychotherapy in the Nineties.* Leuven: Leuven University Press.

Gendlin, E.T. (1997) *Process Model.* New York: Caversham Books.

Levine, P. (2010) *In an Unspoken Voice.* Berkeley, CA: North Atlantic Books.

McGilchrist, I. (2009) *The Master & His Emissary.* London: Yale University Press.

Maturana, H. and Varela, F. (1987) *The Tree of Knowledge.* Boston: Shambhala Publications.

Panksepp, J. (2010) "Brain Emotional Systems and Qualities of Mental Life." In D. Fosha *et al.* (eds) *The Healing Power of Emotion.* New York: W.W. Norton.

Schore, A. (2010) "Right Brain Affect Regulation." In D. Fosha *et al.* (eds) *The Healing Power of Emotion.* New York: W.W. Norton.

CHAPTER 17

Focusing-Oriented Therapy

The Message from Research

Rob Parker

Introduction

Psychology's interest in what we now call the "felt sense" is as old as psychology itself, and formal research into what we call "Focusing" has been going on for over half a century. In this chapter, we will review the history of this research, what recent studies have to say about the relationship between client Focusing and therapy outcomes, and how future research might be improved.

Early research

Psychologists have been interested in the felt sense for about as long as there has been a discipline of psychology. In 1890, barely ten years after Wundt established the first laboratory for psychological research, William James described the experience of a "felt meaning" or "gap" when one tries to recall a forgotten name (James 1890/2009, pp.251–252).

Formal research on what we call the felt sense began in 1958, when William Kirtner, a young PhD student at the University of Chicago, investigated how therapy clients described their problems. Kirtner and Cartwright (1958) created a rating scale with five categories, ranging from the externally focused client who:

> ...[describes] problems as though they are almost entirely external... There is avoidance of discussion of internal feelings...

> even though feeling may be apparent in voice tone, gesture, words used, etc.

to the internally focused client who:

> has a very strong and very apparent drive to generate and examine impulses, thoughts, ideas, despite resultant fear, guilt, sadness, etc. (p.329)

In Kirtner's sample of 24 clients, 6 were in the top two (internally focused) categories and 14 clients were in the bottom (externally focused) categories. This simple scale produced a startling result: *all* clients in the top two categories had successful therapy outcomes, and *all* clients in the bottom two categories had unsuccessful outcomes. Kirtner could predict, after one session, which clients would benefit from therapy and which would not. One might have expected such a finding to be of great interest to anyone practicing or researching psychotherapy, but it was largely ignored until Gendlin and colleagues rediscovered it several years later while pursuing a separate line of research.

The EXP Scale

When Kirtner published his research, Eugene Gendlin was working with Carl Rogers at the University of Chicago Counselling Center. Rogers had already developed a scale to measure client behavior in therapy but, like Kirtner's scale, Rogers' scale focused on the *content* of what the client said. In contrast, Gendlin was more interested in the client's *process*, specifically the extent to which the client focused "on his not yet conceptually clear, but directly felt, experiencing" (Gendlin *et al.* 1968, p.218).

This research led to the development of the Experiencing (EXP) Scale (Klein *et al.* 1970; Table 17.1), a seven-point scale measuring the extent to which clients interact with their felt experience.

Table 17.1 The EXP Scale

Level	Description
1	The content is not about the speaker. The speaker tells a story, describes other people or events in which he or she is not involved or presents a generalized or detached account of ideas.
2	Either the speaker is the central character in the narrative or his or her interest is clear. Comments and reactions serve to get the story across but do not refer to the speaker's feelings.
3	The content is a narrative about the speaker in external or behavioral terms with added comments on feelings or private experiences. These remarks are limited to the situations described, giving the narrative a personal touch without describing the speaker more generally.
4	Feelings or the experience of events, rather than the events themselves, are the subject of the discourse. The client tries to attend to and hold onto the direct inner reference of experiencing and make it the basic datum of communications.
5	The content is a purposeful exploration of the speaker's feelings and experiencing. The speaker pose[s] or define[s] a problem or proposition about self explicitly in terms of feelings...[and] explore[s] or work[s] with the problem in a personal way. The client now can focus on the vague, implicitly meaningful aspects of experiencing and struggle to elaborate it.
6	The subject matter concerns the speaker's present, emergent experience. A sense of active, immediate involvement in an experientially anchored issue is conveyed with evidence of its resolution or acceptance. The feelings themselves change or shift.
7	Experiencing at stage seven is expansive, unfolding. The speaker readily uses a fresh way of knowing the self to expand experiencing further. The experiential perspective is now a trusted and reliable source of self-awareness and is steadily carried forward and employed as the primary referent for thought and action.

Source: Klein *et al.* 1970, pp.56–63

While they were developing the EXP Scale, Gendlin and his colleagues also explored the relationship between EXP levels and psychotherapy outcome. In a series of studies, Gendlin *et al.* (1968) confirmed what Kirtner and Cartwright (1958) had found: that EXP was a strong predictor of who would benefit, and who wouldn't, in therapy.

Gendlin and his team had also expected that therapy would improve clients' EXP levels, but that prediction was not borne out. Gendlin's team was very concerned about this because if clients with low EXP did not benefit from therapy, and there was no way to raise EXP, it meant that some people couldn't be helped by therapy. Gendlin (1964) had already given the name *Focusing* to "the whole process which ensues when the individual attends to the direct referent of experiencing" (i.e., EXP levels 6 and 7). Now, realizing how crucial EXP was for therapy outcome, Gendlin developed a procedure to teach people how to focus (Gendlin *et al.* 1968).

Recent research

After Gendlin's early work in the 1960s, research on Focusing and EXP continued to grow (e.g., Hendricks 2002; Rennie, Bohart, and Pos 2010). Some of the most significant research, both in quality and quantity, has concerned the relation between EXP and psychotherapy process (for a review see Elliott, Greenberg, and Lietaer 2004, and Elliott *et al.* 2013). As we've already noted, this is relevant to Focusing because the EXP scale measures "the extent to which [an individual's] ongoing, bodily, felt flow of experiencing is the basic datum of his awareness and communications about himself..." (Klein *et al.* 1970, p.1); in other words, Focusing.

Numerous studies have found a positive association between EXP and therapy outcome, for a variety of therapies including client centered, process experiential, and cognitive behavioral. In her review of the literature, Hendricks (2002) found that out of 28 studies measuring the correlation between EXP and successful outcome in therapy, 27 studies showed positive correlations. In addition, 23 out of 25 studies found that using Focusing in therapy also correlates with successful outcomes.

In a review of the literature on humanistic-experiential psychotherapies (HEPs), Elliott *et al.* (2013) performed a meta-analysis of 199 outcome studies, including 31 randomized controlled trials. Among many interesting results, two are of particular interest here. First, they found that HEPs (excluding therapies researchers labeled as "supportive" or "nondirective," which are often used as placebos) were as effective as other evidence-based therapies, including CBT (p.855).

Second, they found that EXP levels were consistently associated with successful outcomes, not only in HEPs, but also in many other forms of therapy as well (p.847). This conclusion was based in part on six replications of the Gendlin *et al.* (1968) finding of a strong positive correlation between EXP levels and treatment outcome (pp.847–848).

Elliott *et al.* (2013) also cited a number of researchers who have raised an interesting methodological question about how this research is done. Most studies sample EXP at arbitrarily chosen times such as the beginning, middle, and end of therapy, but some studies have suggested that the relationship between EXP and treatment outcome may be stronger when EXP is measured during critical moments in therapy (Elliott *et al.* 2004, 2013). This makes sense; people don't focus all the time, even in therapy. It is quite possible that a client might have just one or two intense periods of Focusing during an entire course of therapy, and might show considerable improvement as a result. Arbitrary sampling might miss those one or two periods of Focusing, and could thus weaken the statistical correlation between EXP and treatment outcome. We will return to this question later.

Two studies

Two studies (Watson *et al.* 2003; Watson and Bedard 2006) are interesting examples of the kind of research that has been done on psychotherapy and EXP. Both studies were part of a project that compared Cognitive Behavior Therapy (CBT) with Process Experiential Therapy (PET), an experiential therapy that uses Focusing in addition to a number of therapeutic tasks and techniques (Elliott *et al.* 2004, p.179ff).

In the first study (Watson *et al.* 2003) 66 clients were randomly assigned to receive either CBT or PET. All therapists were adherents of the treatment approach they used, all therapists were trained and supervised by an expert in their particular approach, and all therapy sessions were recorded. After 16 sessions, the clients who received PET and CBT had the same improvement on measures of depression, self-esteem, general symptom distress, and dysfunctional attitudes but, in addition, the clients who received PET showed greater improvement on a measure of interpersonal problems. In other words, PET was as effective as CBT for the specific disorder that CBT was originally designed to treat (Beck *et al.* 1987), and also showed additional benefits beyond those provided by CBT.

The second study (Watson and Bedard 2006) was based on the same data. Their procedure was too complex to fully describe here, but basically they used the audio recordings from the previous study to measure EXP levels of 10 good outcome and 10 poor outcome clients in each treatment modality (PET and CBT). For each of the resulting 40 subjects, EXP was rated during three 20-minute segments at the beginning, middle, and end of therapy. Watson and Bedard found that the clients who showed the most improvement at the end of therapy also had the highest EXP ratings at the beginning, middle, and end of therapy. That, of course, was not surprising; it was merely a replication of Kirtner and Cartwright (1958), Gendlin *et al.* (1968), and many others. What was surprising was that the relationship between EXP and treatment outcome held for CBT as well as for PET. This is interesting, because CBT is concerned with dysfunctional thinking (Beck 2011, p.3), not with Focusing or EXP.

Table 17.2 Means and standard deviations of the percentages of modal EXP ratings

Group	Level 2		Level 3		Level 4		Level 5		Level 6	
	M	**SD**	**M**	**SD**	**M**	**SD**	**M**	**SD**	**M**	**SD**
PET										
Total	40.75	15.05	41.25	9.37	9.77	8.61	5.93	7.53	2.13	4.36
Good outcome	37.98	18.05	41.10	9.19	7.75	10.73	9.13	7.07	4.05	5.60
Poor outcome	43.53	11.65	41.75	10.04	11.80	5.68	2.73	6.84	0.20	0.64
CBT										
Total	58.80	16.21	32.66	11.81	5.59	4.91	1.82	3.31	1.13	3.90
Good outcome	52.60	14.72	36.67	12.02	4.90	3.13	3.65	3.97	2.18	5.44
Poor outcome	64.99	15.89	28.65	10.68	6.27	6.32	0.00	0.00	0.08	0.25
Combined therapy										
Total	49.78	17.94	37.04	11.42	7.68	7.23	3.88	6.10	1.63	4.13
Good outcome	45.29	17.70	38.88	10.66	6.33	7.83	6.39	6.25	3.12	5.46
Poor outcome	54.26	17.47	35.20	12.13	9.03	6.50	1.36	4.91	0.14	0.48

Note: EXP = Experiencing Scale, PET = process-experimental therapy, CBT = cognitive behavioral therapy
Source: Data from Watson and Bedard 2006, p.156

Table 17.2 (from Watson and Bedard 2006) shows the results: For both PET and CBT, the average percentage of statements in the good and poor outcome groups was about the same for EXP levels 2, 3, and 4. But subjects with good outcomes have a noticeably higher percentage of EXP 5 statements, and the difference is dramatic for EXP level 6.

I have analyzed their data further to show more clearly the relationship between EXP level and treatment outcome. In Figure 17.1, the height of each bar indicates the average percentage of statements made by clients with good outcomes, divided by the average percentage of statements made by clients with poor outcomes, for each treatment group and EXP level.

Thus, for good outcome clients receiving PET, an average of 37.98 percent of their statements were rated at EXP level 2, while for poor outcome clients the average percentage of level 2 statements was 43.53 percent. The ratio is 0.87, which shows up as close to one on the bar graph. We can see that for levels 2, 3, and 4, the ratio hovers around one, indicating that for each of those EXP levels, good and poor outcome clients give about the same percentage of statements. But at level 5, the ratio is around four, indicating that good outcome clients made about four times as many level 5 statements as did poor outcome clients. And at level 6, the ratio explodes: in PET, good outcome clients made *20 times* more level 6 statements and, in CBT, good outcome made *27 times* more level 6 statements!

Even though the absolute numbers are small, the ratios are impressive. Clearly, it is not just higher EXP levels that predict therapy outcome. It is specifically the percentage of client statements at EXP level 6, in other words *the percentage of time the client spends Focusing,* that predicts successful therapy outcome. And, it doesn't take much Focusing to make a difference.

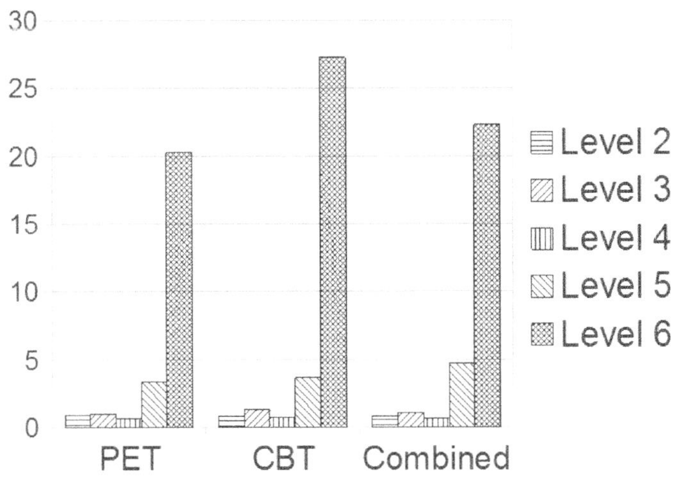

Figure 17.1 Mean percentage of statements at each EXP level, for good outcome clients divided by poor outcome clients

Note: For CBT level 5, poor outcome was changed from 0% to 1% to avoid division by zero (see Table 17.2)

This finding bears on the question of why therapy doesn't appear to raise client EXP levels. An initial clue can be found in the low EXP levels reported in most studies. For example, Gendlin *et al.* (1968, p.226) found that 89 percent of their "neurotic" clients began therapy at EXP level 3 or below (on an early but roughly equivalent version of the EXP scale). Of those, the successful clients increased their EXP levels by an average of about 0.6, while the unsuccessful clients hardly changed at all. Similarly, Watson and Bedard (2006, p.155), found that the average EXP level for good outcome clients started at 2.60 at the beginning of therapy, increased to 2.99 at the middle of therapy, and dropped to 2.87 at the end of therapy. For poor outcome clients, the figures were 2.38, 2.78, and 2.67.

Why are these EXP levels so low? The answer is probably that therapy clients spend most of their time describing their situations and feelings about those situations. Clients are most likely to focus while they are working on some crux issue, but that might not happen very often. Therapy is likely to consist of a considerable amount of EXP levels 2 through 4, punctuated by occasional level 5, and very occasional level 6.

But these numbers are *average* EXP levels, and averages tend to obscure patterns of diversity. Ten minutes of Focusing (EXP level 6) could make the difference between a successful and unsuccessful therapy outcome, yet the average EXP level would show only a very slight increase if the rest of the sample consisted of 50 minutes of level 2 or 3 discussion. Furthermore, if only a few arbitrarily chosen segments of therapy were scored (for example 20 minutes at the beginning, middle and end of therapy) from a total of 12 hours of therapy, 10 minutes of Focusing might not be scored at all, even though it could be decisive in terms of outcome. This could explain why overall EXP levels are so low and why therapy doesn't appear to increase clients' EXP levels: as part of an average, small percentages of EXP level 6 would be washed out by the much larger percentages of EXP levels 2 and 3.

Thus the data in Table 17.2 and Figure 17.1 suggest that instead of asking about the relationship between EXP and therapy outcome, or whether EXP increases during therapy, it would be more relevant to focus specifically on EXP level 6, either throughout the course of therapy or during periods that were judged most significant by the client.

Another way to assess the relationship between EXP and therapy would be to give psychotherapy candidates either Focusing training or relaxation training prior to beginning therapy, and then to measure the effect on treatment outcome. This approach would present some difficulties, for example it might be difficult to keep therapists from guessing which pretreatment their clients had received; but it would have the advantages of being relatively easy to implement, and of producing results that would be of immediate practical use.

CBT and FOT

As noted above, there is strong evidence indicating that EXP is related to outcome in many forms of therapy. CBT is an interesting example because outwardly it is quite different from FOT. CBT has been assumed to be a cognitive approach, not experiential, and presumably not concerned with the felt sense. Why, then, should EXP be related to therapeutic outcome in CBT?

CBT holds that symptoms arise from core beliefs that are inaccurate or dysfunctional (Beck 2011, p.3). These core beliefs are often not verbalized and the patient is often not aware of them. Although CBT generally uses "intellectual" techniques (p.248), in some cases experiential methods may be included, for example (pp.249–250):

Therapist: Do you feel this sadness and incompetency somewhere in your body?

Patient: Behind my eyes. And my shoulders feel heavy.

The purpose, however, is always to challenge and change dysfunctional core beliefs. According to Beck, "the quickest way to help patients... is to facilitate the direct modification of their core beliefs as soon as possible" (2011, p.35). But because challenging core beliefs too quickly can disrupt the therapeutic relationship, therapists must usually approach core beliefs gradually, by first teaching the patient to identify and challenge automatic thoughts that stem from the core beliefs. After the client has learned to challenge automatic thoughts, it becomes possible to challenge the core beliefs which are thought to be the root of the problem.

Focusing-oriented therapists are more concerned with the manner of experiencing than with the content. However, if we consider CBT's core beliefs as a kind of process, it becomes clear that core beliefs have many characteristics of what Gendlin calls *frozen wholes* or *frozen structures* (Gendlin 1964; Parker 2007; Parker in press). These are not contents, but a manner of experiencing in which the client attends only to certain aspects of situations and ignores other aspects. For example, while relating to authority figures the client might notice only the characteristics of an abusive father, while ignoring everything else.

When it is brought into awareness, a frozen structure can be experienced as a felt sense, often from an earlier time ("Oh... *That's* what it was like for me back then!"), and this awareness can be formulated as a statement ("I always felt like it was my fault, that I was no good"). When that happens, it can seem as if the statement had always been there (Gendlin 1964). This can lead to the illusion that the frozen structure was actually a verbal belief waiting to be discovered. This may help explain why CBT assumes that the core belief is a *belief*, such as "I am incompetent" that can be uncovered and completely expressed in words. In FOT, we would say that the frozen structure is a kind of implicit experiencing, a stopped process (Gendlin 1964; Parker 2007).

A focusing-oriented therapist wouldn't normally challenge the automatic thoughts or core beliefs associated with a frozen structure, partly because of the resistance that would entail, but primarily because the problem with them isn't that they are incorrect, but that they are part of a structure bound manner of experiencing. The client is no longer open to all aspects of a situation, but only to the aspect of (for example) personal failure. As FOT helps the client become more open to his/her experiencing, the frozen structure opens and becomes part of that experiencing. Automatic thoughts and core beliefs don't have to be challenged, because they are already interacting with everything else the client knows, and are quickly modified by that interaction.

Thus, core beliefs and frozen structures may represent two ways of thinking about the same basic experience, although, of course, differences in thinking are associated with differences in practice.

Conclusions

The felt sense has been noticed and studied throughout the history of modern psychology, beginning with William James. Research on EXP goes back half a century. Numerous studies, conducted decades apart by independent researchers, have repeatedly shown that high EXP is associated with successful outcome in several forms of psychotherapy and may be an important ingredient in all forms of psychotherapy. On the other hand research has not supported the expectation of Gendlin *et al.* (1968) that therapy would increase client EXP levels.

However, most studies have rated EXP at arbitrary intervals of time. A number of researchers have questioned this approach, suggesting that rating EXP during particularly meaningful moments of therapy might produce more meaningful results, resulting in even higher correlations between EXP and treatment outcome, and perhaps even an increase in client EXP during therapy (Elliott *et al.* 2004, 2013).

In addition, research so far has focused on average EXP levels, which tend to wash out relatively rare episodes of EXP level 6 (or Focusing). Thus the relatively high EXP levels of good outcome clients are still only around 3.0, which is not very high. A reexamination of recent data (Watson and Bedard 2006) suggests that it is not EXP *per se* that leads to successful therapy outcome, but specifically EXP level 6, that is, Focusing. This suggests that research specifically targeting EXP level 6 could lead to new and interesting results.

However, the research available so far already has important implications for the practice of psychotherapy. Clearly EXP is a central factor in successful psychotherapy, and therefore psychotherapists of all persuasions would benefit from learning to focus so that they can support Focusing in their clients and help raise their clients' EXP levels.

Also, therapists no longer need to argue over whether therapy should focus on cognitions, or behavior, or emotions, etc. (Gendlin 1996). All of these "avenues" are intrinsically related, because they are all aspects of the implicit intricacy of the client's experiencing. Thus all avenues can lead to a felt sense, a "feel" of the situation one is concerned about; and when attended to, that felt sense can lead to a new formulation of the problem, so that a resolution is possible.

Finally, therapists don't need to wait years for research to tell them if a particular intervention is likely to help a particular client. A therapist who knows how to focus can tell from moment to moment whether a client's EXP level is going up or down, and can therefore tell almost immediately if the last intervention was helpful or not. Therapists can now be their own researchers, gathering their own evidence for practice with each specific client, in real time.

References

Beck, A.T., Rush, A.J., Shaw, B.F. and Emery, G. (1987) *Cognitive Therapy of Depression.* New York: Guilford Press.

Beck, J.S. (2011) *Cognitive Behavior Therapy: Basics and Beyond,* 2nd edn. New York: Guilford Press.

Elliott, R., Greenberg, L.S. and Lietaer, G. (2004) "Research on experiential psychotherapies." In M.J. Lambert (ed.) *Bergin & Garfield's Handbook of Psychotherapy and Behavior Change,* 5th edn. New York: Wiley.

Elliott, R., Watson, J.C., Goldman, R.N. and Greenberg, L.S. (2004) *Learning Emotion-Focused Therapy: The Process-Experiential Approach to Change.* Washington, DC: American Psychological Association.

Elliott, R., Watson, J., Greenberg, L.S., Timulak, L. and Freire, E. (2013) "Research on humanistic-experiential psychotherapies." In M.J. Lambert (ed.) *Bergin & Garfield's Handbook of Psychotherapy and Behavior Change,* 6th edn. New York: Wiley.

Gendlin, E.T. (1964) "A Theory of Personality Change." In P. Worchel and D. Byrne (eds) *Personality Change.* New York: John Wiley & Sons. Available at www.focusing.org/gendlin/docs/gol_2145.html, accessed November 18, 2013.

Gendlin, E.T. (1996) *Focusing-Oriented Psychotherapy: A Manual of the Experiential Method.* New York: Guilford Press.

Gendlin, E.T., Beebe III, J., Cassens, J., Klein, M. and Oberlander, M. (1968) "Focusing ability in psychotherapy personality, and creativity." *Research in Psychotherapy 1,* 217–241.

Hendricks, M.N. (2002) "Focusing-Oriented/Experiential Psychotherapy: Research and Practice." In D. Cain and J. Seeman (eds) *Humanistic Psychotherapies: Handbook of Research and Practice.* Washington, DC: American Psychological Association.

James, W. (1890/2009) *The Principles of Psychology.* Available at http://ebooks.adelaide.edu.au/j/james/william/principles, accessed November 18, 2013.

Kirtner, W.L. and Cartwright, D.S. (1958) "Success and failure in client-centered therapy as a function of initial in-therapy behavior." *Journal of Consulting Psychology 22,* 5, 329–333.

Klein, M., Mathieu, P., Gendlin, E.T. and Kiesler, D.J. (1970) *The Experiencing Scale: A Research and Training Manual (Vols. 1–2).* Madison: Wisconsin Psychiatric Institute, Bureau of Audio Visual Instruction.

Parker, R. (in press) "Change From the Inside: Focusing Oriented Therapy with an Adolescent Sex Offender." In V. Follette, D. Rozelle, J. Hopper, D. Rome and J. Briere (eds) *Contemplative Methods in Trauma Treatment: Integrating Mindfulness and Other Approaches.* New York: Guilford.

Parker, R.A. (2007) "Making peace from the inside." *The Folio: A Journal for Focusing and Experiential Therapy 20,* 1, 36–47.

Rennie, D.L., Bohart, A.C. and Pos, A.E. (2010) "Eugene Gendlin: Experiential Philosophy and Psychotherapy." In L.G. Castonguay, J.C. Muran, L. Angus, J.A. Hayes, N. Ladany and T. Anderson (eds) *Bringing Psychotherapy Research to Life: Understanding Change Through the Work of Leading Clinical Researchers.* Washington, DC: American Psychological Association.

Watson, J.C. and Bedard, D.L. (2006) "Clients" emotional processing in psychotherapy: A comparison between cognitive-behavioral and process-experiential therapies." *Journal of Consulting and Clinical Psychology 74,* 1, 152–159.

Watson, J.C., Gordon, L.B., Stermac, L., Kalogerakos, F. and Steckley, P. (2003) "Comparing the effectiveness of process-experiential with cognitive-behavioral psychotherapy in the treatment of depression." *Journal of Consulting and Clinical Psychology 71,* 4, 773–781.

CHAPTER 18

Cross-Cultural Focusing-Oriented Therapies

An Approach for a Globalized World

Kevin C. Krycka, Sergio Lara, and Atsmaout Perlstein

To say that the world is beset by challenges would be an understatement. To suggest that we have found an adequate response to the brute facts of violence, discrimination, or poverty, would simply be untrue. While this may seem a rather bleak picture of the state of affairs for many, there is hope.

In many regions of the world practitioners of Focusing-Oriented Psychotherapy (FOT) are charting a new course that brings the concrete expression of one's own experiencing into alignment with the practical need for change at interpersonal, community, systemic, and even cultural levels. These pioneers are developing new approaches that are meaningful for persons while also responsive to the local situation. They constitute an emerging family of what we call experiential social practices.

These new practices can help bridge the gap between personal experience and policy, and between sometimes oppressive cultural structures and freedom. Ultimately, these emerging practices can reduce, even eliminate, the power of entrenched patterns that bind people and situations to dysfunctional or inadequate modes of being and acting. The practices included here are distillations of processes that begin and end with referencing our ongoing experiencing as it intersects with the world in which we live. They are original to the situations that birthed them but they are exemplars of general human processes that can be used elsewhere to better our lives.

This chapter highlights a few of the newly developed experiential social projects. We emphasize their best practices and how each is responsive to local conditions and generative of new steps forward. We end with reflections on how FOT can be used as a model for working in and creating new social change practices in our globalized world.

Let us begin with a brief overview of the foundational philosophical and experiential basis for this work.

The felt-sense engine for cross-cultural and social change

All reality is implicitly much more than it appears to be now.

We believe that referencing one's ongoing experiencing is crucial to social change and is in fact the engine for transformative cross-cultural work in our globalized world. We know ongoing experiencing by its felt sense. The felt sense is the living touchstone of our being and our sense as beings-in-society. The felt sense is the engine of change, personally and socially.

As described in *Focusing* (Gendlin 2007, first published in 1978), persons are taught how to come from their own subjective experiencing and then find, often with a little help, new inner directions and steps forward in life. Without much effort some can connect with the felt sense as deeply subjective in character and also experience it as having to do with more than that subjectivity, as something "about my experience" and about much more. The values of acceptance and openness are central to experience in this manner.

Gendlin (1962, 1968, 1978/2007; Gendlin and Johnson 2004; Gendlin *et al.* 1968) refers to the "felt sense" as the reference point of personal change and the empirical study of ongoing experiencing. As he and others subsequently have found, it is the ability of a client to reference their ongoing experiencing that is at the core of successful psychotherapy (Gendlin 1978/2007, pp.317–352).

Early research studies on psychotherapy outcomes (Gendlin 1961, 1968; Gendlin *et al.* 1968) showed that the people most successful in psychotherapy intuitively access an ongoing practice of zigging and zagging between various subjective, embodied states as they ponder a currently important issue. These studies also showed that many others do not yet know or honor this inner place of searching and discovery. Hendricks (2001) reports on further research supporting the effectiveness of Focusing in therapy.

Focusing-Oriented Psychotherapy contributes to and makes an impact in the world as it brings people from any context (including religious faith, political leaning, socio-economic status, geographic location, etc.) to attend to their felt sense of this moment. We define a "moment" as the simultaneous appearance of one's inner life and social existence in consciousness (Gendlin 1978/2007).

Many individuals across the world who have "translated" FOT into a means of social progress are beginning to fashion new approaches to changing long-standing patterns that have been associated with entrenched violence, poverty, and oppression (see The Focusing Institute website: www.focusing.org/focusing_and.htm). With FOT as its foundation, we are now seeing the development of the values-rich environments in which social change stands the best chance to develop and advance.

Philosophical starting points

Central to understanding the importance of the felt sense in cross-culture and social change work are Gendlin's philosophical writings on human meaning-making as process (Gendlin 1997). Processes are at work in our breathing (e.g., the inhaling process), in our thinking (e.g., cognitive processes), in feeling (e.g., emotive processes), in romance (e.g., the attraction process), and so forth. Beyond these kinds of discrete processes we have already identified through scientific means, for instance, are the situations we want to talk about. The situation itself is another kind of process we can identify and attend to. It includes the subjectively experienced, minute micro shifts that we notice when we learn to attend to the situation as its own event, as an occurring in our existence now. This is a chief basis of an FOT approach to cross-cultural work and the many social change practices emerging from it.

When we do sense the situation itself—bringing along our valuing of openness and acceptance—the experiencing of it talks back. What happens when experience talks back is that the entire situation (involving many other unnamed processes) can change, not just a part of it.

As process, cross-cultural, social and global change involves two main movements: 1) referencing the lived body, and 2) leaning forward into sociality. It is important that we understand that these two movements are another way of describing the doing of the lived body in social change.

1. Referencing the lived body

The role of the lived body in various situations is well established (Galvin and Todres 2012; Giddens 1987; Krycka 2012a, 2012b; Todres 2007). In cross-cultural FOT the body is not merely an instrument or conceptual lens; it is an instance of the double in-dwelling and becoming processes involved in all aspects of thinking and behaving. A doing-lived body is thus as inherent in the entire process of cross-cultural work and social change as breathing is to existence. The doing-lived body is not something to use, but something we are. Through this concept, emergent cross-cultural FOT practices can be better understood as whole, alive processes wherein one's body is "my own" in one sense while subjectively experienced as "not only mine" in another. What was once merely a personal experience is at the same time intimately connected to the larger doing of society. Gendlin's contribution to social change movements lies in giving us a new framework for getting beyond the limitations of starting with objectivity first.

2. Leaning forward into sociality

Perhaps it is amply clear how human experience is not isolated from the very many contexts and processes we can use to describe it. Nonetheless, the process oriented sensibility of FOT reveals something unique about the role of the felt sense in helping one changed process make the other process(es) different. For instance, as practitioners engage people in a particular situation, they attend to multiple channels of information. The skilled person is aware of what is said and what is not yet said, what possible meanings lay behind the words or gestures, and the feel for the next word or gesture to come: for example, the explicit, tacit, and implicit respectively.

Social change does not "float above" this interpersonal level of existence. It will always be change experienced by someone. As communities envision themselves as connected to a larger socio-political space that is freer of the forces that marginalize or create violence, the explicit, tacit, and implicit dimensions of being-in-the-world shift. Together, lived bodily doing and leaning into sociality are complementary ways of seeing the entire process of social change. But how does this happen? Of course this is a reasonable and important thing to ask.

Examples in the world

In the following, we present two key examples of how process thinking found in FOT can in fact be the basis of new approaches to solving our wicked social problems.

Focusing Community Wellness programs

Since 1986, The Focusing Institute has successfully cooperated with other international organizations to build Community Wellness programs in countries in conflict, affected by wars and culture divisions, or inflicted by natural disasters. As reported in Hendricks (2001), the Focusing process was found to efficiently and effectively reduce psychological suffering and increase peaceful existence across ethnic and gender differences. The first Community Wellness program was launched in 2001 in Pakistan and later on in Afghanistan by two Focusing teachers: Nina Joy Lawrence and Patricia Omidian.

The program teaches basic Focusing skills in combination with strategies for increased resiliency and management of stress symptoms (Omidian and Lawrence 2003). Subsequently, participants reported a significant reduction of stress-induced symptoms in their everyday lives, healthier connections with others and increased hope for the future.

An important contribution of this project is the value of using cultural metaphors and communal traditions to facilitate teaching the Focusing process in each unique setting. For example, one of the traditions in Afghan culture is the custom of welcoming any guest into one's home, whether that guest is a friend or stranger.

The Focusing training in Afghanistan includes specific Sufi poetry by Jelaludin Rumi. Rumi was a Sufi poet and leader born in the Balkh Province of Afghanistan 800 years ago. His poetry has strong resonance for the Afghani community.

The Rumi poems used in this model include "Presence" and "The Guest House" (in Barks and Green 1977). They help participants integrate two major Focusing principles to facilitate inner healing. One is "presence," which teaches acknowledgment of all feelings and experiences without being emotionally flooded. The second is how to sit with the "felt sense" of a particular feeling "guest" (e.g., anger, sadness, happiness, and more) and dialogue with it to gain insight into the message and understand its meaning for the person.

Focusing in Afghanistan: a summary story

One villager often fought with his neighbors about whose turn it was to use the irrigation water. One day his neighbor hit him with a shovel. The villager ran home to get his knife and a big stick to fight back. Suddenly, in the middle of his rage, instead of reacting blindly, a thought stopped the villager. "What am I doing? Maybe it is a guest! Maybe I should try the Focusing skills I have learned, and after that I will return to fight."

The villager decided to focus. He became quiet and his body calmed. Afterwards, he felt a new clarity. He decided to leave his weapons behind, went out to meet his neighbor, and apologized for what had happened. "It was a guest, and I have learned to recognize and listen to my guests through Focusing." The whole village rejoiced when they realized that this inner process called Focusing helped bring peace between the neighbors. They decided to construct a Focusing house together. The purpose of this communal house is providing a place to listen to "inner guests" in a Focusing way.

This example points out that instead of having only limited pre-existing behavioral options, such as fighting back, the practice of Focusing can invite new, creative and more positive options. This original Focusing-based program was adapted to fit many other cultures and countries around the world, such as: El-Salvador, Ecuador, Chile, Israel, and the Gaza Trauma Center in Palestine.

In Israel, Atsmaout Perlstein, a Focusing Coordinator, has given workshops to an organization called the Sulha Peace Project; Sulha means forgiveness in Arabic and Hebrew (Sulha Project 2012). This project brings together Israelis, Arabs and Palestinians to engage in encounters that get beyond politics and stigmas. Their goal is to create a meaningful authentic bonding between the children of Abraham/Ibrahim; adults, youth, and children who share a common destiny.

People in the project learned about the "pause"—taking a moment to be quiet to experience the felt sense on a body level beyond thoughts and concepts. Taking a pause has the added benefit of helping participants learn to be patient and sit with unclear feelings until they crystallize and reveal some understanding or meaning.

Clearing a Space, the first movement in Focusing as developed by Gendlin (1978/2007), was experienced by this group as most valuable for their peace project. This skill of clearing the emotional and cognitive spaces before starting any activities allowed each participant to experience relief from stress symptoms while generating more focused energy.

In El Salvador a similar program was started by Beatrice Blake (USA) and Melba Rosenberg, a local social worker who decided to add the approach of Non-Violent Communication (Blake 2007; Rosenberg 2003) to their program. The Community Wellness Focusing model was also implemented in Ecuador, where the poverty level is 39 percent with the population made up of 18 nationalities and a variety of languages and cultures. Edgardo Riveros and William Hernandaze (2009) are both Focusing Coordinators who have created a training program attended by 3500 families. The program's objective is to train community leaders who, in turn, bring the program to their villages. The program is conducted in the native language.

Jerry Conway and Muhamad Altalill brought Focusing to the Palestine Trauma Center in Gaza in 2012. Participants reported that learning to "pause" and take the time to listen to oneself and/or others was most meaningful and surprising. The participants learned to find what is "right" for them and act from an inward source of freedom.

Interchange Groups in Chile

Interchange Groups provide a thought-provoking contribution to our assertion that the adoption of certain values or attitudes exemplified in FOT can be shown to create peace within a process oriented group structure. Sergio Lara, a professor and psychologist, has been developing permanent and regular "Interchange Groups" where people can meet and interact. In style and substance they are reminiscent of the pioneering contributions to this field made by Carl Rogers (Rogers and Rosenberg 1981; Rogers and Russel 2002) and subsequently Eugene Gendlin (Alemany 1997). Interchange groups are built upon an understanding of "felt sense" as that which connects us to individuals, intimate groups and larger social groups. Varela (2000) similarly argues that ones awareness is already a connection to the situations in which we live. Lara's team began developing Interchange Groups with a belief that the practice of making space for the free and spontaneous connection to one's felt sense was critical to finding solutions to problems.

Interchange Group format

WELCOMING: THE FIRST STEP

Welcoming is much more than saying hello or being socially cordial. Welcoming is structured through the use of phenomenological bracketing, or the suspension of assumptions, "the époche." Epoche is from the Greek πoχή, meaning methodologically paying attention to a particular phenomenon. For our purposes époche, the suspension of assumptions, is an ongoing practice of evaluating a situation (or phenomenon) through our experience of it in the present moment. This process, at first a purely philosophical method, was made accessible to psychology (Giorgi 2009) allowing us to empirically investigate subjective experience.

The "suspension" step is strengthened through "clearing a space" as it provides a psychologically safe place for participants to explore their ongoing present experience. Practically speaking, the team found it helped to start leading "clearing a space" (Gendlin 1993) with eyes closed in order to find that calm place where one can open up to the experience.

In Interchange Groups the époche of the welcome stage follows a structured process that occurs in three stages: 1) suspension; 2) re-direction; 3) letting go (Depraz, Varela, and Vermesch 2000). Suspension consists of preparing to open your eyes to what you are telling in a calm, liberating way. This very important step means putting aside anything that could get in the way of this. This could be in the form of concerns or worries, restlessness (physical or mental) or prejudices regarding what surfaces (beliefs, values and ideas). The second stage, re-direction, allows the exploration of that which surfaces, drawing attention to it. Finally the third stage aims at letting go by allowing the surfacing feelings to evolve and come into focus.

SETTING A PLAN: THE SECOND STEP

Proposed activities of the Interchange Groups never followed the same plan as it quickly became apparent that listening carefully to what issues the participant's raised required adjustments to be made to the planned format. The team found that it was helpful for participants to bring problems to the group and first collect them in a list rather than immediately open up the group to discussion of problems.

This stage of the groups included adding teachable processes that helped the group move toward a reasonable stopping place. For instance, teaching self-empathy and how to remain in dialogue while upset arose from the practice of setting a plan. Thus, making a plan evolved into process where participants learned how to explore their subjective experiencing, while, at the same time, moving toward more tangible task completion (e.g., making a list of issues). Often enough, the entire time was spent going around the circle helping the member discern for themselves what was most salient, or important, about what they were bringing to the group that evening.

BRINGING THE PROCESS TO A CLOSE: THE FINAL STEP

Closing begins by inviting the whole group to stop and pay attention to the meaningful lessons that each one has learned. Engaging, rather than defending, becomes a catalyst for how to be in a difficult situation without splitting the experience into good or bad, emotion versus rationality and the like. It is similar to the principle of "wuwei" in Taoism, which states the importance of not fighting or opposing surfacing emotions but going along with them, as they are an agent of change from something aggressive to something creative, constructive, and comfortable.

While it is clear that the Interchange Groups did not always go completely smoothly, the implicit valuing of others' experience and sense of connection to one's own inner life developed through the process, and gave way to harmony for many of the participants. The experience of running several Interchange Groups led the team to adopt small, mobile, and flexible work plans that could be modified partially or completely along the way.

Reflections

Below we summarize how FOT can be used as a model for working in a cross-cultural and globalized world. Developing new social change practices will be the work of many and part of the legacy of Gendlin's work. FOT, Community Wellness programs, and Interchange Groups assume that self-exploration and exploring what surfaces in an interaction or situation between people, requires that participants first be in a psychologically safe environment. Safety is established in different ways depending on the culture, the group, and the social-political context (e.g., inviting a space to silence internal noises, be able to feel the body as a whole, or show kindness and respect to accompany everything that surfaces). Creating an appropriate and psychologically safe space for exploring anything new and fresh, encouraging bodily felt empathy or what Moreno (2009, pp.119–130) calls corporal empathy, is critical to cross-cultural work.

The Interchange Groups and Community Wellness programs provided a structure for new and fresh experiences to emerge, providing greater relief and comfort to the participants. Regardless of the locus of the issue, how the participant or group framed it (i.e., as primarily psychological or situated in society), with the structure and safety provided, the concerns shifted.

Even though group management can be successfully established in FOT cross-cultural work, it is important for the facilitator(s) to embody the generative attitudes (e.g., be peaceful when accompanying a participant who is speaking, be accepting of what is said or revealed, welcome what emerges). Developing bodily empathy (Moreno 2009) showed that positive forward movement could be achieved as the team and group practices patience as they listen.

Another important lesson from our two examples involved observing one´s ethno-location or spiritual tradition as salient aspects of the dialogue. Teams noted how they and participants often reflexively adopted certain critical spiritual or social rules or assumptions. For instance, when considering how to pose questions, suggest actions or make decisions, when deciding who sits where, some participants still assumed their way was "correct." Without attentively listening to what others experience or could feel, without examination of the implicit social contract and attendant spiritual meanings, the groups may not have been able to progress.

Becoming aware of and inspecting personal assumptions drew the teams to question how they dealt with interactions in general. From an observational point of view—the typical stance adopted in most conflict resolution paradigms—objectivity and uniformity are the basis for claiming any truth. However, from a process point of view, these characteristic ways of understanding how interactions begin to shift positively are blurred. Often, the result was that members went back and forth together on a topic until a beneficial stopping place or conclusion was found.

It is in this interactive, felt-sense level conversational space where Community Wellness and Interchange Groups have generated the most pragmatic solutions. There develops a flow of new answers and alternatives to situations that at first may have appeared completely intractable. Welcoming disharmony and discrepancies helps forge environments that invite and foster diversity, something highly valued in FOT work.

This is a potent kind of valuing that stems the tendency of some group members to prematurely act against what they anticipate will be the imposition of another's will upon them. Without making explicit this valuing, participants may feel the pull toward resignation and futility. As a form of unconditional positive acceptance, this approach is generative in that it shows growth toward a more fluid, constructive peace.

A critical issue facing those of us who take interest in cross-cultural and social change is how to bridge the gap between FOT theory and practice and working with communities. A misunderstanding sometimes arises as we recognize that one's social location is already affected by, is embedded in, and a partial product of, a specific set of factors seemingly far from the subjective realm typically associated with Gendlin's work. For instance, today we accept that cross-cultural peace building work must account for factors such as language, cultural customs, religion, political regimes, and economics, to name a few, in that these reflexively create the conditions where the humans who experience them actually live. However, a curious and sometimes dangerous thing happens as we attend to these factors: the more attention we pay to these constituent elements of our existence the more likely that they will overshadow and obscure our lived reality, creating an unnecessary misunderstanding between subjectivity and sociality.

To be fair, learning how to access and speak from one's embodied sense of the present moment is somewhat of an art and likely not appealing to everyone. While we may confidently claim that the process of felt sensing is the most efficient means to understanding the particularities of our own concrete first-person experience, it is difficult to explain how this is so and why "my experience" should matter to anyone else but me. Gendlin and Johnson (2004) have taken this as a challenge to process oriented practitioners, calling on them to create new forms of research based within the first-person perspective.

Undoubtedly there is a significant amount of work that Focusing practitioners and researchers have yet to do to help generate the skill-based educational systems necessary to create the lasting bridges from the intrapersonal to the personal and to the social. It is also not easy to create a safe environment where one can share thoughts and feelings liberally and where this space can be opened up to discussion of broader existential and social issues facing group members. What's more, when there is a desire to expand a new paradigm—for example, the experiential paradigm foundational to FOT—one needs to approach the project with a keen eye to the social foundations present in the locality. In other words, one must continually engage with and return to the communities where real social change occurs.

We can begin to address the myriad potential misunderstandings of the role FOT can play in social change by interrogating the answers to this seminal question, how does one get "beyond" the emphasis on the individual? We suggest that the answer is not to be found in a formula or manual, a reality that may disappoint some. However, what we can say about "how" to bridge the personal and social is that it depends a great deal upon our starting point. In the two practices mentioned above, that starting point was found in the philosophical tenet of *interaction first*. When understanding persons and situations as already interaction, the processes we develop to assist the social change process not only honor the situation's multivocal nature, but also promote a more complex understanding of it.

Conclusions

The main contribution that Gendlin's philosophy brings to cross-cultural work lies in its ability to open up a vast territory from which we can articulate new principles that describe social change as a whole process that includes the many other processes we can distinguish and those for which we do not yet have words. From the simplest form to the more involved and troublesome problems we face, FOT and a process model offers new ways of conceiving, articulating, and demonstrating how the intricate whole relevance of situations are sensed in the body and how they can move forward.

Application of these principles worked out in the field necessitates an entirely novel approach to any of the aspects of cross-cultural work we care to emphasize. As Gendlin suggests, working in this manner brings a vast space within us and within our thinking from which we can speak freshly; speak in a way that helps move the whole situation forward.

As those working in cross-cultural settings, we recognize the importance of shifting the intractable, of midwifing difficulties into openings. At certain junctures in our work, as practitioners we pay very close attention to our embodied sense of the situation. We notice that doing so will generate next steps without much effort, whether we are alone or working with others. The examples we offer describe the importance of pausing to sense the whole situation and the various ways help is brought and successful outcomes are developed. We hope this helps future practitioners create new avenues into their practice that advance cross-cultural exchange and social renewal.

References

Alemany, C. (1997) *Psicoterapia Experiencial y Focusing: La Aportación de E.T. Gendlin.* Bilbao: Desclée de Brouwer.

Barks, C. and Green, M. (1977) *The Essential Rumi.* New York: Castle Books.

Blake, B. (2007) "El Salvador Project Report." *Focusing and Empathic Communication in El-Salvador.* Available at www.focusingnvc.com/focusingnvc/Project_Report.html, accessed November 18, 2013.

Depraz, N., Varela, F. and Vermesch, P. (2000) "The Gesture of Awareness: An Account of Its Structural Dynamics." In M. Velmans (ed.) *Investigating Phenomenal Consciousness: New Methodologies and Maps.* Amsterdam/ Philadelphia: John Benjamins Publishing Company.

Galvin, K. and Todres, L. (2012) "Phenomenology as embodied knowing and sharing: Kindling audience participation." *Indo-Pacific Journal of Phenomenology 12* (Special Issue), 1–9.

Gendlin, E.T. (1961) "Experiencing: A variable in the process of therapeutic change." *American Journal of Psychotherapy 15*, 233–245.

Gendlin, E.T. (1962) *Experiencing and the Creation of Meaning: A Philosophical and Psychological Approach to the Subjective.* New York: Free Press of Glencoe.

Gendlin, E.T. (1968) "The Experiential Response." In E.F. Hammer (ed.) *Use of Interpretation in Therapy: Technique and Art.* New York: Wiley.

Gendlin, E.T. (1993) *Focusing: Proceso y Técnica del Enfoque Corporal.* Bilbao: Mensajero.

Gendlin, E.T. (1997) *A Process Model.* Chicago: Focusing Institute.

Gendlin, E.T. (1978/2007) *Focusing.* New York: Bantam.

Gendlin, E.T. and Johnson, D.H. (2004) "Proposal for an international group for a first person science." Gendlin online library. Available at www.focusing.org/gendlin/docs/gol_2184.html, accessed November 18, 2013.

Gendlin, E.T., Beebe, J., III, Cassens, J., Klein, M. and Oberlander, M. (1968) "Focusing Ability in Psychotherapy Personality, and Creativity." In J.M. Shlien (ed.) *Research in Psychotherapy, Vol I.* Washington, DC: American Psychological Association.

Giddens, A. (1987) *Social Theory and Modern Sociology.* Cambridge: Polity Press.

Giorgi, A. (2009) *The Descriptive Phenomenological Method in Psychology: A Modified Husserlian Approach.* Pittsburgh, PA: Duquesne University Press.

Hendricks, M. (2001) "Focusing-Oriented/Experiential Psychotherapy Research." In D. Cain and J. Seeman (eds) *Humanistic Psychotherapy: Handbook of Research and Practice.* Washington, DC: American Psychological Association.

Krycka, K.C. (2012a) "Peacebuilding from the inside." *Indo-Pacific Journal of Phenomenology 12* (Special Issue), 1–11.

Krycka, K.C. (2012b) "Incorporating research into your experiential and FOT practice: Midwifing the implicit." *The Folio: A Journal for Focusing and Experiential Therapy 9*, 1, 115–129.

Moreno, S. (2009) *Focusing: Descubriendo mi Sabiduría Corporal.* México: Primera Edición.

Omidian, P. and Lawrence, N.J. (2003) "Community Wellness Focusing Update." Available at www.focusing.org/newsletter/may2013/may-2013-newsletter.asp#article, accessed 19/02/2014.

Riveros, E. and Hernandaze, W. (2009) "Focusing and overcoming poverty in Ecuador." Middle of the World Focusing Group. Slideshow Presentation. Available at www.focusing.org/docs/fotconfppt/index.html, accessed 19/02/2014.

Rogers, C. and Rosenberg, R. (1981) *La persona como centro.* Barcelona: Herder.

Rogers, C. and Russel, D. (2002) *Carl Rogers, The Quiet Revolutionary: An Oral History.* Roseville, CA: Penmarin Books.

Rosenberg, M. (2003) *Nonviolent Communication: A Language of Life.* Encinitas, CA: Puddledancer Press.

Sulha Project (2012) "Sulha Peace Project." Available at www.sulha.com, accessed November 18, 2013.

Todres, L. (2007) *Embodied Enquiry: Phenomenological Touchstones for Research, Psychotherapy, and Spirituality.* London: Palgrave Macmillan.

Varela, F.J. (2000) *El Fenómeno de la Vida.* Caracas-Montevideo-Santiago de Chile: Dolmen.

Conclusion

Greg Madison

The chapters collected in this book offer a model based upon immediate resonance with lived experience. This approach saves us from arid intellectualizing and analysis of content that can lead further and further from the person that we know we are, lived from the inside.

Eugene Gendlin's early work in psychology and psychotherapy, and his current work in philosophy, continue to inspire psychotherapists who look to base their practice upon a radical democracy where not only is every client deeply heard, but every aspect of every client has a voice.

The way that the practice of FOT itself has developed is another instance of its own values. Although there is currently one main certifying body, The Focusing Institute, the process of certifying as a FOT can be, like Focusing itself, quite self-directed and non-prescriptive. The diversity of FOT practice is highly prized, as evidenced in the range of topics and interpretations of Gendlin's thinking that you find in this book.

For those interested in knowing more about the practice of Focusing, The Focusing Institute website (www.focusing.org) contains information about many applications of Focusing, including its application to therapy. This site also includes the generous gift of the Gendlin Online Library, where you can retrieve full text articles for free as well as information about the bi-annual FOT international conferences where everyone is welcome. For those interested specifically in FOT, there is the relatively new website by the International Association of Focusing Oriented Therapists (www.

focusingtherapy.org) which is still in development but already hosts articles by many of the authors in this book as well as information about training opportunities around the world.

In this brief conclusion I will not attempt to summarize the preceding 18 chapters or to highlight what I see as common themes and issues. I leave that to the reader, but with a note of caution. You may find that through reading this collection you have been forming, as you read, different felt responses to the ideas and session transcripts you have encountered. Rather than jump right to a cognitive analysis of what you have been offered in these pages, I encourage you to dwell just a little with the feeling of reading these chapters. I think you will find in that feeling, probably located in the middle trunk area of your body, an intricacy that already includes what you might want to say and more than you can easily say... where you felt excited, disappointed, where you disagreed or were inspired to try something new. Those responses in you constitute the leading edge of what can come next in the world of FOT.

CONTRIBUTORS

Peter Afford, MA is a counsellor and psychotherapist in private practice in London. He works as a trainer and supervisor in university and other contexts, specializing in Focusing and in the application of neuroscience to the understanding of psychotherapy.

John Amodeo, PhD has been a licensed marriage and family therapist in California for over 30 years, and is author of *Dancing with Fire: A Mindful Way to Loving Relationships, The Authentic Heart,* and *Love & Betrayal.* He has conducted workshops internationally on couples therapy and relationships, and is an adjunct faculty member of Meridian University.

Zack Boukydis, PhD is visiting professor, Psychology & Pediatrics, Semmelweis Medical School, Institute of Psychology, Eotvos Lorand University, Budapest, Hungary and University of Turku, Finland. He is a focusing-oriented therapist, and Focusing Coordinator at the Focusing Institute of New York, and wrote *Collaborative Consultation with Parents and Infants in the Perinatal Period* (Brookes Publishing 2012).

Helene Brenner, PhD is a focusing-oriented psychologist, national speaker on the psychology of women, and author of I *Know I'm in There Somewhere: A Woman's Guide to Finding Her Inner Voice and Living a Life of Authenticity* (Penguin 2003). Besides her Frederick, MD psychotherapy practice, she provides clinical supervision, workshops, telegroups, and individual phone coaching.

Calliope Callias, PhD is a licensed clinical psychologist in New York, and a certified focusing-oriented and relational psychotherapist. She works as a clinician, supervisor, and as a Focusing trainer. She is an adjunct professor of Psychology at the Derner Institute of Adelphi University in New York, a Clinical Supervisor at the Graduate Center of the City University of New York, and a coach for The Focusing Institute.

Annmarie Early, PhD, LMFT is Professor of Counselling in the Master of Arts in Counselling Program at Eastern Mennonite University. She is licensed as a marital and family therapist and is certified as an emotionally focused couples therapy trainer and supervisor. Her work involves utilizing experiential treatment approaches including attachment, implicit processes, and felt sensing.

Christiane Geiser works as a psychotherapist, Focusing trainer, and supervisor in Zurich. She is a certifying coordinator of The Focusing Institute. She co-founded a training institute (GFK) for person-centered and Focusing-Oriented Psychotherapy, counselling, and bodywork in Switzerland. Currently she is engaged in translating and developing her work into English, together with Judy Moore.

Eugene Gendlin, PhD is Emeritus Professor of Psychology at the University of Chicago and founder of The Focusing Institute. He was founder and editor of the APA clinical division journal, *Psychotherapy: Theory, Research and Practice.* He is the author of numerous articles (accessible through the Gendlin Online Library at focusing.org) and books, including *Focusing* and *Focusing Oriented Psychotherapy.* He is the recipient of a number of awards for his development of experiential psychotherapy and his contributions to contemporary philosophy.

Charlotte Howorth, LCSW is a psychotherapist and Focusing trainer in New York City. She works with individuals and groups in private practice and also is clinical supervisor at a counselling center. Charlotte runs full two-year FOT trainings for The Focusing Institute and is a faculty member of the Focusing-Oriented Relational Psychotherapy training in Manhattan.

Akira Ikemi, PhD is Professor of Psychotherapy at Kansai University Graduate School of Professional Clinical Psychology. He is a focusing-oriented psychotherapist, certifying coordinator of The Focusing Institute and board member of WAPCEPC. He has written books in Japanese and many articles on Focusing, in Japanese and English. He practices part time in medical settings.

Bala Jaison, PhD is a psychotherapist for individuals, couples, and families, director of Focusing for Creative Living, a government-recognized educational Institution, and author of *Integrating Experiential and Brief Therapy: How To Do Deep Therapy Briefly and How To Do Brief Therapy—Deeply.* Her passion is integrating short-term brief therapy with longer-term Focusing-Oriented Therapy.

Anna Karali is a psychotherapist, and Co-founder and Co-director of the Hellenic Focusing Center in Athens, where she acts as trainer and supervisor for client-centered and focusing-oriented experiential psychotherapy. She also holds workshops and seminars and maintains a private practice in individual and group psychotherapy. She is a certified coordinator for The Focusing Institute.

Kevin C. Krycka, PsyD is Professor of Psychology and Director of the Existential-Phenomenological Psychology Masters program at Seattle University where he has taught since 1989. He is also a certified FOT and certifying coordinator with TFI. He uses Gendlin's works, particularly the Process Model, to benefit research, the training and supervision of therapists, and peacebuilding.

Sergio Lara, PhD is a psychologist and certifying coordinator for Focusing in Santiago, Chile. He is the academic director of IFDI Instituto de Formación y Desarrollo Transpersonal Integral.

Larry Letich, LCSW-C is an individual and marital therapist in Frederick and Rockville, MD, providing Focusing-Oriented Therapy and Emotionally Focused Therapy (EFT) for couples. In addition to his general individual and couples work, he specializes in the comprehensive and focusing-oriented treatment of gifted adults with ADHD.

Greg Madison, PhD (editor) is a psychologist and psychotherapist lecturing on doctorate courses in London and on postgraduate university faculties internationally. He works as a supervisor, clinician, and trainer in Focusing and experiential-existential practices. Greg is co-editor of the journal *Existential Analysis* and writes on existential and Focusing themes, including the book *The End of Belonging*, and is co-editor of the recent text *Existential Therapy: Legacy, Vibrancy, and Dialogue.*

Judy Moore is Director of University Counselling at the University of East Anglia, Norwich, UK. She is a certifying coordinator of The Focusing Institute and has facilitated the development of Focusing training at UEA over the past ten years, most recently through an ongoing group project to translate and develop the work of her Swiss colleague Christiane Geiser into English.

Rob Parker, PhD is a licensed psychologist and Focusing trainer who has been studying philosophy with Gene Gendlin since 2003. An expert in the field of psychological trauma and abuse, he has been interviewed twice on national television, published in professional journals, and developed and administered a number of specialized treatment programs.

Atsmaout Perlstein, PhD is a clinical psychologist in private practice treating individuals, couples and families in Tel Aviv, Israel. She co-founded the first Israeli Focusing Center offering a full extensive training to professionals and nonprofessionals. Her vision is to teach Focusing as a way of life and as a language used in daily conversations among family members, in schools and at work.

Lynn Preston, MA, MS, LP has been a focusing-oriented psychoanalyst for over 30 years. She is the director of the New York Focusing-Oriented Relational Psychotherapy (FORP) program and co-director of the Cape Town (South Africa) Focusing-Oriented Therapy (FOT) training program. She is co-director of the Relational Self Psychology (RSP) Study Center in New York City. Lynn has written articles about Focusing and relationality in psychotherapy and is a teacher and supervisor.

Campbell Purton, PhD completed a diploma in Person-Centred Therapy in 1988, having earlier been a lecturer in Philosophy. He has set up university courses in Focusing in the UK and in China. He has published two books: *Person-Centred Therapy: The Focusing-Oriented Approach* (2004) and *The Focusing-Oriented Counselling Primer* (2007).

Laury Rappaport, PhD, MFT, REAT, ATR-BC is the author of *Focusing-Oriented Art Therapy: Accessing the Body's Wisdom and Creative Intelligence* and editor of *Mindfulness and the Arts Therapies: Theory and Practice.* She is a certifying Focusing coordinator, Founder/Director of the Focusing and Expressive Arts Institute faculty at Sonoma State University and is an integrative psychotherapist at Sutter Health Institute for Health and Healing.

René Veugelers, BA is an art therapist, psychiatric nurse, and group social worker, trained in Emerging Body Language (EBL), teaching Children Focusing internationally. He is Coordinator of Children Focusing for the Netherlands, where he works with parents, toddlers, and adolescents emphasizing the non-verbal world.

Pavlos Zarogiannis is a psychotherapist, and Co-founder and Co-director of the Hellenic Focusing Center in Athens. Pavlos offers client-centered and focusing-oriented training and psychotherapy and is a certified coordinator for The Focusing Institute. He has interests in literature, art, and philosophy.

SUBJECT INDEX

Page numbers in *italics* refer to figures and tables.

AUTHOR INDEX

CPI Antony Rowe
Eastbourne, UK
April 17, 2023